TRAINING
HEARTS

TEACHING
MINDS

TRAINING HEARTS

TEACHING MINDS

Family Devotions
Based on the Shorter Catechism

STARR MEADE

PUBLISHING
P.O. BOX 817 • PHILLIPSBURG • NEW JERSEY 08865-0817

Unless otherwise indicated, Scripture quotations are from the New American Standard Bible. Copyright by the Lockman Foundation 1960, 1962, 1963, 1968, 1971, 1973, 1975, 1977.

Scripture quotations marked (NIV) are from the HOLY BIBLE, NEW INTERNATIONAL VERSION®. NIV®. Copyright © 1973, 1978, 1984 by International Bible Society. Used by permission of Zondervan Publishing House. All rights reserved. Italics in Scripture quotations indicate emphasis added.

Questions and answers from the Shorter Catechism are from *The Westminster Shorter Catechism in Modern English* © 1986, Reformed Theological Seminary of Jackson, Mississippi.

Page design by Tobias Design
Typesetting by Michelle Feaster

Printed in the United States of America

Library of Congress Cataloging-in-Publication Data

Meade, Starr, 1956–
    Training hearts, teaching minds : family devotions based on the shorter catechism / Starr Meade.
        p. cm.
    Includes bibliographical references.
    ISBN 0-87552-392-7
    1. Westminster Assembly (1643–1652). Shorter catechism. 2. Presbyterian Church—Catechisms—English. 3. Reformed Church—Catechisms—English. 4. Christian education of children. 5. Devotional calendars. I. Title.

BX9184.A5 M43 2000
248.8'45—dc21

00-037511

INTRODUCTION

In the first manual of pastoral practice ever written, the apostle Paul defined the church as "the pillar and support of the truth" (1 Tim. 3:15). For many of today's churchgoers, a pillar and support of truth is not necessarily what they seek when they look for a church. The first concern may be the warmth of the welcome, the style of a church's music, or the number of weekly activities from which to choose. Faithfulness to biblical doctrine is becoming increasingly rare as the first thing people seek in a church.

The supreme test of a church, however, at least from the perspective of the New Testament writers, is this: Is the church the pillar and support of the truth? Is it thoroughly acquainted with the truth of the gospel as given in the Scriptures? Does it exalt God's Word, giving it the place of preeminence in all its worship and in all its activities? Does it defend the truth at whatever cost, proclaiming it without compromise in a world of confusion and falsehood? Does it call its people to *know* God's Word for the purpose of faithfully *living* by God's Word?

THE CHURCH'S TASK

In each generation, the church's most critical task is to uphold and proclaim the truth as it was delivered to her by her Lord. One important aspect of this task is the diligent preparation of the church's children to continue to be the support and pillar of the truth in the generation to come. God calls the church of each generation to "contend earnestly for the faith which was once for all delivered to the saints" (Jude 3). When our children replace us as contenders for the faith, will they have a clear grasp of the faith they must defend? When they replace us as supporters of the truth, will they know the truth well enough to articulate it clearly and to recognize counterfeits?

Wise and godly men of another day understood the need for standards of truth and Christian doctrine. They saw the value such standards would have in presenting the fundamental teachings of

Scripture in a concise and systematic manner and in providing a grid through which to sift all teaching and all ideas. With great care and much prayer, they worked together to formulate creeds and confessions to define the basic doctrines of the Christian faith. Aware of the importance of passing these doctrines on to their children, they also prepared catechisms for the instruction of the young.

A catechism is simply an instructional guide. It is a handbook of questions and answers designed to teach principles of religion. To "catechize" children is to teach them to memorize the answers found in a catechism, so that when the catechism questions are asked, the children can reply with the correct responses. Because a good catechism is at the same time concise and thorough, when children have learned it well, their understanding of the basic doctrines of the Christian faith can be tested and found to be complete. One excellent catechism is the Westminster Shorter Catechism. In concise fashion, it gives children key biblical teachings about God, Scripture, the Lord Jesus Christ, the Holy Spirit, salvation, the sacraments, the Ten Commandments, and the Lord's Prayer.

Once, catechisms were used routinely. Church and family worked together to provide the most effective teaching possible for children growing up in Christian circles. Parents would work with their children at home, requiring them to memorize the answers to the catechism (and memorizing the answers themselves, as well). Families would discuss together the meaning of the questions and answers. Pastors would preach on topics addressed in the catechism and would systematically visit each church family, asking the questions to see how well family members had learned the answers.

Puritan Pastor Richard Baxter made it his practice to visit each of the eight hundred families in his church in a year, centering his visits on the instruction given in the Westminster Shorter Catechism. Besides examining children and adults to see how well they knew the catechism, he would ask additional questions to see if the answers had been understood. He would then go on to encourage all the members of the family to live in the light of the truth of each memorized answer. Baxter claimed to have more outward signs of success in demolishing the kingdom of darkness among his church members through this practice than through all his public preaching to them.[1]

Unfortunately, the practice of catechizing children has fallen out of favor, both in families and in churches. One reason for this is a fascination with new educational techniques that stress experience, student participation, and choice. Rote memorization has fallen out of favor. Yet, the things I remember best from my childhood are the things I memorized. The "ABC" song we all sing when we have items to alphabetize, the multiplication tables, common nursery rhymes, even lines from Shakespeare that I memorized just because they were beautiful, long before I understood what they meant—all these are indelibly fixed in my memory. I can call them up any time I need them, confident that they will be there to serve me.

It is said that if we require our children to memorize by rote, they will only memorize meaningless sounds and words without understanding them. Certainly we do a disservice to our children if we insist that they memorize words they do not understand, while we fail to take the time to discuss, teach, and explain the meanings to them. The solution, however, is not to discard memorization as a teaching method, but to faithfully supply meaning by discussing and explaining.

THE CHURCH'S FAILURE

There is, however, another, graver reason catechisms have fallen out of favor. It is that doctrinal instruction in general, for anyone and especially for children, has become unpopular. In an attempt to attract nonbelievers, the church has occupied herself with providing the things the world finds attractive. In doing so, she has lost sight of her true purpose of being the pillar and support of the truth.

From the pulpit, comfort, inspiration, and "spirituality" are acceptable; doctrine is not. In a misguided attempt to maintain unity at any cost, doctrinal teaching is shunned because "doctrine divides." Churchgoers criticize sermons stressing doctrine as not be-

---

1 J. I. Packer, *A Quest for Godliness: The Puritan Vision of the Christian Life* (Wheaton, Ill.: Crossway, 1990), 45.

ing practical enough, without understanding that a truly changed life flows from a truly changed mind. Eager to meet people's demands, more and more churches offer warm, inspiring messages that never clearly define the gospel at all. In a growing number of worship services and church programs, entertainment is replacing the substantive teaching of Christian doctrine.

Nowhere are these things more apparent than in the children's and youth departments of the average American church. In my decade of service as Director of Children's Ministries for a local church, I sampled many curriculums and received numerous advertisements for others. Commonly, the colorful, glossy promotional materials promised "better games, new crafts, fun experiences your children will really enjoy." Certainly, there is nothing wrong with "games, crafts, and fun experiences" for children. Those of us who love children want them to enjoy learning. However, when page after page of promotional material describes the fun, while the curriculum's content is only hinted at in an obscure corner of a brochure, priorities are clearly misplaced.

Advertisers appeal to what research tells them people want. What are the church's priorities for its children? The advertising for children's curriculum makes the answer all too clear. That the children are entertained and that they have fun—these are the primary goals to which everything else seems to be subservient.

Even where teaching the Bible to children is a priority, teaching Bible *doctrine* seldom is. Children hear the same Bible stories repeatedly, almost always as moral lessons on how to behave. Typical Sunday school lessons reduce Bible stories to moral tales much like Aesop's fables. The focus is on the human being in the story, who becomes its main character. So the teacher comes to the end and concludes, "And you must be like David and God will bless you," or "You must not act as Ahab did or you will find trouble."

When Bible stories are used in this way, God sits on the periphery of the narrative, like the genie in a fairy tale, blessing human actors for good behavior or cursing them for failures. Children seldom learn to see that God Himself is the main character of every Bible story. They do not learn to ask about each account they read, "What does this story tell me about God?" They never learn to read all the biblical narratives in the light of God's overall purpose to redeem a people for Himself. All they learn is: Be good and God blesses; be bad, and He does not. Not only is this a faulty representation of the gospel, it is not the gospel at all! What a tragedy!

God in His grace and condescension loaded Scripture with stories, concrete illustrations of abstract truth. But we must use the Bible stories as God intended them to be used. He gave them to us for the same reason He gave us all of Scripture—that we might know what He, the only true God, is like, and that we might understand the salvation He has provided for His people through His Son. Bible stories illustrate Bible doctrines. We who work with children should be grateful for that and should use the Bible narratives to help our children understand the doctrines of our faith. We waste Bible stories when we only use them to moralize or to equip our children to win Bible trivia contests.

Is the church equipping its children to be the support and pillar of the truth in the next generation? Several years ago, I heard a radio broadcast featuring on-the-spot interviews with Christian authors and publishers at a large Christian convention. Interviewers repeatedly asked attendees two key questions: "What is justification?" and "What is the gospel?" Most of those interviewed proved deplorably incapable of giving a lucid, biblical response to these questions. Yet Christianity *is* the gospel. The central issue of our faith is that of sinners being justified before a holy God. These things are essential to an understanding of the Christian faith.

If those being interviewed had been taught the Westminster Shorter Catechism, they would have had this response ready: "Justification is the act of God's free grace by which He pardons all our sins and declares us righteous in His sight. He does so only because He counts the righteousness of Christ as ours. Justification is received by faith alone." How simple and yet how thorough! Is there any reason people must wait until they go to Bible college or seminary to learn such a simple definition, one so basic to our faith?

Today, we are often content with "God" words and with warm feelings about Him. In a society rife with faulty ideas of God, we fail to give a definition to the word when we use it. Eager to include and to think the best of everyone, we rejoice when we hear those "God" words, assuming the person using them is one of us. When we combine this failure to discriminate with our natural sympathies toward children, we are even quicker to assume children are Christians when, in reality, they have no idea at all what it is to be one.

One summer, at a Christian camp for children from troubled homes, a counselor reported to me a conversation she had with a ten-year-old camper. "I asked him if he had ever asked Jesus into his heart and he said he did that when he was six," she said. She went on to tell me that they were thumbing through his new Bible together when he saw a picture of the three crosses on Calvary. "What is that story about?" the boy asked, curiously. The result of the discussion with the child was comfort for the counselor, who was convinced that the boy was "saved" because of whatever he had done when he was six. Evidently, however, it never occurred to her that whatever "decision" children may have made, if they have absolutely no knowledge of the crucifixion of Christ, it is not safe to assume they are believers.

A PROPOSED SOLUTION

Those of us who care about passing on the baton of historic Christian truth must awaken to the importance of faithfully imparting its doctrines to our children. We cannot depend on haphazard, hit-or-miss Bible stories and memory verses, hoping that somehow our children will distill from them Christianity's important teachings. Rather, we must provide careful, systematic instruction in doctrine. Children need a grid through which to sift all that they see and hear. We must provide this for our children while they are still young. Doctrine cannot wait until children are teens, because adolescents are making major life decisions. The theological framework on which to base those decisions, the biblical worldview, must already be in place.

The purpose of this book is to provide a tool for Christian parents and churches who take seriously this task of imparting doctrinal instruction to their children. Questions and answers come from *The Westminster Shorter Catechism in Modern English,* but the older version of the catechism may be used if preferred. Each question and answer of the catechism has six days' worth of devotional readings for families to share together. The readings are simply written, with elementary and junior-high children in mind. They are brief, out of consideration for children's short attention spans and for the busy schedules of contemporary families.

Each reading gives biblical support and simple explanations for the catechism answers. Every day for a week, the same question should be asked and the answer recited several times, followed by the reading provided. By the end of the week, the answer will be memorized. Prizes of some kind can be decided upon in advance, to be awarded after a certain number of questions and answers have been successfully learned. If one answer is memorized weekly, the entire catechism will be finished in two years. Because it contains such a wealth of information and because we remember best what we review repeatedly, I recommend taking children through the entire catechism more than once.

The apostle Paul called Timothy his "true child in the faith." He instructed Timothy thoroughly and faithfully, then set him loose to carry on the ministry Paul himself had begun. This is what we as parents must do for our children. It is what we, the church, must do for the church that follows us, the church of the next generation. We must fulfill our responsibility now, so that we will be able to say with assurance, as Paul said to Timothy, "Retain the standard of sound words which you have heard from me, in the faith and love which are in Christ Jesus. Guard, through the Holy Spirit who dwells in us, the treasure which has been entrusted to you" (2 Tim. 1:13–14).

Q.1. WHAT IS MAN'S PRIMARY PURPOSE?

A. ✑ *Man's primary purpose is to glorify God and to enjoy Him forever.*

MONDAY

What happens when you use something for a purpose other than its *real* purpose? For example, what if you wanted whiter teeth, so you tried to brighten them up with white shoe polish? Would it work? Of course not! Shoe polish is for whitening shoes, not teeth. What would happen if you put marshmallows in your toaster? You would have a terrible mess, because toasters are for toasting bread, not marshmallows. Things work best when we use them for the purpose they were intended.

God had a purpose in mind for human beings when He created them. God intended for people to know and enjoy Him. Rocks and trees and kittens cannot enjoy God—but people can!

Read Psalm 16:11. This verse describes the joy and the pleasure people have in God when they live according to the purpose God has for them. Some people live as though their purpose were to have a good time or make a lot of money. People like this are never satisfied. They find that the joy of fun times or of having new things wears off. That is because they are not living according to the purpose God has for them. When we live to enjoy God, we are doing what God made us to do and our joy in Him will last.

TUESDAY

Since God created us to enjoy Him, it is important to know how we can do that. You cannot fully enjoy a flower unless you stop and take a good look at it to see how beautiful it is and take a deep breath to see how wonderful it smells. You cannot fully enjoy an apple until you take a bite of it and find out how crisp and sweet it tastes. If you are going to enjoy God, you have to spend time finding out how wonderful He is.

Read Luke 10:38–42. Mary was enjoying Jesus. Martha was confused about the purpose God had for her. She seemed to think that her purpose was to work hard and be a good housekeeper. Jesus said Mary had made a better choice by choosing to spend time enjoying Him. The more time we spend getting to know how wonderful God is, the more we will enjoy Him.

WEDNESDAY

One of the good things about living for the purpose God intended when He made us is that, no matter what is going on around us, we can still enjoy God. If I live for the purpose of having and pleasing friends, when my friends are gone I have nothing to live for. If I live for the purpose of being beautiful and healthy, once I grow old or become sick, I have no reason to live. If I live to make money to buy things, something may happen that causes me to lose everything. Then what will I do?

One of God's Old Testament prophets was Habakkuk. Habakkuk lived in Jerusalem, where he and his neighbors had comfortable homes and were at peace. Habakkuk lived to enjoy and glorify God. His neighbors, though, lived to please themselves. Because Habakkuk was a prophet, God showed him what would happen in the future. Enemy soldiers would destroy Jerusalem in a war. They would burn the comfortable houses, and Habakkuk and his neighbors would be left with nothing. Of course, Habakkuk did not look forward to losing everything. Since his purpose was not to enjoy *things,* but to enjoy God, listen to what he could say. **Read Habakkuk 3:16–18.**

THURSDAY

God made everything for the purpose of glorifying Himself. That means that He made everything to show how wonderful He is. Right now, there are people who do not know much about God's glory; there are others who know about God but will not admit how wonderful He is. But God promises that someday everyone everywhere will know of His great glory. **Read Habakkuk 2:14.**

Although some people refuse to see it, every created thing was created to show us something of God's glory, to show us something of what God is like. **Read Psalm 104:31 and Psalm 19:1.** When you look up at all the millions of stars in the night sky, what do you think about God? When you look at the strong, solid mountains that have stood for thousands of years, what do you think about the God who made them?

God's creation glorifies Him. It shows something of what He is like. We are God's creatures too. It is God's purpose that we glorify Him too.

FRIDAY

What are some ways in which we can glorify God? How can we show how wonderful He is? One way is by praising and worshiping Him. **Read Psalm 29:2 and Psalm 50:23a.**

Jesus said we glorify God by doing good deeds. God is good, kind, and holy. When our actions are good, kind, and holy, we're showing people what God is like. **Read Matthew 5:16.**

The Bible tells us that we should do everything we do, even the simplest and most ordinary things, in a way that will glorify God. **Read 1 Corinthians 10:31.**

SATURDAY

A strange thing happened to Belshazzar's dad. Belshazzar's dad ruled over the greatest kingdom in the world. He became very proud of his kingdom. God warned Belshazzar's dad that, if he did not give glory to God for his kingdom, God would take it away from him. Belshazzar's dad continued to be proud and, just as God had said, his kingdom was taken away from him for seven years. Not only that, but the king basically lived like an animal for seven years. At the end of the seven years, Belshazzar's dad got both his man's mind and his kingdom back again. Then he gave glory to God.

You would think that Belshazzar learned from what had happened to his dad. You would think that he would have understood that his purpose for living was not to please himself or to be a great king but to give glory to God. But Belshazzar had not learned.

11

When he was king, he lived to make himself happy. He used the cups from God's temple for wine for getting drunk. One night, at one of his parties, a hand appeared out of nowhere and wrote on the wall of Belshazzar's palace. Frightened, Belshazzar sent for Daniel, God's prophet, to explain what the writing meant. Daniel reminded Belshazzar of what had happened to his father.

Read Daniel 5:22–23 to see what else he said to him. That very night, enemy soldiers attacked, killing Belshazzar and taking his kingdom. God created us to give glory to Him, not to ourselves.

Q.2.

WHAT AUTHORITY FROM GOD DIRECTS US HOW TO GLORIFY AND ENJOY HIM?

A. ⚘ *The only authority for glorifying and enjoying Him is the Bible, which is the word of God and is made up of the Old and New Testaments.*

MONDAY

Our primary purpose is to glorify God and to enjoy Him. But how do we do that? Where can we find out how to do it? The only One who really knows how to glorify God is God Himself. He is the only One who can tell us how to glorify Him.

God could have spoken to us any way He chose. He has chosen to speak to us through His Word, the Bible. Everything we need to know about God in order to glorify and enjoy Him is found in its pages. If we were to ask someone how to glorify God or if we were to look it up in a book other than the Bible, we could not be sure we were getting right information. But we can trust the Bible because it is the Word of God, who is never wrong. **Read 2 Timothy 3:16–17.**

TUESDAY

The Bible is a wonderful book. Inside it are letters people wrote to friends, songs, stories, and poetry. There are laws and sermons and predictions (hundreds of these predictions have already come true). Many different people wrote the Bible, including kings, fishermen, a farmer, and a doctor. All these people wrote what God wanted them to write because the Holy Spirit directed them. **Read 2 Peter 1:20–21.**

WEDNESDAY

God first gave His Word in written form to the Israelites. They were on their way from Egypt, where they had been slaves, to the land God had promised them. God met them on Mount Sinai. He wrote the Ten Commandments on two pieces of rock and gave them to Moses. He also gave Moses many other laws and teachings that Moses wrote down. Even though this was only a small portion of the Bible compared to what we have now, the Israelites were aware of what a wonderful privilege it was to have God's Word to read and to keep. **Read Deuteronomy 4:5–8.**

God is so much greater than we are that we could never discover Him by ourselves. He had to tell us what He is like and how to glorify Him or we would never know. God is good! He gave us His Word in the Bible so we could know and please Him. **Read Deuteronomy 29:29.**

THURSDAY

Many things that we have are important, but we could do without them if we had to. God's Word is so important that we could never do without it. Without God's Word, we could only imagine what God is like and we would certainly be wrong. Without God's Word we would have to guess about how to live wisely and how to know right from wrong—and each person's guess would be different from every other person's! Of all God's good gifts to us, the Bible is one of the very best. Ask God to give you a thankful heart that appreciates the value of His Word. **Read Psalm 119:97–105.**

FRIDAY

The Bible is the only authority on how to glorify and enjoy God. That means the Bible has the final word; it is always right. If a person or a book ever disagrees with what the Bible says, it is the person or the book that is wrong. The Bible is always right. That is because it is from God who is never wrong and never makes a mistake. The apostle Paul wrote that if someone were to teach something other than what the Bible teaches—even if that someone were an angel from heaven—he was to be accursed! **Read Galatians 1:8.** That is how important it is to reverence God's Word as higher and more important than anything else.

God commands people not to tamper with His Word. They are not to add anything to it, nor are they to take anything away from it. **Read Deuteronomy 4:2.** God becomes very angry with those who say something is God's Word when it is really just their own teaching or opinion. **Read Jeremiah 23:31–32.**

SATURDAY

Even though God commands people not to do it, people *do* add to God's Word and they *do* take away from it. People do say "God says" and go on to say something that God does not say at all! Sometimes, even preachers will say things about God that are not true. It is very important to make sure that what people say is in the Bible really is in the Bible. In New Testament times, people in the city of Berea checked everything the apostle Paul said to see if it agreed with the Scriptures. **Read Acts 17:10–11.**

Since the Bible is God's Word, we should value it very highly. We are never to argue with it. Rather, we must study to know it as well as we can, respect it, and obey what it says. **Read 1 Thessalonians 2:13.**

Q.3. WHAT DOES THE BIBLE PRIMARILY TEACH?

A. ❧ *The Bible primarily teaches what man must believe about God and what God requires of man.*

MONDAY

Imagine an artist who has worked secretly for months on what is to be his greatest masterpiece. Everyone is anxious to see what he has done. Finally the day comes when the artist plans to show his painting. A crowd gathers in a room where the painting sits, covered with drapes. At the right moment, a man opens the drapes and everyone sees the painting. What was hidden has been revealed.

To reveal something is to make known what was hidden before. The Bible reveals what God is like and what He requires of man. **Read 1 Corinthians 2:7–12.** What does verse 7 say was hidden? In verse 11, who is the only One who knows the thoughts of God? Look in verse 10 to see how we come to know the thoughts of God and His hidden wisdom.

TUESDAY

Read Job 11:7 and Romans 11:33. God had to reveal Himself to us if we were ever to know what He is like. God is so much greater than we are that we would never find out about Him on our own. He is more wonderful than anything we could imagine. Left to ourselves, we would never know God. The knowledge of him would have remained hidden forever. God is loving and good. He wanted us to know Him so we could love and enjoy Him. So God gave us the Bible to tell us all those things about Him that we would never have known otherwise.

One of the most important reasons for knowing what the Bible says is so we will believe what is true about God. Many people—even

Christians—believe ideas about God that are not at all correct. The only way to be sure that what we believe about God is true is to be sure that all we believe about God comes from the Bible alone.

WEDNESDAY

God gave us His Word in bits and pieces over hundreds of years. We call the very first part of God's Word the Books of the Law. In these first five books, God reveals something of what He is like, and gives laws concerning how He wants people to act. There are so many laws in the first part of the Bible and those laws are so hard to keep that none of us could ever obey them all—not even for one day. This is because we are sinful on the inside—we naturally want to do things our way instead of God's way. God knew when He gave His law that we are sinners and could never keep it. So why did He give it?

All along God had planned to give His Son to save His people from sin. But He knew His people would not believe they needed a Savior unless they understood how sinful they are. By giving us His perfect and holy law, He showed us that it is impossible for us to be pleasing to Him by ourselves. **Read Romans 7:7.** How did Paul know he was wrong for coveting? **Read Galatians 3:22.** What does this verse say that the Scriptures tell us about all men? The verse also gives a reason for Scripture telling us that. What is the reason?

THURSDAY

The Bible tells us what God is like. The main way in which it does this is by showing us who Jesus Christ, the Son of God, is and what He has done for His people. Many different men wrote the Bible over hundreds of years. Since God gave them what they should write, they all wrote about the same all-important truth: God provides salvation for His people through His Son. This is the one story of the whole Bible. The Old Testament looks ahead to the Savior who was coming; the New Testament looks back to the Savior who came. **Read 2 Timothy 3:15.** This verse says the Scriptures can make you wise. What does that wisdom lead to? **Read John 5:39.** Jesus is speaking in this verse. What does He say the Scriptures bear witness of (or testify about or tell about)?

John is one of the men God used to write the Bible. **Read John 20:31** to see why he wrote what he wrote.

FRIDAY

First, the Bible shows us what we are to believe about God. Then it shows us what He requires of us and helps us see that we could never do what He requires; we need a Savior! Scripture shows us who that Savior is (Jesus), what He has done to save us, and what God requires of us (that we believe in Jesus). Finally, God shows His people who have believed in Jesus what He requires of them—not to be saved, but to show how thankful they are for being saved. Once we have believed in Jesus, we are afraid to do what would displease Him because we love Him so much. Getting to know the Bible and how it tells us to live is the best way to be sure that we are living in a way that is pleasing to Jesus. **Read Psalm 119:9, 11.**

SATURDAY

Read Matthew 7:24–27. Who is like a man building on a rock? Who is like a man building on sand? To learn what God's Word says without *doing* what it says is foolish.

If we know and love Jesus, we will want to do what He wants us to do. To know what He wants us to do and how to do it we need to know the Bible. It will give us all we will ever need for knowing who God is and what He requires of us. **Read 2 Timothy 3:16–17.**

Q.4. WHAT IS GOD?

A. *God is a spirit, Whose being, wisdom, power, holiness, justice, goodness, and truth are infinite, eternal, and unchangeable.*

MONDAY

Read John 4:24. What is God? **Read 1 Timothy 1:17.** Can God be seen?

God is a spirit. He has no body and He cannot be seen. God is different from everyone and everything else in the universe. For one thing, God alone was never created. God created every person and every thing that has ever existed. Only God has always been. He is eternal. That means He has no beginning and He has no end. **Read Psalm 102:24b–27.**

God is also infinite. Infinite means having no limits. People are finite; they have limits. People can do many things, but there is a limit to what they can do. God can do anything; His power is infinite. People are limited to being in one place at a time. God is infinite; He is in all places at the same time. When King Solomon built a magnificent temple for God, he knew that a building cannot hold all there is of God, so he prayed this prayer. **Read 1 Kings 8:27.**

God is unchangeable. He cannot become better than He is because He is already perfect. He cannot become worse or less than He is or He would stop being God. **Read Malachi 3:6.**

God is infinite, eternal, and unchangeable. Everything about Him—His love, His holiness, His power, everything—is infinite, eternal, and unchangeable as well.

TUESDAY

Read Romans 11:33 and Psalm 147:5. What does Psalm 147:5 say about God's understanding? Infinite means having no limits.

God's wisdom is infinite. Wisdom is knowing and doing what is best in every situation. Because God knows all things, He always knows what is best and that is what He does. Because God's wisdom is infinite, we can trust what He tells us. We can do what He tells us to do, confident that it is the wisest thing we could possibly do.

Since God's wisdom is infinite, eternal, and unchangeable, we know that the Bible, which is His Word, is truth. Everything it says is absolutely true. **Read Psalm 19:7–9.**

WEDNESDAY

Read Isaiah 40:25–26. Why are none of the stars missing? What keeps them from falling out of the sky?

God's infinite power keeps all of creation going. His power is eternal—it has always been, and it will never run out or become weaker. God's power is unchanging. Having all power, He will never become any stronger than He is. His power is infinite—nothing can limit it. **Read Jeremiah 32:17.** What does this verse say is too difficult for God? **Read Daniel 4:35.** According to this verse, who can stop God from doing what He intends to do?

THURSDAY

The prophet Isaiah saw a vision of heaven. Around God's throne, he saw seraphim or angels who praise God all the time. **Read Isaiah 6:3** to find a word the angels repeat three times to describe God. **Read Revelation 15:4.** Why will all people fear the Lord and glorify His name?

God is absolutely holy. He never thinks, speaks, or does anything that is evil. All that God is and does is good, right, and perfect. **Read 1 John 1:5.** Not only does God never sin Himself, He also hates sin in any of His creatures. The word "holy" is used of God more times than any other word in the Bible. God is eternal, infinite, and unchangeable in His holiness.

FRIDAY

There would be something very wrong with a police officer who saw a robbery taking place and ignored it. There would be something very wrong with a judge who let murderers go free. God would not be God if He ignored sin. God hates sin and will always punish it. Right now, we see many horrible things all around us. Every day the news is full of stories of people doing terrible things to other people and sinning against God. Sometimes news of crime and hatred can trouble us. But **Psalm 96:11–13** gives us a reason to rejoice. What is it?

The Bible assures us that God is a God of justice. He will not allow evil to go on forever. When Jesus comes again, all evildoers, those who have already died as well as those who are alive, will be judged and will receive what their wicked deeds deserve. **Read 2 Peter 2:9.**

God's justice is infinite, eternal, and unchangeable. Even the best human police officers and judges sometimes make mistakes because they are unable to see everything that happens and there are secrets they cannot know. God sees everything and knows all secrets. He can even judge what we are thinking and feeling when we do something, because He can see into our hearts.

SATURDAY

If God is holy and hates sin and if He will judge and punish all sin, we have a serious problem. Every one of us sins every day. None of us wants to face God's judgment and punishment.

But God is also infinite, eternal, and unchangeable in His goodness. That does not mean simply that God is nice. Because of God's goodness, He is always at work to do wonderful things for the good of His people, even though they are sinners and do not deserve it. **Read Psalm 86:5.** God's goodness makes Him willing to forgive. He is holy and cannot ignore our sin, but because of His infinite goodness, He gave His Son to be punished in our place. All who believe in Jesus are protected from God's justice and will have His blessing instead. **Read Psalm 34:8.**

Praise the LORD!
Oh give thanks to the LORD, for He is good;
For His lovingkindness is everlasting. (Ps. 106:1)

Q.5. IS THERE MORE THAN ONE GOD?

A. ⁓ *There is only one, the true and living God.*

MONDAY

Read Deuteronomy 6:4. When the first people were created, they knew that there was only one God. But the first people sinned and passed that sin on to their children so that everyone since is born with a sinful heart. Because people are sinful they do not want to believe that there is a holy God who requires them to live a certain way. So, early in history, people began to make up their own gods who would be less holy and easier to live with than the one true God. Nonetheless, there is only one God and no one is like Him. **Read Isaiah 45:18, 22.**

TUESDAY

Throughout history, people have worshiped the things God made instead of worshiping God. Often, people would make little statues from gold or silver or wood to represent the god they worshiped. These statues were called idols. In Old Testament times, almost everyone in the world worshiped idols. God had set apart the nation of Israel as His own special people who were to worship Him and were never to worship idols. Psalm 115 compares the God of Israel to the idols of the neighboring nations. **Read Psalm 115:1–8.** Name the things this psalm says that idols *cannot* do. What does verse 3 say that God *can* do?

WEDNESDAY

God had called the Israelites to be His special people. He had commanded them to build the Tabernacle where they were to come to worship Him. Inside the Tabernacle was the Ark of the Covenant, a box in which were placed the Ten Commandments. Sometimes God had commanded the Israelites to carry the Ark of the Covenant with them into battle, as a reminder that God was with them. One time the Israelites were beaten by their enemies, the Philistines. The reason was that they were living very wickedly, refusing to obey God. When the Philistines defeated them, the Israelites should have turned from their wicked ways. Instead, they decided that they would win the next battle if they took the Ark of the Covenant along with them.

They went to fight the Philistines again, this time carrying the Ark of the Covenant into battle. God was still not with them, though, because of their disobedience to Him. The Philistines defeated the Israelites again and captured the Ark of the Covenant. The Philistines were thrilled! They thought this proved that their idol Dagon was more powerful than the God of Israel! They took the Ark of the Covenant to Ashdod, one of their cities, and put it in the temple of Dagon, like a trophy to Dagon's greatness. **Read 1 Samuel 5:2–5** to see what happened.

THURSDAY

The Israelites did not always faithfully worship only the one true God. All the nations around them had many gods and they often became like their neighbors. When Ahab was king of Israel, he and his wife Jezebel worshiped an idol called Baal and caused the rest of Israel to worship him too. Many people continued to worship God, but they worshiped Baal along with Him.

Elijah, a prophet of the true God, challenged the prophets of Baal to a contest. (There were 450 of them and only one of him!) Elijah gathered the Israelites and Baal's prophets. He proposed that both he and the prophets of Baal each build an altar and prepare a sacrifice on it. Neither of them could set their sacrifices on fire, however. They would pray to their God and whichever God answered by sending fire from heaven to burn up the sacrifice would be recognized as the true God.

Baal's prophets began. **Read 1 Kings 18:26–29** to see what they did. How long did Baal's prophets work at getting Baal to answer? What was the result?

Then it was Elijah's turn. He dug a ditch around his altar and ordered that four large pitchers of water be poured all over his offering and the wood. He had this done two more times until water was flowing off the altar and had filled the ditch. Then he prayed. **Read 1 Kings 18:37–39** to see what happened.

FRIDAY

Like Elijah, Jeremiah was a prophet of the one true and living God. Like Elijah, he spoke out against Israel's worship of idols. In Jeremiah 10, Jeremiah describes how people make idols. Someone cuts down a tree and carves an idol from it, then decorates the idol with gold and silver. **Read Jeremiah 10:5.** What does it say about idols? **Now read verses 6–7, 10.** List all the things it says about God. **Read verse 11.** What will happen to idols?

SATURDAY

Is idolatry—the worship of idols—a thing of the past? **Read Colossians 3:5.** What is called idolatry in this verse? When people want more and more money and more and more things, they are being greedy. Greed is a form of idolatry for two reasons. First, it makes money and things most important, when really God is most important. Second, greedy people are trusting in their money and their things to meet their needs when really only God can meet our needs. Do you think many people in our society are idol-worshipers? **Read 1 Thessalonians 1:9,** where Paul describes what happens when people become Christians.

Q.6.

HOW MANY PERSONS ARE IN THE ONE GOD?

A. ✒ *Three persons are in the one God, the Father, the Son, and the Holy Spirit. These three are one God, the same in substance and equal in power and glory.*

MONDAY

Question 5 tells us that there is only one God. Yet we know from Scripture that the Father is God, Jesus is God, and the Holy Spirit is God. Doesn't that sound like three Gods? This week's question and answer tell us that there is only one God, but that God is in three persons. This is one way in which God is different from human beings. A human being is one human being and one person. There is one of you and you are only one person. There is one God, but He is three persons.

Do you find that hard to understand? You are not alone! The wisest Christians and the best Bible students of the church have never been able to fully understand how God can be one God in three persons. Remember that God is infinite. He has no limits. Human minds are finite and limited. We can only go so far with our limited minds in understanding the limitless God. **Read Job 11:7–8.** Over and over again, the Bible insists that there is only one God. At the same time, the Bible tells us that there are three persons—Father, Son, and Holy Spirit—each of whom is God. We must believe what Scripture requires us to believe, even when we cannot fully understand it.

TUESDAY

The first of the three persons who are God is God the Father. He is Father to Jesus, who is God the Son, and He sends the Holy Spirit to His people. **Read 1 Corinthians 8:6a.** It was the Father's purpose to create all things for His glory (although the Son and the Spirit were involved in creating too). It was also God the Father who planned to save His people from sin by providing a Savior, His own Son, to die in their place. **Read 1 John 4:14.**

WEDNESDAY

The second of the three persons who are God is God the Son or Jesus. God the Son has always been alive. When He was born as a human baby in the stable, He was taking on a human nature too. He was not beginning His life though. He had always been alive as God. Because the Son was born as a human being, we can see what the invisible God is like. (Those of us who were not alive when He was on earth can read about Him in the Bible and see what God is like in that way.) **Read Colossians 1:15–16** to see what God the Son, or Jesus, created. Yesterday we saw that God the Father planned to save His people from their sin, or reconcile them to Himself (make peace with them). God reconciles His people to Himself through His Son, Jesus. **Read Colossians 1:19–20.**

THURSDAY

The Holy Spirit is the third of the three persons who are God. He is sent by the Father and the Son. The Holy Spirit was also involved in creating and He is the One who inspired the writing of the Bible. (That means that He so directed the men who wrote that what they wrote was the Word of God.) The Holy Spirit is very active in God's work of saving His people. He is the One who causes a person to be born again so that he or she is able to believe in Jesus. **Read John 3:3–5.** The Holy Spirit lives inside His people and causes them to grow more and more like Jesus. **Read Galatians 5:22–23.**

FRIDAY

What does "same in substance" mean? Down through the years, people have given different explanations of the three persons who are God. Some have said that only the Father is God and that Jesus, while very special, is not God in the same way that the Father is. "Same in substance" means that each of the three persons is fully

God. Jesus, the Son, is just as much God as the Father is. The Holy Spirit is as fully God as the Father and the Son are. Father, Son, and Holy Spirit are equal in power and glory. One is not stronger or more worthy of worship than the other two. We worship Father, Son, and Holy Spirit as God.

The Bible tells us that the Father is God and that we are to give Him worship. **Read Ephesians 4:6 and John 4:23.**

SATURDAY

Jesus, the Son of God, is fully God. All glory and power are His and He deserves our worship. **Read Matthew 1:23 and Psalm 2:10–12.**

The Holy Spirit is also fully God, deserving worship and praise. **Read 2 Corinthians 3:17–18.**

Q.7.

WHAT ARE THE DECREES OF GOD?

A. ✍ *The decrees of God are His eternal plan based on the purpose of His will, by which, for His own glory, He has foreordained everything that happens.*

MONDAY

God had a purpose for everything He made. He has a purpose for everything that happens: God's purpose is to glorify Himself. Before He began to create, God planned how every single thing He would create would fit together and how all of it together would bring Him glory. To be certain that everything would happen just as He had planned it, He foreordained, or gave orders in advance, for everything that would ever happen. We call these orders God's decrees.

Read Psalm 33:11. We often make plans and have to change them. We might plan a picnic, then have to change our plans because of rain. When we made our plans we did not know it would rain and rain is outside our control. God never changes His plans. Nothing surprises God because He knows everything. Nothing is outside His control because He is all-powerful. God's plan is eternal. It is based on His purpose, which never changes.

TUESDAY

God's purpose for all He has made and for everything that happens is to make His glory known. By doing things that demonstrate how wonderful He is, God makes His glory known. God tells us His purpose in **Habakkuk 2:14.** God makes a similar promise in **Isaiah 40:5.**

What did you learn in the first catechism question? What is man's primary purpose? Man is not the only creature whose purpose is to glorify God. God created all things for the purpose of making His glory known.

WEDNESDAY

The purpose of all of creation is to give glory to God. The heavens, with all the stars and galaxies, give glory to God. **Read Psalm 19:1.** God created His people for His own glory. **Read Isaiah 43:7.** God's people are to give Him glory and to declare His glory among the nations. **Read Psalm 96:3, 8.**

THURSDAY

A decree is an order issued by a king that everyone in his kingdom must obey. God is the King of the universe. His decrees control everyone and everything in it. Even God's enemies carry out His purposes, though they do not mean to.

God created or decreed the creation of all things. **Read Psalm 148:1–12.** God decreed that His Son would be the Ruler of all things. **Read Psalm 2:6–8.** God orders the things that take place in people's lives by His decrees as well. King Nebuchadnezzar lost his mind for seven years. **Read Daniel 4:24** to see why this happened.

FRIDAY

God foreordains—plans and orders in advance—everything that happens. Nothing happens unless God has decreed it. Even the things that seem to be contrary to God's purposes—sad things and bad things—still fit into His plan. **Read Isaiah 45:6–7.**

God foreordains what people will be and do. **Read Jeremiah 1:5.** God foreordains that His people will believe in Jesus. **Read Acts 13:48.** All things happen because God has foreordained them to happen so His purposes will be accomplished.

SATURDAY

Read Isaiah 46:9–10. Some people think that God looks ahead into the future, sees what is going to happen, and then makes His plans around it. The Bible teaches that God does not just *know* what is going to happen; He is the One who *causes* it to happen. Scripture is full of prophecies. Many of them have already come true in every detail. The reason God can tell His prophets exactly what will happen in the future is because He will make it happen. Whatever God has decreed to happen will happen, and nothing can prevent it from happening.

Sometimes we say that certain things will happen, like "our team's going to win" or "I will never do that again!" What we say may or may not happen. God's Word has the power to actually *cause* things to happen every time He speaks. **Read Isaiah 55:10–11.**

Q.8.

HOW DOES GOD CARRY OUT HIS DECREES?

A. ⚘ *God carries out His decrees in creation and providence.*

MONDAY

God always works to carry out His eternal plan and to cause all things to happen exactly as He has foreordained that they will. God carries out His decrees in two ways. He carries out His decrees in creation. He created all that is so that it would work exactly as He wanted it to. God also carries out His decrees in providence. He works out all the events, big and small, of everyday life so that they accomplish His purposes. We call these two ways "creation" (God's creation of all things) and "providence" (God working out all the details of all of life according to His will). **Read Psalm 135:5–6.** What does the Lord do? Where does He do this? **Read Daniel 4:35.** With what two kinds of creatures does God do whatever He pleases? Who can stop Him?

TUESDAY

What happens when you drop something? It falls. Always. What happens to water when it is at freezing temperatures? It hardens into ice. Always. The stars follow the same paths across the sky year after year; summer follows spring and spring follows winter every year; every day the sun rises and sets. All these things do what they do because God has decreed that they are to do them. The ordinary, everyday things of nature that are so familiar to us are the working out of God's decrees. What we call the "laws of nature" are really the decrees of God.

The reason scientists can do science is that the universe is so dependable. We can count on certain things to always happen under certain circumstances because that is what God has decreed. He built these laws into His universe when He created it and all of His creation obeys Him. (However, whenever God wants to, He can cause nature to do things it does not usually do. This is what we call a miracle.) **Read Psalm 104:5–9.**

WEDNESDAY

Read Psalm 104:10–30 and answer these questions. Where does the water come from that the wild animals drink? (vv. 10–11) How do mountain plants get the water they need? (v. 13) Wild animals hunt in the nighttime. What would happen if darkness did not come? Why does darkness come? (v. 20) Where do lions get their food? (v. 21) All creatures depend on God for each breath they take! When God does not give a creature breath, what happens to it? (v. 29) All these things in nature—and many more as well—are examples of God carrying out His decrees in creation.

THURSDAY

When we study science, we study God's decrees in creation. When we study history, we study God's decrees in providence. From the very first moment of time, God has been at work to carry out His decrees and to accomplish His purposes through every event that happens. God created all the different nationalities of people—Polish people, Germans, Africans, Jews. Any time in history when one nation grew powerful, it was because God had decreed that nation would be powerful. It remained powerful exactly as long as God had decreed it should be powerful, and then another nation rose to power.

God chose where on earth each nation would be located and established the natural boundaries—mountains, oceans and rivers—that kept them there. **Read Daniel 2:21a and Acts 17:26.** Some people have said about God that all of history is "His story." How incredibly wise God is to plan every detail in all of history to accomplish His purposes. How powerful God is to be able to cause everything to happen just as He has planned!

FRIDAY

It is amazing to think of how many different things God works out according to His plan. God works out every detail in the life of each individual person. Not only that, He is also causing all of those details to accomplish His plans for whole nations as well. In all of it, God is causing things to work together for the good of His people.

Joseph's jealous, hateful brothers sold him as a slave. He was taken far away to Egypt. Joseph had some difficult times in Egypt but everywhere he went, God caused people to like him and to give him positions of honor. Finally, Joseph was the second highest ruler in Egypt. God foreordained each detail of Joseph's life for his good. While Joseph was a ruler in Egypt, he stored great amounts of food in preparation for a famine. When the famine came, there was food in Egypt because Joseph had stored it. Joseph's own family—the first Israelites—came to live in Egypt during the famine. In this way, they survived the famine.

God had foreordained each detail of this story for the good of the nation Israel. Israel was the nation from which Jesus the Savior would come. That is why it was so important that these first Israelites survive the famine. God foreordained each detail of this story for the good of His people and for His own glory. **Read in Genesis 50:20** what Joseph said to his brothers who had sold him as a slave. **Then read Romans 8:28.**

SATURDAY

It can be difficult to believe that God is working out His decrees. This is true when very sad things happen to people or when we see evildoers getting away with evil actions. Jesus' disciples certainly felt that way when Jesus was crucified. The disciples were certain that God had sent Jesus to be the Messiah He had promised. But jealous Jewish leaders arrested Him, lied about Him, said He was guilty, and had Him sentenced to death. The disciples must have thought that surely God would do something! He would not let His Messiah be killed. Yet, after cruelly torturing Him, the soldiers crucified Jesus. He died and He was buried.

The disciples felt hopeless. God's Messiah was dead; God could not accomplish His purpose. What they did not understand was that God had planned all along that Jesus would be killed as a sacrifice for the sins of His people. God used even the most wicked plans and actions of His enemies to carry out His decrees. The disciples understood this after Jesus rose from the dead. **Read** what they prayed to God in **Acts 4:27–28.**

Q.9. WHAT IS CREATION?

A. ✎ *Creation is God's making everything out of nothing by His powerful word in six days—and all very good.*

MONDAY

Because God made people in His image, people can create. Other creatures make things, but only human beings create. Bees make hives and birds make nests, but birds and bees can only make what their instincts tell them to make. Human beings can create all kinds of things—buildings and music, stories and inventions, furniture and clothing. What people create is far better than what animals make by instinct. But God's creation is much more wonderful than anything man makes because God creates from nothing. If you were going to create a painting, you would need paints and paper or a canvas. If you wanted to create a beautiful sweater, you would need knitting needles and yarn. When God created, He created all that is *out of nothing*. No one else can create something from nothing. Only God can do that. **Read Hebrews 11:3 and Revelation 4:11.**

TUESDAY

How did God make everything out of nothing? By His word or by His command. He only had to speak and things came into being. All through the creation story we read the words "And God said." "And God said, 'Let there be light.'" "And God said, 'Let there be lights in the expanse of the sky.'" "And God said, 'Let the land produce living creatures'" (Gen. 1:3, 14, 24 NIV). After the commands of God, we read, "And it was so." Each time God spoke, something new was created.

God is amazing! Not only can He create something out of nothing, He does not have to work at creating at all—He only has to speak. That is why the answer to this week's question calls God's Word "powerful." When God wants something to happen, His Word alone is enough to make it happen. **Read Psalm 33:6–9.**

WEDNESDAY

God made all that He made in six days. Write the numbers 1 through 6 on a piece of paper and see if you can write (in order) what God made on each of the six days of creation. (No peeking at answers!) **Then read Genesis 1:1–27** and see how close you were to being right.

THURSDAY

Look at Genesis 1:1–24 again. How many times do you find the sentence, "And God saw that it was good"? After He had created each different kind of creature, God saw that it was good. After He had completely finished making everything, what did He think of it all? **Read the answer in Genesis 1:31.** The world we see around us is no longer the way God made it. God made everything good, but now we see things around us that are not good—things like pain and evil and sadness and death. God did not create these; they entered the world when the first human beings chose to sin.

We still see much of the beauty and the good left over from God's creation, but when He first created, it was better and more beautiful than it is now. Things are not ruined for God's creation though. Sin did not take God by surprise. He has promised to destroy evil someday and to undo all the ugly things sin brought into the world. God will do this when Jesus comes back for His people. Everything will be perfect and good again and there will be no more sadness or sin.

FRIDAY

Why is a day always twenty-four hours long? Why does the sun come up every day? Why do the leaves fall off the trees every autumn and new ones grow every spring? Because God has decreed that these things should happen. How good it was of God to order everything so that it would all be so dependable. Farmers know when to plant seeds so that their crops will grow at the best time. God's decrees in creation show us how faithful He is to care for His creatures. His faithfulness continues, century after century. The "laws of nature" that obeyed God when your great-grandfather was a child still obey God today. **Read Psalm 119:89–91.**

SATURDAY

Read Psalm 147 and answer these questions.

What does God call by name (v. 4)?

What does God give (v. 8)?

What does He provide for birds and animals (v. 9)?

Verses 16 and 17 talk about the snow, ice, and hail. What causes those things (v. 15)? What melts them (v. 18)? All these are God's decrees in creation.

Q.10. HOW DID GOD CREATE MAN?

A. ❧ *God created man, male and female, in His own image and in knowledge, righteousness, and holiness, to rule over the other creatures.*

MONDAY

God created people last. He had created the universe, made a beautiful world, and filled it with birds, animals, and fish. Then God made man. Was it because He was lonely and wanted someone who could love Him back? Absolutely not! God has all He needs in Himself. He does not need anyone or anything to make Him any happier or any more satisfied than He already is. All through eternity, before anything else existed, God the Father, God the Son, and God the Holy Spirit shared perfect love among themselves. God is never lonely. He chose to create man for the same reason that He chose to create everything else—for His own glory. **Read Psalm 100:1–3.**

TUESDAY

Do you remember what God said about each thing that He created? "It is good." **Read Genesis 2:18.** What did God say was *not* good? God did not intend for people to live alone. He wants people to live together in loving relationships. Men need women and women need men. Adam and Eve, the first husband and wife, were the first family. God's purpose is for new human beings to be born into families where they will learn how to love and get along with other people. God also planned for children to learn about God in their families. Families are gifts from God that show His wisdom and His goodness. **Read the first line of Psalm 68:6.**

WEDNESDAY

God created human beings different from all other creatures. **Read Genesis 1:27** to see how man is different. What does it mean to be created in the image of God? **Read Genesis 5:1** to see another way of saying it. To be created in God's image is to be like God in ways that other creatures are not. Of course, no one and nothing are *really* like God. God is infinite (having no limits) and everything else is finite (limited). God created all that is, while He alone was never created. But God made people so that, in some ways, they show a little bit of what God is like. People can communicate what they think and feel to others. They can think of creative things to make and do. They can plan ahead. God created man as the highest and best of all His creatures. What a privilege it is to be made in the image or likeness of God!

THURSDAY

One way people show the image of God is in their ability to gain knowledge. Fish, birds, and animals act by instinct. God has built into each of these creatures wonderful orders that tell them how to do what they need to do to survive. Beavers know to build dams to make places to live in the water. Birds know to migrate hundreds of miles to warmer places every year. But animals and birds do not choose to do these things after thinking and planning. They do them by instinct.

Man alone is different. He can think and know things. Man can learn and keep adding more knowledge to the knowledge he already has. God created us with the ability to know and learn so that we could know Him. No animal can know God. Since sin came into the world, people have used their ability to know for many wrong purposes. Some people want to have a lot of knowledge just so they can be smarter than other people. Other people want to gain knowledge that will make them rich. People even use their ability to learn for learning to do evil. **Read Jeremiah 9:23–24** to find the best way to use our ability to know.

FRIDAY

There is another way in which people bear the image of God. They have the ability to choose between right and wrong. God did not give that ability to other creatures. Animals that kill or that take things from other animals are acting by instinct. They have no sense of right or wrong. Human beings are like God in that they know and choose between right and wrong. All people are sinful on the inside. That causes them to choose to do wrong, to choose their way instead of God's way.

God did not make the first people like that. He made them righteous and holy with nothing evil in them at all. God gave them the ability to choose between right and wrong, though, and Adam and Eve chose to do wrong. This made them sinful on the inside. They passed that sinfulness on to all humans born after them. Because people know the difference between good and evil, they are better than all the other creatures on earth. They are also responsible for what they do. God will not judge animals that act selfishly or that hurt other animals. He will judge people for choosing to do what they know is wrong. **Read Ecclesiastes 7:29.**

SATURDAY

When God created man, He gave him two commands. The first was to increase and fill the earth with people. What was the second command? **Find it in Genesis 1:28.** The earth and everything in it belong to God, but He has given it to mankind to use to meet his needs. Because the earth and everything in it are the Lord's, we should glorify God in how we use it. We should not be selfish or greedy or wasteful with what God has made.

People today are concerned about how we use creation. They worry about water and air pollution. They are concerned about using up the things God has made for us. We should use God's gifts wisely. We also need to remember that God gave the right to rule over creation to man. People who say that man is just one more part of creation, no more important than bugs, are wrong. For instance, some people may be concerned about killing baby whales or baby dolphins, but they see nothing wrong with abortion, the killing of unborn human babies. What *is* the difference between a human baby and a whale baby? **Read Psalm 8.**

Q.11. WHAT IS GOD'S PROVIDENCE?

A. ✒ *God's providence is His completely holy, wise, and powerful preserving and governing every creature and every action.*

MONDAY

God plans everything that happens in advance. Then He causes everything to happen just as He planned. We call this providence. God is holy. Every plan He forms, as well as the way in which He carries it out, is completely holy. God is perfectly wise. He never makes a mistake in what He plans or does, but always chooses the very best. God is powerful. Since all power belongs to Him, nothing can keep Him from doing exactly as He has planned.

All of history tells of God's providence. Every story in every history book tells of God, even when it never mentions His name. He is the One who caused every event in history to work out just the way it did. **Read** these examples of large and small things decided by God: **Proverbs 16:9, 33 and Proverbs 21:1.** Esther is a history book in the Bible that never mentions God's name. All through the book of Esther, we clearly see God's providence.

TUESDAY

The book of Esther gets its name from Queen Esther. It tells the story of a wicked plot to kill all the Jews. Remember that God had promised to send the Messiah to save His people from sin. God had said that the Messiah would be one of Abraham's descendants, or a Jew. If all the Jews were killed, God's Messiah could not come from the Jewish nation and God could not keep His promise. The book of Esther tells how God kept this wicked plot from being carried out, protected His people, and punished His enemies. Esther tells the story of God's providence.

The story begins when the king of Persia, the ruling power of that time, needed a new queen. The king held a giant beauty contest to find a queen. **Read Esther 2:5–7.** What was Esther's nationality? Who made her so beautiful? **Read Esther 2:17–18.** Who caused the king to care more for Esther than for all the other women?

WEDNESDAY

Esther had a cousin named Mordecai. One day two men were plotting to kill the king. **Read Esther 2:21–23** to find out what happened. How did it happen that Mordecai overheard the plot so he could warn the king through Esther? Pay attention to where the king recorded what Mordecai had done—it will be important later!

Haman was a very important man, second only to the king. Nonetheless, Mordecai would never bow when Haman walked by. This made Haman so angry that he hated Mordecai and wanted him killed. Not only that—when Haman learned that Mordecai was a Jew, he wanted all the Jews killed as well. Haman paid the king to issue an order saying that, on a certain day throughout the whole kingdom, people were to kill all the Jews.

THURSDAY

When the Jews learned about the king's order, that they were all to be killed, they mourned and wept. Esther had not heard about the king's order. She sent a message to Mordecai asking what was wrong. He sent a message back, telling about the king's order and begging her to go ask the king not to allow the Jews to be killed. **Read Esther 4:11** to learn how Esther answered.

Mordecai understood the providence of God. He knew that God would preserve the Jews so that He could accomplish His plan to send a Jewish Messiah. He also understood that nothing happens by accident. It was not an accident that Esther, a Jewish woman, was queen at just this dangerous moment in time. **Read** what Mordecai said to Esther in **4:13–14** and Esther's decision in **4:15–16.**

What happened when Esther went to see the king, without having been called? **Read Esther 5:1–3** to see. Why did the king welcome Esther? Do you remember the verse we read Monday that says

God turns the king's heart wherever He chooses (Prov. 21:1)? Esther invited the king and Haman to a banquet. When they came, she invited them to another banquet. It was at that second banquet that she would ask the king to save her people.

FRIDAY

Esther's invitations thrilled Haman! Only he and the king were invited. Haman bragged about it to everyone. "There's only one thing that ruins it all for me," Haman complained, "and that is that Jew, Mordecai! Every time I see him standing when he should be bowing to me, I get so angry!"

"Don't wait until all the Jews are killed to be rid of Mordecai," Haman's wife told him. "Build a gallows right now and ask the king, first thing in the morning, if you can hang Mordecai on it." Haman loved this idea. He had the gallows built and eagerly waited for morning. God not only saved Mordecai from hanging. He also had him honored and humbled His enemy, Haman. **Read Esther 6:1–12.**

SATURDAY

Read Esther 7 to learn almost-the-end of this story. The *very* end of the story is this. The king could not change his order about killing the Jews, but he made a new order allowing the Jews to defend themselves. God caused people throughout Persia to fear the Jews. On the day that the Jews would have been killed, they killed their enemies instead. Mordecai was honored and given Haman's high position.

The book of Esther gives us just one small example of God's providence. Ever since the world began, God has been faithfully at work to cause everything that happens to bring good to His people and glory to Himself.

WHAT DID GOD'S PROVIDENCE SPECIFICALLY DO FOR MAN WHOM HE CREATED?

A. ✑ *After the creation God made a covenant with man to give him life, if he perfectly obeyed; God told him not to eat from the tree of knowledge of good and evil or he would die.*

MONDAY

Because God created people, they belong to Him and He may deal with them however He chooses. In His grace, God has chosen to deal with people through covenants. A covenant is an agreement that promises certain benefits if certain conditions are met. When people make covenants, the covenant has to be exactly what both of them want before they agree on it. Then each person promises to do certain things for the other person. Both of them must keep their promises. If one of them fails to keep his or her part of the covenant, the other person is freed from keeping it.

When God makes a covenant with people, the covenant is not between two equal people. God is much greater than we are. He made us and we belong to Him. In the covenants God makes, He promises blessings to people and requires that they keep His commandments. As you read the Bible, you will find many times when God makes covenants with people. The first covenant God made was with Adam. **Read Psalm 103:17–19.**

TUESDAY

When God created the first man, He gave him everything he could possibly need and more. God made man in His image, with abilities to do many things no other creatures could do. God placed man in a perfect world, telling him he could use anything in it he liked. He held only one thing back from Adam: the Tree of the Knowledge of Good and Evil. God told Adam not to eat the fruit from this tree. God warned Adam that if he ate the fruit from this tree, he would die. This was God's first covenant with man. The requirement was that Adam obey God. He would die if he failed to obey; he would live if he obeyed. **Read Genesis 2:8–17.**

WEDNESDAY

Human beings are wonderful creatures—but they are only creatures. Man can do many things the other creatures cannot do, but he cannot live without God. He must remember that he depends on God for everything he has—including life itself. **Read Psalm 104:27–30.**

God's covenant with Adam required him to trust God's Word enough to obey it. God wanted Adam to trust Him completely. When God told Adam not to eat the fruit from the Tree of the Knowledge of Good and Evil or he would die, Adam should have trusted God enough to believe and obey Him.

THURSDAY

God's covenant required perfect obedience from man. Obeying most of the time would not meet God's requirements. When people talk about a good person, they usually mean someone is good when compared to others. When we call someone "a good girl," we do not mean that she is perfect; we mean that she behaves better than many other children. "A good man" is someone who does more good things than other people do, but we do not think he is perfect.

God's idea of "being good" is different from ours. God does not consider someone good unless he or she perfectly obeys all His commandments. That is because God is holy. He never does what is wrong and He hates all wrongdoing in His creatures. **Read Leviticus 19:2 and Deuteronomy 18:13.** God made man able to do good and then required that he do good—not sometimes, not most of the time, but all the time. If Adam disobeyed God one time and ate the forbidden fruit, he would die as God had warned.

FRIDAY

Read Genesis 2:7. The first man came to life when God breathed the breath of life into him. Physical life is a gift from God. The ability to breathe and walk and think and laugh is a wonderful gift from God. God not only gives physical life, He gives spiritual life as well. Spiritual life is the ability to be at one with God. Those who have spiritual life know they are God's friends, not God's enemies. To have a right relationship with God is to have spiritual life. **Read Proverbs 22:4 and Psalm 36:9.** God also gives eternal life, life that lasts forever and is perfectly happy and good. **Read John 17:3 and John 11:25–26.** In His first covenant with man, God promised all three kinds of life—physical, spiritual, and eternal—if Adam would obey God's commandment.

SATURDAY

Wages are what people earn for work that they do. **Read Romans 6:23.** To disobey God is to earn death. God warned Adam that if he disobeyed God's command and ate fruit from the Tree of the Knowledge of Good and Evil, he would surely die. Just as there are three kinds of life, there are also three kinds of death man would experience if Adam sinned.

If he sinned, his body would die—not at the very moment he ate the fruit, but beginning then. His body would start to age and weaken until, finally, he would die of old age or sickness. If Adam sinned, man would die spiritually. His sin would separate him from God and make him God's enemy because God hates sin. **Read Ephesians 2:1.** If Adam sinned, he would earn eternal death for man as well. Eternal death is being cut off from God and being punished in hell forever. **Read Revelation 21:8.**

God promised man he would live if he obeyed Him and warned him that he would die if he disobeyed. God also gave man everything he needed to make a right choice and obey.

Q.13.

DID OUR FIRST PARENTS REMAIN AS THEY WERE CREATED?

A. ✍ *Left to the freedom of their own wills, our first parents sinned against God and fell from their original condition.*

MONDAY

What a privilege God had given to man! He alone, of all the creatures, was made in the image of God. Only man could worship God and communicate with Him. Man alone could think, remember, and plan. Only he could make choices, instead of simply doing things from instinct. But with such a high privilege comes responsibility. God had given man the ability to choose. Man was to use that ability to choose to obey God. **Read Deuteronomy 10:12–13.**

TUESDAY

God had told Adam that if he ate from the Tree of the Knowledge of Good and Evil, he would die. God had created man and everything else. Surely Adam could trust what God said about His creation. God had given Adam every good thing to enjoy. Surely when He gave him a commandment, Adam could trust that it was for his own good.

Yet when Satan came and told Adam and Eve, "You won't die when you eat that fruit; you'll become like God!" they believed and obeyed *his* word instead of God's. Instead of bowing to God and fearing to disobey His Word, Adam and Eve tried to be their own gods. Many years later, Satan tempted Jesus to take care of Himself instead of trusting God. Jesus' answer showed that He believed and trusted God's Word. **Read it in Matthew 4:4.**

WEDNESDAY

When Adam and Eve sinned, they sinned against God. Sin is always against God. When we sin, it may seem that we are simply doing something we want to do. Yet if what we do breaks God's law, we sin against Him. It may seem that we are doing something against a person with whom we are angry. Yet if what we do breaks God's law, we sin against God. Whenever we sin, whether or not we are thinking of God at the time, our sin is a crime against Him. When we choose to sin, we are telling God that we do not care what He wants; what *we* want is more important to us. **Read Psalm 51:3–4.**

THURSDAY

"The Fall" is the name that we give to the first sin of the first human beings. We call it that because when Adam and Eve sinned, all mankind fell from being perfect and good into being sinful. God had given man the ability to create, but now man uses that ability to invent wicked things and ways to hurt people. When God made man, He made man able to love God and other people, but now man loves himself more than anyone else. Man has a mind, a gift from God setting him above the other creatures, but now man uses his mind to choose evil and plan ways to do it. Man alone was created able to know and worship God, but now man worships other things or says there is no God at all. **Read Psalm 14:1–3.**

FRIDAY

In Question 10, we learned that God created man in knowledge, righteousness, and holiness. God created man so he could know God and His will. Since the Fall, man can no longer know God on his own or understand spiritual truth. **Read 1 Corinthians 2:14.** Man was created righteous, able to do what pleases God. Since the Fall, even man's best deeds are not righteous in the eyes of God. **Read Isaiah 64:6.** God made man holy, so man could love God and want what is good. Because of the Fall, man has become God's enemy. Now he refuses to love God and chooses to love things and evil instead. **Read Romans 1:21–23, 25.**

SATURDAY

When God created man, God told him to rule over the other creatures. This was a high privilege and a great responsibility. Man would rule over creation, taking care of it and using it wisely for God's glory. Since the Fall, man wants to rule in evil ways. He rules over creation with greediness, wasting it instead of caring for it. Men selfishly try to rule over each other, even killing each other to get their own way. Since the Fall, man can no longer control even himself. **Read James 4:1–3.**

Man was created in the image of God, so he could know and love God, choose good, and rule all other creatures. Now man cannot know God and His truth. Man fights against God and chooses evil. He harms and kills by ruling for his own pleasure rather than for God's glory. How far man has fallen because of sin! How greatly do we need a Savior!

<table>
<tr><td>## Q.14.</td><td>WHAT IS SIN?</td></tr>
</table>

A. ✑ *Sin is disobeying or not conforming to God's law in any way.*

<table>
<tr><td>## Q.15.</td><td>BY WHAT SIN DID OUR FIRST PARENTS FALL FROM THEIR ORIGINAL CONDITION?</td></tr>
</table>

A. ✑ *Our first parents' sin was eating the forbidden fruit.*

MONDAY

God's perfect law gives us the rule for deciding what is right and what is wrong. God's law is absolute. That means it is the same at all times and in all places. Anytime someone disobeys one of God's laws, that person sins. A person may feel that circumstances were such that he or she just could not help breaking God's law; but it is still sin. **Read 1 John 3:4.** Not conforming to God's law means not agreeing with it and not obeying it.

There are two ways we sin. We sin when we do what God has told us *not* to do. We also sin when we fail to do what God has told us *to do.*

TUESDAY

Sin is doing what God has told us not to do. The answer to Question 14 says that sin is disobeying God's law *in any way.* That means that disobeying God's law even once is sin. God is holy and His law is holy and absolute (the same at all times and in all places). Even if we obeyed every other command God had ever given, and only disobeyed *one,* the Bible says we would be as guilty as if we had broken all of God's laws. **Read James 2:10–11.**

WEDNESDAY

Doing what God has commanded not to do is sin. We not only sin when we *do* what God has commanded us not to do. We sin when we *want to do* what God has told us not to do. When we love, or long for, or even wish we could try what God hates, we sin. When we think or when we plan sin without actually carrying it out, we are still sinning. **Read Matthew 5:21–22.**

THURSDAY

When we do *not* do what God has commanded us to do, we sin. We may fool ourselves into thinking that we are obedient to God when we do not break any specific law. However, when we fail to do what is *right,* we also sin. **Read James 4:17.** Sometimes we think we are holy and Christlike because we know God's will. To know God's will and not do it is no better than not knowing it at all.

FRIDAY

When someone asked Jesus what was the most important of all God's commandments, Jesus said that it is this one: *"Love God with all your heart, mind, soul, and strength."* Jesus said that the second most important commandment is *"Love your neighbor as yourself."* If we always loved God and others perfectly, we would never sin. If we always put God and others before ourselves, we would do no wrong. We would never break any of God's laws that way. But, of course, all of us put ourselves first, again and again, every day. So all of us sin over and over every day. **Read Romans 13:8–10.**

SATURDAY

The Bible says that doing wrong is sin. Failing to do right is also sin. God is perfectly holy. He never does anything wrong. He only does what is right. God requires the same of His creatures. Whenever people do not measure up to His requirements, they sin. The writers of the New Testament wrote in the Greek language. The Greek word our Bibles translate "sin" means "missing the mark." It was a term used for people who shot arrows with a bow. The word meant that you had missed the target. To not quite hit the target of God's perfect righteousness is to sin and fall short of His glory. **Read Romans 3:23.**

Q.16.

DID ALL MANKIND FALL IN ADAM'S FIRST DISOBEDIENCE?

A. *Since the covenant was made not only for Adam but also for his natural descendants, all mankind sinned in him and fell with him in his first disobedience.*

MONDAY

Adam was a real man like any man you might see on any day of the week. In several important ways, however, Adam was different from other men. For one thing, Adam was the only man who was never born and never grew up. God created him fully grown. For another thing, Adam was the very first human being. Every other human being came from Adam. Even Eve was made from one of his ribs. For at least a little bit of time, Adam was the only human being in the whole world.

One of the most important ways that Adam was different from other men was this: Adam was the representative of the whole human race that would come after him. A representative takes another person's place. Whatever a representative does, it is as though the people he represents had done it. For example, if two countries want to make a peace treaty, it would be impossible for all of the people living in both of the countries to get together for a meeting. So each country sends a representative to the meeting. Whatever the representative says, his country is saying. If the representative signs a peace treaty, his country has signed it.

Sometimes people choose their own representatives. Sometimes someone in authority chooses the representative for them. God chose Adam to represent all mankind. Because we know that God possesses all wisdom and all that He does is good, we know that this was the best possible choice. **Read Romans 11:33 and Psalm 145:17.**

TUESDAY

The answer to Question 12 says that God made a covenant (or an agreement) with man to give him life if he perfectly obeyed. If he disobeyed and ate the fruit God had told him not to eat, he would die. Adam was the representative for all the human beings who would come from him. So when God made that covenant, He was not making it only with Adam. God made that covenant with all Adam's natural descendants—all of Adam's children and grand-children and great-grandchildren—all who would come from Adam. If Adam had chosen to obey God, it would have been as though all mankind had been obedient. Not only Adam, but the whole human race would have had peace with God and eternal life. But if Adam disobeyed, all mankind would experience death as God had promised. **Read Romans 5:12.**

WEDNESDAY

Adam was our representative. When he sinned, "all mankind sinned in him." When Adam took the forbidden fruit from Eve and bit into it, it was just as though you and I were eating that fruit and sinning with him. God always keeps His promises. Even though Adam did not drop dead on the spot when he ate the fruit, he died spiritually. He was no longer right with God and able to please Him. His body began to weaken and grow old in preparation for the day when it would die too.

The image of God in Adam became twisted. Adam had fallen and because he was our representative, all of us "fell with him." All the consequences Adam earned for his disobedience happened to us as well, before we were even born! **Read Romans 5:14.**

THURSDAY

The good news is that God had already chosen another repre-sentative for His people. God had planned that His own Son would become a human being. As a human being, Jesus Christ would live a life of perfect obedience. He would never fail even once to keep all the commandments of God. Jesus lived that life of perfect obe-dience *in the place of* all who would believe in Him. God calls us to put our faith in Jesus Christ as the only One who can make us right with God. When we do, God counts Jesus' life of perfect obedience, as if we had lived it ourselves! **Read Romans 5:15, 18.**

FRIDAY

Even if I believe in Jesus, and all of His perfect obedience is counted as if I had done it, what about all my sins? God is holy and always punishes sin. He can never just "let it go this time." This is another wonderful thing Jesus did in the place of His people. All of us deserved to die because of our sin, just as God had promised Adam. Jesus died in the place of His people. He took the punishment their sins deserved. **Read Isaiah 53:5–6.**

SATURDAY

Read Romans 5:19. The first time this verse says "the one man," it is talking about Adam. The second time it says "the one man" (or "the One"), it is talking about Jesus Christ.

Adam represented the whole human race. When he sinned and fell by disobeying God, all of us "sinned in him and fell with him." Jesus represents all of His people. When He obeyed perfectly, He did it in the place of all who believe in Him. When He died on the cross, He died in the place of His people, to take the punishment for their sin.

How very thankful we should be to God for giving us Jesus! How thankful we should be to Jesus for all He has done in our place! We need to make certain that we are trusting Him and His life of perfect righteousness and His death in our place. This is the only way we can have peace with God and please Him!

Q.17. WHAT HAPPENED TO MAN IN THE FALL?

A. *Man fell into a condition of sin and misery.*

MONDAY

God had warned Adam that he would die if he disobeyed. Adam and Eve did not fall down and die when they bit into the fruit. But they did become spiritually dead on the inside and their bodies began to die. When Adam and Eve disobeyed, they and everyone who would ever come from them became sinful and miserable. As we go on reading the story, we see the sin and the misery that come from ignoring what God says. **Read Genesis 3:6–10.**

As soon as Adam and Eve ate the forbidden fruit, they felt embarrassed about being naked. They felt guilty and ashamed—feelings they had never had before. When they knew God was coming, they were afraid of Him and hid. They had never been afraid of God before. They had always loved Him and had enjoyed Him more than anything in the world. Now sin had ruined that.

God made us to be holy and happy, and to enjoy Him. Instead, because of Adam's sin, we are sinful and guilty, feeling ashamed and trying to keep away from God. We need a Savior who can take away our sin and make us friends with God again!

TUESDAY

Read Genesis 3:8–13. Because Adam and Eve were now guilty and afraid of God, they tried to hide from Him. Of course, they could not hide from God. He is everywhere at the same time and He sees everything. Adam told God that he had hidden because he was ashamed of being naked. God knew Adam had disobeyed Him, but He wanted Adam to face what he had done. So God asked him if he had eaten the forbidden fruit.

Trapped, Adam admitted he had eaten it—but not before blaming everyone else for what he had done! "The woman You put here with me—she gave me the fruit and I ate," he said. It was as if Adam were saying, "It was Eve's fault; she gave me the fruit." Or maybe, "It was God's fault; He gave me Eve!"

God had created Eve as a wonderful gift for Adam. Now Adam complained about God's gift. God had meant for Adam to protect and care for his wife. Now Adam was trying to blame her to protect himself.

God created us to live happily in our families, being a blessing to each other. Instead, because of Adam's sin, husbands and wives quarrel and hurt each other. God created us to enjoy His many gifts to us and to praise Him for them. Instead, because of Adam's sin, we complain against our good and perfect God. We need a Savior who can make us able to love each other as God intended and to enjoy God's wonderful gifts.

WEDNESDAY

Read Genesis 3:16–19. God is holy. In the world He made, sin always has consequences. God told Adam and Eve what would happen to them, to their children, and to the rest of the world because of their sin. He told them there would be pain. Have you ever been badly hurt? Have you ever had to stand by and watch when someone you loved was hurting? Sometimes our bodies hurt because of sickness or accidents—or maybe even someone hurting us on purpose. Sometimes our feelings hurt on the inside. That kind of pain cannot be seen, but it can hurt just as badly. Pain would not exist at all if Adam had never sinned.

God also said there would be hardship. There would be stickers and thorns. Sometimes the weather would be dangerously hot and sometimes it would be dangerously cold. There would be earthquakes and floods and other natural disasters. The whole world would still be like the Garden of Eden if Adam had obeyed God.

Because of sin, there would also be death. Most people are more afraid of dying than of anything else. Most people feel more sadness over the death of someone they love than over anything else. We would never lose people we love through death, and we would never need to worry about dying ourselves if Adam had obeyed God perfectly.

God created us to be happy and healthy. Instead, because of Adam's sin, we feel pain and sadness. God made all creation as a gift for us. Instead, because of Adam's sin, nature often fights against us. God gave us life, but now all have to die. We need a Savior who can take away sorrow and pain and can cause the creation to serve man and glorify God again. We need a Savior who is stronger than death and can give us life that lasts forever.

THURSDAY

Read Genesis 4:1–10. The Bible tells us that children are gifts from God and that the family with many children is a happy family. God gave Adam and Eve children, but because of sin, their family was not a very happy one. After Adam's sons, Cain and Abel, grew up, Cain grew jealous of his brother Abel. He became so angry with him that he attacked and killed him.

God meant for people to keep each other company. God created us to love and enjoy each other. He planned for people to need each other and to help each other. Instead, because of Adam's sin, people are selfish and think of themselves first. We grow angry with one another over little things, usually because we do not get our own way. We quarrel with each other and say things that are unkind to and about each other. People try to hurt each other and they kill and go to war with one another. We need a Savior who can change our hearts and make us able to love God and others more than ourselves.

FRIDAY

Read Genesis 5:1–3. In whose image or likeness did God create man? But when Adam's son Seth was born, in whose likeness or image was Seth? God created man good and righteous. If Adam had obeyed God, all his children and grandchildren would have been born in God's image, good and righteous. We still have the image of God, but since Adam's disobedience, it is damaged. Now we also are born in the image of Adam. That means that all of the guilt and hiding from God and blaming others that we read about in Adam and his family are in us too.

The sadness, the pain and death, the selfishness and anger and hatred of Adam's family are ours as well. The story of the first family ever created could have been such a happy one! Instead, it is sad and disappointing. Instead of showing the rest of creation what God is like, Adam's family and all of us have become sinful monsters. We live for ourselves and cause every kind of ugliness. We need a Savior who can repair the image of God in us and make us able to reflect His glory again.

SATURDAY

The first two chapters of Genesis tell the beautiful story of God creating all things, including man. The next few chapters tell the sad and ugly story of Adam's sin and its consequences. It is the story of Adam and Eve becoming enemies of God and of each other. It is the story of one of their sons killing his brother. The story goes on to tell how Adam's descendants were born sinful and miserable like Adam and how all of them had to die in the end. Finally, the story tells of the whole world and everyone in it becoming so wicked that God destroyed it all with a flood. He protected only Noah and his family.

But in the middle of all these sad happenings, God made a very happy promise. Right after Adam and Eve had sinned, before God told them of the consequences, God made this wonderful promise. He made it while He was talking to Satan, who had tempted Eve to take the fruit and eat it. **Read this wonderful promise in Genesis 3:15.**

God promised that someday a baby would be born to a woman. This baby would destroy Satan and would undo all his work. This baby would take away sin and make people friends with God again. He would be a Savior who would change our hearts so that we could love God and each other. He would restore the image of God in us, take away pain and sadness, and destroy death so that we could live forever with God. Thank God for keeping His promise and giving us Jesus to be our Savior!

Q.18.
WHAT IS SINFUL ABOUT MAN'S SINFUL CONDITION?

A. ✑ *The sinfulness of that fallen condition is twofold. First, in what is commonly called original sin, there is the guilt of Adam's first sin with its lack of original righteousness and the corruption of his whole nature. Second are all the specific acts of disobedience that come from original sin.*

MONDAY

The answer to this question tells us the two ways in which every human being is sinful. We are sinful because of what we are on the inside and we are sinful because of what we do on the outside. Not only do we do things that are sinful, we *are* sinful. The reason we sin on the outside is that we are sinners on the inside. Many people today believe that people are born good. People like to think that every human being, if just left alone, would always act kindly and with love and never do anything wrong. People say that people do bad things only because others have mistreated them. Every child starts life as a good person, they would say, but if he was poor or if he did not have good parents, he behaves badly.

The Bible teaches something else. The Bible says that because of the Fall, all people are born sinful on the inside. All of us are sinners and none of us are naturally good. We *do* what is sinful because we *are* sinful. **Read Psalm 58:3 and Matthew 15:18–19.**

TUESDAY

We are guilty before God because of what we do and we are guilty before God because of what we are. We are human beings. Adam acted as the representative of all human beings when he rebelled against God, so all human beings became guilty. Adam passed on his guilt to all who came from him. We are all born guilty because of Adam.

Not only are we born with Adam's guilt, we are also born without something because of Adam. When God created human beings, He created them righteous. This is what we call "original righteousness." It is the righteousness God gave man when He made him. With this original righteousness from God, human beings could have done things, on their own, that pleased God.

When Adam chose to sin, he lost the original righteousness God had given him. He could no longer do what pleased God. He could only do wrong. Adam lost original righteousness for himself and for the whole human race. No ordinary human being would be born with original righteousness. All humans would be born guilty before God and unable to do what is pleasing to Him. "Original sin" means the guilt we are born with, combined with our inability to act righteously. **Read Psalm 14:2–3 and Isaiah 64:6.**

WEDNESDAY

Because of Adam's sin, our whole nature has become corrupt. That means that every part of us has something wrong with it now. God made man as the most wonderful of all His creatures, but man turned himself into something much less wonderful by his sin. Sin damages every part of every one of us. Sin has damaged our bodies so that now we become sick or hurt, or we have body parts that do not work perfectly. Because of sin, our bodies grow old and die.

Sin has damaged our minds as well. God gave us minds so we could learn about Him. Because of sin, we use our minds now to think evil thoughts and form wicked plans. Our minds are so damaged that they cannot, by themselves, understand the things God says in His Word. **Read 1 Corinthians 2:14.**

Our hearts have also been damaged by sin. God gave us feelings so we could love Him and love and want what is good. But our hearts and our feelings are sinful now, so we love what we should hate and we hate what we should love. We enjoy and want to do things that God has said not to do. We do not like to pray or to go to church or to do things for others. Because our hearts are sinful, we use our feelings for all the wrong things. **Read John 3:19.**

God gave man the ability to choose between right and wrong, an ability that animals, birds, and fish do not have. Man has a will so he can choose to do good. Sin has damaged our wills so that we use them to choose to do wrong. We make bad choices not just because we do not know any better; we choose to do wrong because we are sinful. **Read John 5:39–40.**

THURSDAY

Although there is still much about us that is good, we are damaged by sin in every part—body, mind, emotions, and will. We use all that God has given us to sin instead of using it to serve God. We cannot do anything to change ourselves. By ourselves, we cannot understand the spiritual truth of God's Word. Even if our minds understood it, our hearts would not love and desire it. On their own, our wills have no power to choose God's will. **Read Jeremiah 13:23.** Because of sin, no human being can turn to God and begin to love and live for Him.

We are hopeless as we are and we are helpless to change and become something different. How very much we need a Savior! How thankful we can be that God has given us a Savior in Jesus who can do for us all that we cannot do for ourselves.

FRIDAY

The past few days we have spent looking at what we are as sinners. We are born into a sinful, fallen condition. We are born guilty because of Adam's sin, and we have no righteousness of our own with which to please God. We are also born corrupt—or damaged by sin—in our whole nature, in every part of us. This is only one part of our sinfulness. All these things come from Adam's sin and are passed on to us.

The other part of our sinfulness is that part we commit every day as we choose to sin and do what is wrong. Like Adam, we choose to disobey God ourselves. If we sinned only once every day all the days of our lives, we would be very guilty sinners. We do not sin only once a day, of course. Each of us sins many times a day. All the specific acts of disobedience each of us commits make up the other part of our sinfulness. **Read how Romans 3:10–18** describes all human beings.

SATURDAY

People do not like to think about their sin. They prefer to think that God loves everyone and does not mind when they sin. The Bible tells us that God is holy and cannot accept or love anyone when sin is in the way. We are sinful in two ways. We are sinful with Adam's sin and we are sinful because of all the wrong things we choose to do. It may feel better to us when we do not think about sin, but God will not accept and bless us as we are. When we think about our sin, we see how much we need a Savior. **Read 1 John 1:8–9.**

Q.19. WHAT IS THE MISERY OF MAN'S FALLEN CONDITION?

A. ✍ *By their fall all mankind lost fellowship with God and brought His anger and curse on themselves. They are therefore subject to all the miseries of this life, to death itself, and to the pains of hell forever.*

MONDAY

People are not only guilty and sinful because of Adam's Fall; they are now also in a state of misery. The most miserable thing about the condition of man after the Fall is that he is separated from God. Do you remember the answer to the very first catechism question: "Man's primary purpose is to glorify God and to enjoy Him forever"? Because of sin, man cannot do the very thing God created him to do. God hates sin and as long as sin is in the way, God will have nothing to do with man. **Read Isaiah 59:2 and Ephesians 2:12.**

TUESDAY

Not only will God have nothing to do with man because of his sin, God is very angry with man because of his sin. People do not like to talk about God being angry. They like to think of God's love and of His goodness, but God's anger is just as much a part of who He is as love and goodness are. The Bible makes it very clear that sin makes God angry. When *we* get angry, it is usually selfish and wrong. God's anger is righteous anger. His anger always causes Him to act. That is why God *always* punishes sin. **Read Nahum 1:2–3, 6.**

Sometimes people will say, "God gets angry at *sin,* but not at people." This is not true either. The Bible tells us that, before we were believers in Christ, we were just like everybody else—we were "objects of wrath" to God. God was not only angry at our sin; He was angry with *us,* the sinners.

WEDNESDAY

Man is miserable because he is separated from God. He is also miserable because God is angry with him. All of the fierce and severe wrath of God that can melt mountains and destroy worlds is directed against man because of his sin. What a frightening thought: the great and holy God who possesses all power angry with us! The Bible tells us that "it is a dreadful thing to fall into the hands of the living God" if He is angry with us (Heb. 10:31 NIV). The book of Revelation describes the judgments for sin that God will bring at the end of the world. All who have never trusted in Christ to save them from sin will be terrified. They will know that Christ is coming and that He is angry with them. **Read Revelation 6:15–17.**

THURSDAY

Read Ecclesiastes 2:22–23. Part of the misery of man's fallen condition is made up of all the problems, sorrows, and hardships of life on this earth. After Adam sinned, God told him, "Cursed is the ground because of you" (Gen. 3:17). This means that the whole earth is different now because of sin. As God first made the earth, nothing would have caused sadness or pain. Plants had no stickers. Work was only enjoyable and never difficult. Nothing would ever hurt anyone. Now, because of sin, sad things often happen to people.

People's bodies get hurt and people's feelings get hurt. Sickness attacks our bodies and sickness can attack our minds. Troubles of all kinds face people all through life. Some of these troubles simply annoy us. Some of them make us so sad we feel that we do not want to live any longer. All these hurts and sorrows and hardships are a part of the curse that is upon all the earth because of sin. All this misery comes to man because of his fallen condition.

FRIDAY

Read Psalm 49:10 and Psalm 103:15–16. One of the miseries that all people face is knowing that someday their lives must end. Everyone knows that they will die, and no one wants to die. If Adam had never sinned, we would have had life that never ends. People worry about dying. They worry about how they will die and when they will die. They wish that they did not have to die. People are sad when someone they love dies and they cannot be with that person any longer. Death exists because of sin. It takes what God created to be good and beautiful and makes it sad and ugly. Death brings misery to all mankind.

SATURDAY

Death makes people so miserable because they fear what will happen after it. The person who has not believed in Jesus Christ as the only Savior really has something to fear. The Bible tells us that man's sin against God is so serious that God has a place of punishment prepared for him after he dies. This is hell, a place of torment and misery that lasts forever. **Read 2 Thessalonians 1:8–9.**

Man's misery is complete. He lives a life of hardship and sadness, separated from the God he was created to enjoy. He dies, and after he dies, he goes to a place of punishment forever. How much damage sin has done! How greatly we need a Savior to rescue us from our misery!

Q.20. DID GOD LEAVE ALL MANKIND TO DIE IN SIN AND MISERY?

A. ✒ *From all eternity and merely because it pleased Him God chose some to have everlasting life. These He freed from sin and misery by a covenant of grace and brought them to salvation by a redeemer.*

MONDAY

Almost as soon as Adam and Eve fell into sin and misery through their disobedience, God made them a very comforting promise. God promised that someday Someone would be born of a woman who would crush the head of Satan, who had deceived them.

The Fall, with all its terrible consequences of pain, death, and the judgment of God, did not take God by surprise. He had always planned that His people would be His people because of what He would do for them, not because of what they would do for themselves. For centuries after the Fall, God's people waited for the birth of the One whom God had promised. The whole Old Testament looked forward to His coming. It contains many prophecies that Jesus fulfilled perfectly. Some of these Old Testament prophecies tell of what this Promised One would do for His people. He would save them from their sin and misery by taking the judgment their sin deserved and by living a life of perfect obedience to God in their place. For just one example of such a prophecy written hundreds of years before Jesus came, **read Isaiah 53:5–6, 11.**

TUESDAY

God has made a covenant of grace with His people. A covenant is an agreement that promises good things if certain conditions are met. Grace is goodness and blessing that people do not earn or deserve in any way. So when God made a covenant of grace with His people, He agreed to give them many wonderful gifts and blessings that they never deserved. In this covenant, as in all covenants, there were conditions that had to be met if God's people were to receive the blessings. God promised that He Himself would meet those conditions.

Do you remember the answer to this question: "How many persons are in the one God?" ("Three persons are in the one God, the Father, the Son, and the Holy Spirit. These three are one God, the same in substance and equal in power and glory.") All three persons had a part in making and keeping this covenant. God the Father chose certain human beings to be His children.

Although these human beings, like all human beings, deserved God's anger, God chose to love them. Although they deserved death for their sins, He chose to make a way to give them life that would last forever. God the Father did not *have* to choose anyone. He chose to give His love and everlasting life to some people just because He is a God of grace, a God who gives people wonderful things that they do not deserve. If you have believed in Jesus as the Savior God provides, how thankful you should be to God the Father for choosing you to be His child. **Read Ephesians 1:3–6.**

WEDNESDAY

God the Son had an important part in the covenant of grace that God made with His people. He became man and met all the requirements of the covenant so that God's people could receive all the benefits. Long before a single person had been born, even before the world had been created, God chose those people who would be His own special people. He entrusted those people to God the Son who would save them from sin.

Jesus came to earth to accomplish the will of God for His people. Jesus came to die so that every one of the people of God could have life (John 6:37–40). If you have trusted in Jesus to save you from your sin, His life of obedience to God was for you. He earned all the blessings of God's covenant of grace for you, since you could never have done it for yourself. You had earned God's wrath and judgment, and Jesus took that for you when He died on the cross. How thankful you should be to God the Son for coming to earth to keep all the requirements of the covenant for you so that you could enjoy all its blessings! **Read Ephesians 1:7–12.**

THURSDAY

God the Holy Spirit also has an important part in the covenant God made with His people. Sin has blinded our minds so we cannot understand the gospel on our own. The Holy Spirit gives spiritual understanding so God's people will understand the gospel when they hear it. Left to themselves, people like their sin. They do not worry about God's anger toward it. The Holy Spirit changes the hearts of God's people so they hate their sin and turn to Christ to save them from it. God the Son earned all the blessings of the covenant of grace for His people. God the Holy Spirit takes those blessings and applies them to the specific people whom God has chosen.

Some of the blessings Jesus earned for His people will not be given until Jesus comes again. Until then, the Holy Spirit lives inside them. He is the promise that they finally will receive everything Jesus earned for them. If you have believed in Jesus as your Savior, how thankful you should be to the Holy Spirit for giving you understanding of the gospel and for changing your heart so you could believe in Christ! **Read Ephesians 1:13–14.**

FRIDAY

If God only chose some to have everlasting life, why did He choose them instead of others? Did He choose those who were smarter than other people, or those who behave better? The Bible answers "no." There was nothing about anyone God chose that would make Him want to choose that person. No one can be proud that God chose him. God chooses someone just because He wants to choose him, not because there is something especially good about that person.

The Bible tells about two twin brothers, Jacob and Esau. Although God was good to both of them, He chose Jacob for special blessings. God chose Jacob to know God and to be one of the ones from whom the Messiah would come. Before the twins were even born, God told their mother, Rebecca, that he had chosen Jacob to love in a special way. Since neither baby had been born yet, neither one had done anything to make God want to choose him. God chose Jacob simply because He wanted to choose Jacob. **Read Romans 9:10–17.**

SATURDAY

Read Romans 8:28–30. These verses talk about God predestining, or choosing ahead of time, some to be His children. It says that God predestined or chose those whom He foreknew. This does not mean that God looked ahead into the future, saw who would believe in His Son, and chose those people to be His children. That is not what "foreknew" means. It does not mean that He knew what His people would *do* ahead of time; it means that He knew *His people* ahead of time. Long before any of His people were born, God knew them, the way you know a good friend. He could know His people before they were born because He was the One who would create them. Of course, God knew His people would believe in His Son. But He did not choose them because they would believe; they would believe because He had chosen them.

Q.21. WHO IS THE REDEEMER OF GOD'S CHOSEN ONES?

A. ❧ *The only redeemer of God's chosen is the Lord Jesus Christ, the eternal Son of God, Who became man. He was and continues to be God and man in two distinct natures and one person forever.*

MONDAY

In Old Testament times, land was very important to people because most people were farmers. A farmer has to have land in order to farm. Sometimes, though, a person would become so poor that he would have to sell his land. In Old Testament times, a family member called a redeemer would buy back the poor person's land, and then return it to him. A redeemer paid a price to buy something back for someone who had originally owned it.

Jesus is the redeemer of God's people. God's people have always belonged to Him, but sin separated them from Him so they could not be called His people. With His own blood, Jesus paid the great price to buy God's people back for the One to whom they really belonged. **Read** what is sung to Jesus in heaven in **Revelation 5:9.**

TUESDAY

Did Jesus Christ begin His life when He was born in the stable? Did His life start when He began to grow inside Mary? The Bible tells us that Jesus is the Son of God. Since He is God, His life never began. He has always lived. Long before He came to earth as a man, long before there *was* an earth, the Son of God existed. **Micah 5:2** is a famous prophecy. Hundreds of years before Jesus' birth, it told in exactly which small town God's promised King would be born. Read that verse to see what it says about the origins (or beginnings) of God's promised Ruler. **John 1:1–2** speaks of Jesus

Christ as "the Word." Read it to see what it says about how long He has existed.

WEDNESDAY

Jesus has not always been man, but He has always been God. He limited Himself in many ways when He became a man and lived on earth, but He never stopped being God. Scripture gives us many wonderful names for Jesus. One of them is "Immanuel," which means "God with us" (Matt. 1:23).

All His life, Jesus did things that showed Him to be God. He showed that He is the Creator when He commanded the storm and it obeyed Him. He demonstrated that He knows all things whenever He said something to answer what someone was thinking before he or she had said it. Jesus proved that He has all power when He healed people and when the demons obeyed Him. He showed that He is holy when He lived His whole life without ever sinning. Jesus most clearly showed Himself to be God when He rose from the dead. By His own power as God, Jesus came to life again after He had died. No one else has ever done that because no one else is God. **Read Romans 1:3–4.**

THURSDAY

Jesus has always existed as God. On a particular day in history, He also became human. He took a human body and soul and began to grow inside the woman chosen to be His mother. He grew inside His mother for nine months, like every other human being, and was born just as all humans are born. Jesus grew as a little child and became a teenager, then an adult, as all humans do.

We see that He was a human just like we are when we read of Him sending His disciples for food because He was hungry or sleeping through a big storm because He was exhausted. We see He had human feelings like we have when we read of Him wishing His disciples would stay awake to keep Him company when He felt lonely. The only way in which Jesus was different from us as a human being living on earth was that He never sinned. He was often tempted like we are, but because He is God He was unable to sin. **Read Hebrews 4:14–15.**

FRIDAY

Once the Son of God took a human nature and a human body, He never stopped—and never will stop—being human. Jesus is always and completely God and He is always and completely man. He still has His human nature and body in heaven and He always will have them. While He lived on earth, too, Jesus was always completely God and always completely man. As God, He knew all things. As man, He grew in wisdom. Because Jesus was God, He possessed all power. Because He was man, He grew tired and hungry and felt weak. As God, Jesus was eternal and unchanging. As man, He was born, grew up, and died.

It may not be possible to understand fully how one person could be both God and man at the same time, but it is very important that we believe it. We must believe it because it is what the Bible teaches. Jesus could not save us from sin if He were not *both* God and man.

Some people teach that Jesus was only a man—a very good man, but nothing more. If Jesus were only a man, His death would not be worth enough to pay for the sins of other people. Because He is God, when He died in the place of His people, His death could pay for all their sins.

Some people have said that Jesus was God, visiting us, but not a real human being like we are. God cannot die; if Jesus had not been man, He could not have died for our sins. Only God who had become man could be a Savior for sinful human beings. **Read Philippians 2:5–11.**

SATURDAY

Since Jesus is both God and man, He could be our Redeemer. Because He was man, He could die, paying the price to buy us. Because He was God, His death had enough value to pay for the sins of His people. Since Jesus is the only person to ever be both God and man, only Jesus could be our Redeemer.

The Bible tells us that Jesus is also our mediator. A mediator is someone who comes between two people who are angry with one another and helps them to work out their disagreements. Jesus is the mediator between God and human beings, because He is both God and a human being. He alone can be our mediator. He is the only one who can wash us clean from our sin so that our sin no longer keeps God from accepting us. Jesus is the only one who could die for us, taking all of God's anger at our sin, so that God would no longer be angry with us. Many people today say that Jesus is one of many ways to know God. This is wrong. He is the *only* mediator between sinful men and a holy God. Jesus is the only Redeemer. **Read 1 Timothy 2:5–6.**

Q.22.   HOW DID CHRIST, THE SON OF GOD, BECOME MAN?

A. ✎   *Christ, the Son of God, became man by assuming a real body and a reasoning soul. He was conceived by the power of the Holy Spirit in the womb of the Virgin Mary, who gave birth to Him; yet He was sinless.*

MONDAY

Animals, fish, and birds all have bodies we can see. There is also a part of animals, birds, and fish that we cannot see. This part we cannot see is what is there when the animal is alive and is not there when the animal's body is dead. Human beings also have two parts, a part we can see, called a body, and a part we cannot see, called a soul. The human soul is capable of knowing and worshiping God.

When Jesus became a man, He was not just God in a human body. He assumed or took to Himself a human body *and* a human soul. Jesus continued to be God in every way. He was also completely man just like every other human being. Jesus lived a life of perfect obedience to God in the place of those who would believe in Him. To do that, He had to be fully human just as we are. **Read Hebrews 10:5–7.**

TUESDAY

A new human being begins when a cell from a human father and a cell from a human mother come together inside the mother. A new tiny human being then begins to grow. It grows inside the mother until it is big enough to be able to live on its own and then it is born. Christ never began. Because He is God, He has always existed. The human part of Him had a beginning, though. Like all human babies, Jesus grew inside His mother until He was big enough to be born. There is one very important way, however, in which Jesus was different from all other humans. Jesus had no human father. When the angel first told Mary, Jesus' mother, that she was going to have a baby, she wanted to know how that could be since there was no human father. The angel told her that the power of the Holy Spirit would come upon her and that is how this baby would begin. God alone would be His Father. **Read Luke 1:26–35.**

WEDNESDAY

Read Romans 5:19. What does this verse say happened to many because one man (Adam) was disobedient? Every human being ever born after Adam was born in his image. Every one of us is born a sinner. Mary, Jesus' mother, was a sinner who needed a Savior. Jesus alone was born without sin. He was not sinful on the inside like we are, so He never wanted to do what was wrong. Do you remember what Jesus said to His Father when He prayed in the garden right before He went to the cross? He said, "Not My will, but Yours be done." Jesus wanted God's will through His whole life on this earth. All other human beings are sinners, wanting their own way, not God's. Jesus alone always put God's will before His own.

THURSDAY

Jesus was the only human being ever born who was not sinful on the inside. He was also God. Because He was God, He was the only human being ever born unable to sin. God is absolutely holy. He hates all sin and He never sins. Because Jesus is God, sinning is impossible for Him. This does not mean that He was never tempted to sin.

The Bible tells us that Jesus *was* tempted. He never wanted to sin, though, not even once. Satan often tried to get Jesus to sin. He knew that Jesus would not be able to save us from *our* sin if He Himself were a sinner. The greatest temptation Jesus ever faced was the temptation to *not* bear our sin and die on the cross. Jesus knew that Satan would try hard to stop Him from doing this, but Jesus also knew that He would go ahead and die on the cross just as God wanted Him to do. He knew He would not sin because He was the Son of God and could not sin. Jesus spoke to His disciples about this at the last meal that He ate with them. **Read John 14:30–31.**

FRIDAY

Read John 8:29. How much of the time did Jesus say that He did what was pleasing to God? Could anyone else say that without being called a liar? In another place, Jesus asked, "Which one of you accuses Me of sin?" and not even His enemies could think of anything He had done wrong. Peter, one of Jesus' disciples, followed Him and lived with Him almost all the time. If Jesus had ever sinned, Peter would have seen it. **Read** what Peter said about Jesus in **1 Peter 2:22.** Jesus' whole life was one of perfect, sinless obedience to God.

SATURDAY

Read Hebrews 4:14–15. Adam represented the whole human race. When he sinned, we all sinned. Jesus represented all God's people. When He obeyed God perfectly, He did it in our place. God counts all His perfect obedience to us, as though we had obeyed God perfectly ourselves. That is why it is so important that Jesus be fully human like we are, so He could represent us. He had to live a human life without ever sinning once. He did it for us. When Jesus died on the cross, too, it was very important that He had never sinned. If He ever sinned, He would deserve to die for His own sins. Because He had never sinned, He could die to take the punishment for the sins of His people. **Read 2 Corinthians 5:21.**

Q.23. HOW IS CHRIST OUR REDEEMER?

A. *As our redeemer, Christ is a prophet, priest, and king in both His humiliation and His exaltation.*

MONDAY

God's people waited hundreds of years for Him to send the One He had promised to send. This One would destroy Satan and his work. As they waited, God gave His people three kinds of special people: prophets, priests, and kings. These three kinds of people helped God's people know and do His will while they waited. They were also pictures of the One whom God had promised. Jesus would be the perfect prophet, the perfect priest, and the perfect king all combined in one Person. This would be true during His humiliation, or the time of His living and suffering on earth. Jesus' humiliation is over now and the time of His exaltation has begun. Jesus' exaltation is the time of His being honored as He deserves because of what He has done for sinners. During His exaltation as well, He is also the perfect prophet, priest, and king. **Read Hebrews 2:9.**

TUESDAY

Prophets took the Word of God exactly as God had given it to them and passed it on to God's people. This was how the people would know what God was like and what He wanted from them. One of the first prophets was Moses. God would meet with Moses and talk with him. Then Moses would tell the people what God had said. Once, the people heard God themselves. At the sound of His voice, the mountain from which He was talking shook and fire and smoke came from it. The people found it so frightening to listen to the holy and awesome God that they begged Moses to go listen to

Him and talk with Him for them. At that point, God promised that one day He would give them a prophet who would be a human being like them and who would be faithful to reveal all God's will. He was speaking of His Son, who would be the perfect prophet. **Read Deuteronomy 18:15–19.**

WEDNESDAY

During His humiliation, or life on this earth, Jesus was the best prophet ever. All other prophets had spoken their own words most of the time, speaking God's words only when He gave them to them. Everything Jesus ever said was the Word of God because He Himself was God. Jesus not only taught God's will. He *showed* people God's will by His perfect and sinless life. Now that Jesus is exalted in heaven, He still makes God's will known to us through the Bible, where His words and life are recorded. He sends His people His Holy Spirit to give them understanding of His Word. **Read Hebrews 1:1–3.**

THURSDAY

It was the job of the priest to offer sacrifices for the sins of God's people. The people would confess their sins and bring an animal to kill and offer to God. In this way, people admitted that they deserved to die for their sin. They trusted God to provide Someone to die in their place. The animal sacrifices did not take away sins, but they pointed ahead to the death of Jesus that would take away sins forever. God appointed the priests to kill the animals and offer them as sacrifices.

Jesus came to earth to die in the place of His people. He was the perfect priest. All the other priests simply pointed to Him. Jesus offered His own body and blood as a sacrifice. This sacrifice is so valuable that it has the power to wash away all sin forever. This is how Jesus was a priest in His humiliation, or life of suffering. Now that He is exalted, Jesus is still the priest of His people. Whenever Satan accuses one of God's children of sin, Jesus is there as a reminder that His death paid for all the sins of God's people. Jesus lives forever to pray for those for whom He died. **Read Hebrews 7:24–27.**

FRIDAY

Because He is God, Jesus is and always has been the greatest King of all. During the time of His humiliation on earth, He did not always look like a king. He was born to a poor family and lived as a poor man all His life. People hated and killed Him as a criminal. But there were many times when it was clear that Jesus is the highest King of all and that all creatures must obey Him. **Read** these two stories to see examples: **Mark 1:23–27 and Mark 4:35–41.**

SATURDAY

After Jesus had accomplished the will of God by dying for His people, God raised Him from the dead and exalted Him over all. God raised Jesus higher than any other thing. **Read Ephesians 1:20–23.** What things is Jesus over now? What is under Jesus' feet (or under His control)? God gave Jesus to the church as head over what? This means that, as King, Jesus controls all that happens for the good of His people, the church.

Q.24. How is Christ a Prophet?

A. ✍ *As a prophet, Christ reveals the will of God to us for our salvation by His word and Spirit.*

MONDAY

Sometimes a prophet would predict what was going to happen in the future. When he did that, it was a sign that he was speaking God's message since only God would know the future. A prophet's main task, though, was to reveal God's will to His people. To reveal is to make something known that was hidden before. God is much greater than we are. Our minds are sinful and cannot, by themselves, understand spiritual things.

We would never figure out God's will for ourselves. It is hidden to us and God must make it known. God used Old Testament prophets to reveal bits and pieces of His will, but all the prophets who came before Christ pointed ahead to Him. Jesus is the perfect Prophet, the One who perfectly reveals God's will to us. As long ago as the days of Moses, God promised to send this perfect Prophet. After Jesus had risen and returned to heaven, the apostle Peter preached a sermon. In it, he said that Jesus fulfilled that promise to Moses. **Read** part of Peter's sermon in **Acts 3:18–24.**

TUESDAY

When Jesus was on earth, He revealed the will of God through His teaching. The people of Jesus' day were used to being taught. The scribes and the Pharisees taught them what the law of God said. When Jesus taught God's law, however, it was different. The crowds were amazed at His teaching, because He taught as One who had authority (Matt. 7:28–29). He taught as though He really knew what He was talking about. And He did! When Jesus spoke of heaven, He spoke of a place He had seen. When He spoke of the Father, He spoke of Someone He knew well. **Read John 3:31–32.** Jesus always said exactly what the Father had given Him to say. **Read John 12:49–50.**

WEDNESDAY

Jesus revealed the *will of God* by His teaching. He also revealed *God* to us by His life. His life on earth gave us the perfect example of what God wants us to do and to be. God's will for His children is that they be like Jesus. When we look at Jesus' life, we see exactly what God wills for us. Jesus shows us what *we* are to be like, but He also shows us what *God* is like. When Jesus became man and lived among us, He did not stop being God, so His human life made God known to us. By never sinning, He showed us that God is holy. He became angry at wrongdoing and showed us that God hates sin. When He healed the sick, He showed us that God is compassionate. By caring for sinners whom no one else wanted, He showed that God is a God of love and of grace. **Read John 1:14–18.**

THURSDAY

Jesus revealed God's will so that His people could be saved. God had chosen some to have everlasting life. He had sent His Son, the perfect Prophet, to make it possible for those whom He had chosen to have that everlasting life. Jesus said something about Himself that no other prophet could ever have said. **Read John 14:6** to see what it was. People recognized Jesus as a prophet and a teacher and so they asked Him what God's will for them was. They were thinking of things God would want them to *do*. Jesus told them that God's will for people is that they believe in Jesus, the Savior God provided, so their sins could be forgiven and they could have everlasting life. **Read John 6:28–29.**

FRIDAY

The Lord Jesus no longer lives here on earth in His human body, so we can no longer watch what He does to see how we should live or to see what God is like. We can no longer go to hear Him teach and preach. Does that mean that Jesus has stopped being a Prophet? Not at all. Jesus still reveals the will of God to us.

Before Jesus went back to heaven, He chose certain men to be apostles. These men had been with Jesus all along, had watched Him, had heard His teaching, and had seen Him alive after He had died. Jesus gave the apostles the job of passing on to others what they had seen and heard, so that others could also have everlasting life. They had to pass on the message exactly as they had seen and heard it, without changing it at all. This was a heavy responsibility! What if they made a mistake? What if they forgot something important?

Jesus knew this could happen, so He promised to send them the Holy Spirit. The Holy Spirit is God and never makes a mistake. He would make them able to remember what they needed to say. The Holy Spirit would help them to better understand the things Jesus had taught them, too. Because of the Holy Spirit's work, the apostles could be sure that what they passed on to others was the Word of God, with no mistakes in it. **Read John 14:26 and John 16:13–14.**

Not only were they sure that what they *said* was the perfect Word of God; they could be sure that what they *wrote* was the perfect Word of God as well. God used these apostles to write the entire New Testament, so that those of us who live today can also have God's Word and know His will. This is how Jesus is a Prophet to us today. He speaks to us from His Word.

SATURDAY

Read Hebrews 1:1–2. Everything God had to say to us He said in Jesus Christ. Jesus called men to be apostles and sent the Holy Spirit to reveal His will through them. These apostles wrote about the life and teachings of Jesus. They wrote about the importance of who He was and what He had done. Their writings make up the New Testament. Once the last apostle had died, God's revelation was finished. Everything He had wanted us to know He had told us through His Son and through the holy men who wrote of Him. To-day, the perfect Prophet, Jesus, speaks to us only through His Word.

One more way that Jesus is the perfect Prophet is this. Sin has darkened our hearts so that we do not rightly understand what God's Word says. Jesus has provided a way to be sure that we understand what God reveals to us in Scripture. He has sent His Holy Spirit to live in each believer. The Holy Spirit makes us able to rightly understand and to receive what Jesus has to say to us in the Bible. **Read John 14:16–17 and 1 Corinthians 2:12.**

Q.25.   HOW IS CHRIST A PRIEST?

A. ✍ *As a priest, Christ offered Himself up once as a sacrifice for us to satisfy divine justice and to reconcile us to God, and He continually intercedes for us.*

MONDAY

Read Hebrews 5:1–4. Almost as soon as Adam and Eve had sinned, God graciously promised to send Someone who would save His people from sin and its miserable results. But He did not send that Someone right away. He wanted to teach His people that sin is terrible and separates them from Him. To teach them this, God commanded His people to bring Him sacrifices for sin. They were to bring sheep or goats or calves to the tabernacle, kill them, and offer them as sacrifices. The person bringing the animal would lay his hands on it to show that his sins were being laid on it. Then the priest would kill it. This demonstrated that the person bringing the animal deserved to die, but the animal was dying instead. Bringing many sacrifices a year, year after year, taught God's people that their sins were very serious and deserved to be punished by death.

God also commanded His people to have priests, men whom He had chosen to offer the animals as sacrifices. Not just anyone could offer a sacrifice, but only the priests. In this way, God taught His people that sin separates people from God and makes them His enemies. He taught them that they needed a mediator, someone to come between them and God and make peace. Of course, the death of an animal did not have enough value to pay for our sin against God. And a priest, a sinful human being just like the rest of us, could never be good enough to mediate between God and man.

Old Testament sacrifices and Old Testament priests pointed

ahead to the One whom God had promised. They showed people how much we need a perfect Priest to offer a perfect sacrifice.

TUESDAY

Priests burned incense and offered sacrifices day after day, year after year. As God's people watched this happening, they came to understand that their sin stood between them and God. They learned that they could not come directly to God themselves, but had to come to someone chosen by God who would come to God for them. Of course, the Old Testament priests were only human. They, too, were sinners. They had to offer sacrifices for themselves and their own sins before they could offer sacrifices for others. God never intended for these priests to be the mediators between sinners and Himself. They were simply pictures of the perfect Mediator who would come.

Jesus lived a life of perfect obedience to God in every way. He never sinned, not even once. He had no sins of His own to confess or for which to offer a sacrifice. Jesus is human like we are, and was tempted in every way just as we are, so He can understand our needs and our weaknesses. But He never sinned and He always pleased God perfectly. Because He is fully God and fully man, Jesus alone is the perfect priest. **Read Hebrews 7:26–28.**

WEDNESDAY

Imagine that someone gave you a beautiful masterpiece worth thousands of dollars, painted by an artist who was no longer alive. One day, a guest in your home took a marking pen and scribbled all over it, ruining it. When your guest realized how angry this made you, he clipped a photograph out of a newspaper advertisement, handed it to you, and said, "Here. This is to make up for your painting." Would you feel any better about your painting? Of course not. In addition, you would feel insulted that your guest thought it was that easy to make up for ruining the masterpiece.

When we sin, we sin against God who is absolutely holy. Our sin is ungrateful rebellion against a Creator who has been very good to us. The offering of an animal could never make up for what we have done to God—not even the offerings of thousands and thousands of animals. Even the death of a human being could not pay for the terrible thing we have done by sinning against God. Only the death of the Son of God would be of enough value to pay for what we have done.

But the Son of God, being God, could not die. So Christ became man so He could die. He offered Himself as the only sacrifice worth enough to God to be able to pay for man's sin. Jesus Christ, the perfect priest, offered to God the perfect sacrifice—His own body and blood. This sacrifice was so valuable that it had to be offered only once and it would pay for all the sins of all of God's people for all time. **Read Hebrews 9:11–14.**

THURSDAY

Those who love Jesus feel sadness when they think of Him having to suffer and die on the cross. Was there no other way to save us? The Bible teaches us that because God is holy, He hates all sin. Because He is just (always perfectly fair), He always punishes all sin. If God let any sin go unpunished, He would not be holy and just. *Someone* had to be punished for the sins of God's people. God's people could only escape punishment if God punished someone else in their place. When we say that Jesus' sacrifice was "to satisfy divine justice," that is what we mean.

Divine justice is God's justice. God's justice could only be satisfied if someone took the punishment for the sins of His people. Once sin has been paid for by being fully punished, it no longer separates God and His people. By paying for our sin, Jesus reconciled us to God or made us right with Him again. **Read Romans 5:1, 8–10.**

FRIDAY

Once Jesus had offered Himself as a sacrifice for His people, had He finished being a priest? Not at all. He still serves as a priest for all those who believe in Him. Besides offering sacrifices, priests offered prayers for the people as well. Jesus is in heaven now, at the right hand of God, where He intercedes or prays for His people. Jesus rose from the dead and will never die again, so He will be our priest forever. Old Testament priests kept changing. One would grow old and die and another would replace him. Jesus remains our priest forever. **Read Hebrews 7:23–25.**

SATURDAY

In every way, Jesus is a better priest than the priests in the Old Testament, who were only meant to be pictures of Jesus, the perfect priest. Those priests were sinners themselves; Jesus is sinless. Those priests offered animal sacrifices; Jesus offered His own blood. Those priests offered thousands of sacrifices, day after day; Jesus offered one sacrifice for all time. Those priests were only pictures of God's forgiveness and cleansing from sin; Jesus actually accomplished it. Those priests all died and had to be replaced; Jesus will never die and will continue as our priest forever. **Read Hebrews 10:11–14.**

Q.26. How is Christ a king?

A. ✑ *As a king, Christ brings us under His power, rules and defends us, and restrains and conquers all His and all our enemies.*

MONDAY

God had promised to send One who would be the greatest Prophet of all to reveal Him and His will to us. He had promised that this One would also be the perfect Priest, offering a sacrifice valuable enough to pay for all our sin and make us right with God. God had also promised that this One would rule as the highest King of all, whose kingdom would last forever. **Read Isaiah 9:6–7.**

Before Jesus came, God gave kings to His people. Again, they were only to be pictures of His chosen Ruler and to show the need for a perfect King. Some Old Testament kings were better than others. The best one was David, a man after God's own heart. He wanted to rule for God's glory and to protect and defend God's people. In this, he was a picture of Christ, God's perfect King. Even so, at times he sinned miserably. At times he put what he wanted for himself before the will of God. He did some foolish and even sinful things that put his people in danger to get what he wanted for himself. In this, he showed the need for a sinless King who would always seek the will of God and the good of God's people without ever failing.

TUESDAY

The first thing King Jesus does to each of God's people is to bring us under His rule. Every human being ever born is a rebel against God. We want nothing to do with Him or with His chosen King. We want to live our own lives and do things our own way. But if we are among those whom God has chosen for eternal life, Jesus is determined to have us as His subjects. Left to our own, we would never obey Him as our King. So Jesus sends His Holy Spirit, who convicts our hearts of sin and shows us our need for a Savior. He changes our rebel hearts so that we can believe in Jesus as our Savior from sin and obey Him as our King. Read this story of how Jesus brought a very rebellious enemy under His rule so that he became one of Jesus' most faithful servants. **Read Acts 9:1–7.**

WEDNESDAY

Today we will finish the story we began yesterday. **Read Acts 9:10–19a.** Ananias called Jesus "Lord." We call someone whom we obey "Lord." Ananias did not want to go to Saul, because everybody knew that Saul wanted to hunt and hurt Christians. But Ananias went. He understood that Jesus ruled over him. Jesus was his King. A servant does not argue with a king; he obeys him. In verses 15 and 16, Jesus told Ananias some things about Saul that showed him that now Saul the rebel would begin to obey Jesus as Lord. Jesus had chosen him for a specific purpose and Saul *would* fulfill Jesus' purpose for him. In carrying out Jesus' purpose, Saul would suffer. Even so, he would do as Jesus wanted him to do because Jesus would be his King from now on. Jesus would rule over Saul as He rules over every one of His people.

THURSDAY

A king rules his people and can command them to do whatever he wishes. A good king always cares about the welfare of his people. Jesus is the best King, so He never fails to defend us. Sometimes Jesus defends or protects His people from sickness or physical harm. Every time we recover from an illness, even if it is just a cold, God in His providence has healed us. Every day of good health we enjoy is a gift from God who protects us from all the sicknesses we could get. Whenever we are in an accident—or almost in an accident—and escape serious injury, Jesus our King is protecting us.

Sometimes, though, the followers of Jesus *do* get sick—even very sick—and do not get well. Sometimes Jesus' servants *are* badly hurt or even killed. So when we say that Jesus is a King who always perfectly defends or protects His people, we are not talking about physical things. Jesus has promised to always keep His people safe from spiritual enemies. Nothing will ever draw us away from Him so that we are His enemies again. Nothing can cause His people to turn away from Him or to so sin against Him that He will no longer love and keep them. Left to ourselves, we would never be strong enough to resist Satan's attacks and our own sinful hearts for a whole lifetime. But King Jesus has promised to keep those over whom He rules. He will never lose one of them. **Read Romans 8:31–39.**

FRIDAY

When we look at the history of the church down through the ages, we see that in many times and in many places, it looked like her enemies had won. Even today, the church's enemies often seem more powerful than the church. In many countries, Christians cannot get jobs and feed their families if they admit that they are Christians. In other places, Christians are put in jail or even killed for their faith. In these countries, the church is almost completely invisible and it seems like her enemies have won. In other countries, sin has weakened the church, so that it looks like the world. You may see many church buildings and find many people who say they are Christians. It is much harder to find people who study what King Jesus says in Scripture so that they can obey Him.

Whenever it looks like our enemies are winning, we need to remember that Jesus has promised that nothing will destroy His church. Our enemies are His enemies. As King over all, He restrains them for us. That means He keeps them from doing all the evil and all the harm to us that they could do. He only allows them to do as much harm as will make us stronger and be for our good in the end. As King, Jesus orders all things so they work out for the good of His people, the church. **Read Ephesians 1:20–23.**

SATURDAY

None of Jesus' enemies can stand against Him. He conquers all of them. And the day will come when He will destroy them all. **Read** this description of King Jesus in **Revelation 19:11–16.** Revelation describes Jesus' enemies too. It describes them as strong and terrible and cruel. All of them are described as gathering together to make war against Jesus. **Read Revelation 17:14.** We who have Jesus as our King can rejoice and be glad that our King is so great. He can protect us from all our enemies and will someday destroy them all.

Q.27. HOW WAS CHRIST HUMILIATED?

A. *Christ was humiliated: by being born as a man and born into a poor family; by being made subject to the law and suffering the miseries of this life, the anger of God, and the curse of death on the cross; and by being buried and remaining under the power of death for a time.*

MONDAY

God the Father, God the Son, and God the Holy Spirit had agreed together that Jesus Christ would save God's chosen ones. This plan for saving God's people had two parts: the humiliation of Christ and the exaltation of Christ. Christ's humiliation includes all the difficult things Jesus endured for us. His humiliation includes His suffering and death. Exaltation means the honor and glory God gave to Jesus after His death. God gave Jesus honor for His obedience. He restored Him to the glory He had always had as God. This week, we will be learning about Christ's humiliation. **Read Philippians 2:5–11.**

TUESDAY

Read Isaiah 40:14–17. This chapter speaks of the greatness and glory of God. This greatness and glory belonged to Christ before He became man to live among us. According to this passage, if you took all the people of all the nations of the world and added them together, what would they be like to God? God is much greater than man. If you changed from being a human being to being a one-celled creature in the sea, it would not be nearly so big a step down as for God to become man. That is because you and the one-celled creature are both finite (having limits) and you are both creatures.

The Son of God is infinite (having no limits) and uncreated. To become a man, Christ limited Himself for a time so He could live on this earth. He is God, needing nothing, but by becoming man He took on a created body with ordinary human needs. Taking on a human body and soul, with all of the weaknesses and suffering that come from the Fall, was the first step in Christ's humiliation.

WEDNESDAY

Read Psalm 95. This psalm praises God as the great King over everything. It tells how all things and all people belong to Him to do with as He chooses. The psalm reminds us that we must obey this great King because He will judge those who do not. Since Jesus is God the Son, all that this psalm says of God is true of Jesus. Part of Christ's humiliation was that, although as God He is King over all, He became a servant to us who should have been serving Him. As God, He was the One who made the law for His creatures to obey. By becoming man, He became subject to the law Himself—He now had to obey the laws that He had made for His creatures.

THURSDAY

Because of the Fall, every human being ever born experiences some suffering and misery. Jesus experienced suffering and misery too. Jesus felt all of the things that make our lives less than perfect—hunger, exhaustion, pain, loneliness, and sorrow. In addition, Jesus' life on this earth had misery added to it that ordinary human beings do not face. As the sinless Son of God who hated sin, it would have caused Jesus great suffering to live on earth among people who were sinful. Satan knew how important Jesus' work was. Although all of us face temptation, Satan attacked Jesus with special strength.

Even Jesus' closest friends and relatives constantly misunderstood Him—and many people hated Him. Jesus suffered loneliness. He knew who He was. He knew He had the awesome responsibility of taking the punishment for the sins of God's people in order to save them. **Read** the following verses to see just a few of the special miseries Jesus endured: **John 7:1; 7:5; 8:48; 8:59; 12:27.**

FRIDAY

Surely the hardest thing for Jesus in His humiliation was bearing the sins of God's people and taking God's anger for them. As God, Jesus is perfectly holy and hates all sin. Having all of our sins laid on Him as He went to the cross would have filled Him with horror. As God the Son, Jesus had always enjoyed perfect fellowship with God the Father. They had never been separated in all eternity. When Jesus bore our sins on the cross, God the Father poured all His anger out on Him and turned His back on Him, causing Jesus to cry out, "My God, My God, why have You forsaken Me?" **Read Isaiah 53:4–6, 10a.**

SATURDAY

As God, Jesus is eternal. He has no beginning and no end. Death could not touch Him. Even as man, Jesus did not have to die, because He alone was sinless. Death comes from sin. Because Jesus lived a sinless life, He did not have to die. Death is a part of the curse on mankind because of the Fall. Jesus did not have to experience that curse but He did, in our place. A human ruler (whom Jesus Himself had created) judged Jesus and condemned Him to die the kind of death reserved for the worst criminals. Hanging on the cross, He took the curse we deserved. Although He is the most holy God, He endured death, the punishment due to disobedient creatures, and remained dead in the tomb for three days. **Read Galatians 3:13.**

What a wonderful Savior we have! How very, very good is our God who suffered humiliation in all these ways for us His people, when we deserved only His anger and punishment. We could spend every minute of every day praising Him and we would not be praising Him enough! **Read 2 Corinthians 8:9.**

A. Christ is exalted by His rising from the dead on the third day, His going up into heaven, His sitting at the right hand of God the Father, and His coming to judge the world at the last day.

MONDAY

To exalt someone is to lift him up to a place of high authority and honor. In His humiliation, Jesus was brought low so that He could save His people. Afterward, God exalted Him. God raised Jesus from the dead as the first step in His exaltation. Wicked men had killed Him and left Him dead in a tomb. But Jesus could not remain dead. He was God's honored Son who had perfectly obeyed His Father. So God raised Him on the third day. **Read Acts 2:22–24.**

TUESDAY

Read John 2:19–22. There are many ways in which Jesus is unique—unlike anyone else. One important way in which Jesus is unique is that He is the only One who ever died and rose again. In Bible stories, God sometimes gave prophets the power to raise people from the dead. Jesus raised others from the dead during His life on earth. Jesus alone rose from the dead by His own power. Only Jesus is God. As God, He has power over death. It is very important to us that Jesus rose from the dead, because that is how we know that He really is God. Nothing that Jesus did during His lifetime would matter at all if He had stayed dead like any other human being.

Jesus is our Prophet. He had claimed to be God and He said He would come back to life. If He had not risen from the dead, He would be a false prophet. Jesus is our Priest. If He had not risen from the dead, He would have been just another ordinary human being. His death would not have been of enough value to pay for anyone's sin. Jesus is our King. If He had not risen from the dead, He would be a dead king, unable to rule over and defend His people. Jesus' resurrection is a cause for celebration!

WEDNESDAY

Forty days after Jesus rose from the dead, He ascended into heaven. He received a place of highest honor. This was the second step in His exaltation. As God, Jesus had great glory before He became man. When He returned to heaven, He returned to the glory that had always been His. Now He also received glory for conquering sin and death. **Read John 17:5 and Hebrews 2:9.**

THURSDAY

Not only was Jesus exalted when He ascended into heaven. In heaven, He was also given the highest and best place. He sat down at the right hand of the Father. Exalted in heaven, Jesus still cares for His people here on earth. As prophet, Jesus teaches His people by means of His written Word and sends the Holy Spirit to teach and to live inside all who believe in Him. **Read Acts 2:32–33.** As priest, He intercedes for us with the Father. That means that He asks for things for us so that we will receive all He has earned for us. **Read Hebrews 7:24–25.** As king, Jesus rules over us, His church. He protects us and gives us all that we need. **Read Colossians 1:13–14.**

FRIDAY

Jesus will be further exalted at the end of time when He returns. At that time Jesus will judge everyone who has ever lived for all they did during their lifetimes. Those who lived in rebellion against God and never repented will be condemned to punishment that lasts forever. Those who rebelled against God but repented and put their faith in Christ will go to spend eternity with Him in heaven. They will be rewarded for their righteous deeds. The Bible teaches that Jesus is the One whom God has appointed as Judge. He will judge those who are still alive at His return as well as those who have already died. **Read Acts 17:31 and John 5:22–23.**

SATURDAY

Read 1 Corinthians 15:24–28. Jesus is Lord of all even now. But He waits patiently for people to repent. As He waits, His enemies—demons, death, rebellious human beings—fight against Him. One day, Jesus will destroy all His enemies. Only those who love and serve and honor Him will live with Him. This will be the final step in Jesus' exaltation. He will forever stop all His enemies from resisting His will. Voices in heaven will celebrate, saying, "The kingdom of the world has become the kingdom of our Lord and of His Christ and He will reign for ever and ever" (Rev. 11:15).

Q.29. HOW ARE WE MADE TO TAKE PART IN THE REDEMPTION CHRIST BOUGHT?

A. *We take part in the redemption Christ bought when the Holy Spirit effectively applies it to us.*

MONDAY

Imagine that you are a prisoner of the most wicked ruler in the universe. Imagine that this ruler keeps you as a captive in his kingdom always, a kingdom of darkness and sorrow. Not only that, but imagine that this ruler has power over you to make you do his evil will. Day after day, he causes you to do things that hurt both you and those you love. What a miserable way to live! All of us live like this before we believe in Christ. We need someone stronger than our powerful enemy, Satan, to rescue us from his power and place us in the kingdom of the wise and good King, Jesus.

Because of our sin, Satan has power over us. To free us from his evil rule, someone must pay the price for our sin. Jesus frees us from the rule of Satan and places us in His own kingdom. Jesus bought our redemption, or paid the price for our sin, to set us free from Satan. **Read Colossians 1:13–14.**

TUESDAY

Do you still remember the answer to Question 20, Did God leave all mankind to die in sin and misery? The answer begins: "From all eternity and merely because it pleased Him, God chose some to have everlasting life." Before any of them were even born and before Adam had ever sinned, God planned to redeem His people. **Read Ephesians 1:11.**

Whatever God plans, He always accomplishes, exactly as He had planned. None of those whom God has chosen can "die in sin and misery." Many people seem to think that Jesus died on the cross to make it *possible* for people to be saved. Now they think He waits to see who will believe in Him, hoping that people will. The Bible teaches that *all* whom God has chosen *will* believe in Jesus and be saved. The Holy Spirit makes sure that all of God's chosen ones will trust in Christ as their Savior. God the Father chose people to save; God the Son died to redeem or save those people; and God the Holy Spirit works in the hearts of those people to cause them to trust in Christ.

WEDNESDAY

Many people think that all God can do to save people from their sin He has already done: He gave His Son to die to pay for sin. Now, these people think, God can do nothing but hope that people will trust in His Son as Savior. Each person must decide whether he or she will be saved. The Bible teaches that God planned to save specific people and that He will save every one of those people. God *always* accomplishes His purposes and no one can stop Him.

More than that, the Bible teaches that, left to themselves, no one would ever believe in Jesus. The Holy Spirit must first work in people's hearts to make them sorry for their sin. Only then can they believe. In the all-important work of salvation, God does not do a part of it, or even most of it, and then we must do the rest. God plans our salvation. He gave His Son to save us. He makes us able to believe. God does it all. **Read Romans 9:15–18.**

THURSDAY

God is one God in three persons: Father, Son, and Holy Spirit. All three of the persons who are God are always agreed on everything. In everything that God does, each of the three persons has an important part. This is true of our redemption. God the Father, God the Son, and God the Holy Spirit each participated in redeeming us. God the Father chose people and willed or planned to redeem them. God the Son took on a human body to live a life of perfect righteousness in the place of God's people and to die to pay for their sins. **Read Galatians 1:3–5.**

FRIDAY

The Holy Spirit also plays an important part in the redemption of God's people. Jesus' death was worth enough to pay for the sins of the whole world. However, it only counts for those who believe in Him as the Savior from sin. The Holy Spirit is the One who works in the hearts of people to cause them to believe in Jesus. That is what the answer to this week's question means when it says that "the Holy Spirit effectively applies" Christ's redemption to us.

Because of sin, our hearts are hardened against God. Left to ourselves, we want only what we want, not what God wants. On our own, we cannot understand our need for a Savior. Left to ourselves, we would not choose to believe in Jesus. Our hearts must change *first* and then we can repent for our sin and believe. Only the Holy Spirit can change a heart. The change in a heart that the Holy Spirit causes is so great a change that the Bible speaks of it as being born all over again. This change of heart is what Jesus meant when He spoke of being born again or being born of the Spirit. **Read John 3:3–6.**

SATURDAY

God alone saves His people. If certain people are God's chosen ones, they will repent and believe, no matter how far from God they have wandered. God does everything necessary to save His people. No sin and no stubbornness on the part of His people can keep God from saving them. We do not have to worry that some of God's people will continue to rebel and will never turn to Christ. Since God is the One who saves His people, we know that all of them will be saved. **Read John 6:37–39.**

<table>
<tr>
<td>

Q.30.

</td>
<td>

HOW DOES THE HOLY SPIRIT APPLY TO US THE REDEMPTION CHRIST BOUGHT?

</td>
</tr>
</table>

A. ✒ *The Spirit applies to us the redemption Christ bought by producing faith in us and so uniting us to Christ in our effective calling.*

MONDAY

Because Adam was the father of the whole human race, all of us are united to him. Just by being born, we are united to Adam, the first human being. We are united with him in his sin. When Adam disobeyed God, it was counted as though *we* had disobeyed God. We are united with Adam in his sinful nature. Each of us is born sinful inside, wanting our own way instead of God's way. We are united with Adam in the death that his sin brought into the world.

If we are to be saved, we must be united with Christ. His life of perfect obedience must become ours. His death for sin must become ours. His victory over death must become ours. **Read 2 Corinthians 5:17.** Faith unites us to Christ.

TUESDAY

Read Hebrews 11:6. We must have faith to please God. **Read Romans 8:8.** The person controlled by the sinful nature cannot please God. On our own, we do not have the faith that pleases God. We are not able to believe in Jesus and so be united to Him. If we cannot have faith by ourselves, where does faith come from? **Read Ephesians 2:8–9.** Faith is God's gift to His people.

God the Father gave His Son to redeem us. God the Son lived a life of perfect obedience and died to pay for sin. His obedience and death only count for those who are united to Him. Only those who have put their faith in Jesus are united to Him. The Holy Spirit produces the faith in God's people that makes them able to believe in Jesus and be united to Him.

WEDNESDAY

Read Galatians 2:20. One way we are united with Christ is in His death. His death on the cross was God's punishment for sin. When we put our faith in Jesus, God counts it as though we ourselves had died on the cross with Him. Now all our sins have been punished once and for all. When a judge condemns a criminal, he pronounces the criminal guilty and tells him what punishment he must suffer for what he has done wrong. **Read Romans 8:1.** There is no condemnation for those who are "in Christ Jesus," or who are united to Him.

THURSDAY

We are also united with Christ in His life and in His resurrection. Jesus spent His whole life on earth perfectly doing the will of His Father. By faith, His perfect righteousness becomes ours. **Read 2 Corinthians 5:21.** As Jesus rose from the dead, so our bodies will also one day rise from the dead. **Read 1 Corinthians 15:22.** By faith, we also become united with Jesus in a new life of holiness. Jesus lived His whole life seeking to please God. When we are united with Him, we want what He wants. The Holy Spirit, who lives inside us, gives us the power to desire God's will and seek to follow it in our lives. **Read Romans 6:4–7.**

FRIDAY

Sin and rebellion against God have consequences. Adam earned these consequences by his disobedience. All of Adam's descendants, who are united to Adam by birth, experience those consequences—sorrow, pain, death, and God's anger. Righteousness and obedience also have consequences: God's blessing, God's favor, eternal life, and everlasting joy and peace. Jesus earned these blessings by His perfect righteousness. All believers in Jesus, who are united to Christ by faith, experience the rewards of obedience. **Read Ephesians 1:3 and Ephesians 2:6–7.**

SATURDAY

Another wonderful way we are united to Christ is in His glory. When He returns, the Bible tells us that we will share in His glory. When He rules over everything, we will reign with Him. **Read Colossians 3:4.** Christians are people who are united to Christ. They are united to Him in His death, in His life, in His resurrection, and in His glory. They are united to Christ by their faith and their faith comes from the Holy Spirit.

Q.31. WHAT IS EFFECTIVE CALLING?

A. ✍ *Effective calling is the work of God's Spirit, Who convinces us that we are sinful and miserable, Who enlightens our minds in the knowledge of Christ, and Who renews our wills. This is how He persuades and makes us able to receive Jesus Christ, Who is freely offered to us in the gospel.*

MONDAY

Read (or repeat from memory!) **John 3:16.** What does this verse say that those who believe in the Son of God will have? What would have happened to those people if they had *not* believed in Jesus? According to this verse, why did God send His Son? Who will have eternal life?

God's love is so great that He gave His only Son. All anyone has to do to have eternal life instead of perishing is simply to believe in Jesus. Then why doesn't everyone believe in Jesus? The answer is that, because of their sin, people cannot trust Christ to save them. Sinning comes naturally to us. Doing what God tells us to do—such as trusting Christ for salvation—is unnatural to us. In the gospel, God freely offers Jesus Christ to us as a Savior. Left to ourselves, we cannot receive Him. God makes sure that all of His people receive Jesus Christ through effective calling.

TUESDAY

At dinner time, a mother whose children are playing in the yard might stand at the back door saying, in a loud voice, "Dinner's ready!" The children may obey their mother and come in—or they may not. That would be one kind of calling. That is not "effective calling." "Effective" means to cause an effect, to make something happen. Effective calling is calling that *causes* the person being called to respond. In effective calling, God calls a person to receive Jesus Christ as He is offered in the gospel. At the same time, God actually *causes* that person to do what He has called her or him to do. The Holy Spirit effectively calls God's chosen ones so that they respond in faith to the gospel. **Read 2 Thessalonians 2:13–14.**

WEDNESDAY

Imagine that you were having a great time swimming when along came a person who had a fear of water. He saw you in the pool, cried, "I'll save you! I'll save you!" and dragged you out of the water. Would you appreciate that? Of course not. You did not need saving. You were having fun.

God offers His Son to people as a Savior from sin. People do not see their need for a Savior unless they believe there is something dangerous from which they need to be saved. Left to ourselves, we would never turn to Christ to save us from sin because, by ourselves, we do not see our need for a Savior. We enjoy the things that God calls sin. We do not see sin as dangerous, but as pleasant. **Read John 3:19.**

People will not ask Jesus to save them from their sin until they realize how sinful and miserable they are without Christ. One thing the Holy Spirit does in effective calling is to convince us that we are miserable sinners in need of a Savior. **Read** what Jesus said about the Holy Spirit to His disciples in **John 16:7–8.**

THURSDAY

Even if people understand that they are sinful and need to be saved, that is not enough. They must also understand *how* to be saved. All over the world and all through history, people have invented many ways of trying to be right with God. But because man's mind is sinful, he can think as long and as hard as he likes and he will never understand how to be saved. That is because he has a sinful mind and cannot understand spiritual truth. **Read 1 Corinthians 2:14.** The natural man thinks the things of the Spirit of God are foolishness. **Read 1 Corinthians 2:12.**

People will not trust Jesus to save them from their sin unless they believe that Jesus can save them. But the god of this age (Satan) does something to keep people from seeing who Jesus really is. **Read 2 Corinthians 4:4.**

In effective calling, the Holy Spirit shows us our need for a Savior. He also enlightens our minds. He makes us able to understand that God has provided a Savior from sin and that the Savior is Jesus. **Read 2 Corinthians 4:6.**

FRIDAY

Yesterday we saw that our sinful minds need the Holy Spirit so they can understand the salvation God provides. That means too that our sinful wills need the Holy Spirit. Left to ourselves, we would never choose what pleases God. **Read John 5:39–40.** Jesus spoke these words to Jews who did not believe in Him. These Jews studied the Scriptures and the Scriptures clearly teach that Jesus is the Savior. Yet the Jews refused to come to Him. Our sinful wills must be renewed. They need to be made capable of choosing to trust in Christ and serve Him as Lord. In effective calling, the Holy Spirit renews our wills so that we can make the choice to obey God's command to believe in Jesus. **Read Romans 8:5–6.**

SATURDAY

The Holy Spirit persuades God's people to believe in Jesus. That is wonderful to know. Those people who preach or teach can know that whether or not people trust Christ does not depend on how good a job they do. It would be terrible for anyone to think, "That person may not go to heaven because I did not speak well enough." It is the Holy Spirit who persuades people to believe in Jesus, not a speaker. Also, since the Holy Spirit is the One who persuades people, we can be sure that not one of God's people will be left out of His kingdom. The Holy Spirit will provide whatever is needed and will work in hearts, even when the people who explain the gospel are not very good speakers.

Those who believe in Jesus get no credit for helping to save themselves. Those who explained the gospel to them get no credit for saving them either. All of the praise and all of the glory for any person's salvation go to God alone. **Read 1 Corinthians 2:4–5.**

Q.32.

WHAT BENEFITS DO THOSE WHO ARE EFFECTIVELY CALLED SHARE IN THIS LIFE?

A. *In this life those who are effectively called share justification, adoption, sanctification, and the other benefits that either go with or come from them.*

MONDAY

If you have put your faith in Jesus to save you, you have received certain benefits. A benefit is something that makes things better for you. Often, we earn benefits. ("If you turn in all your homework this week, you can stay up half an hour later on Friday.") Sometimes we buy benefits. ("If you buy an all-day pass to the water park, you may use all the slides as often as you like that day.")

The benefits we have when we have been effectively called have been given to us for free! God the Father planned, long before we were born, to give us these benefits. They had to be bought, but God the Son bought them for us with His blood. The Holy Spirit applies them to us. These benefits make us much better off, not just when we die and go to heaven, but now in this life as well. **Read Ephesians 1:3–8.**

TUESDAY

The biggest problem we have ever had is that we are sinners while God is holy. Somehow we must get rid of our sin and become right with God. Justification is God's solution to this problem. In justification, God forgives our sin because Jesus has already been punished for it. In justification, God counts the righteousness of Jesus' perfect life to us, as if we had lived that perfect life ourselves.

If we could have kept the law of God ourselves, we would be righteous and we would have earned for ourselves eternal life.

Read Galatians 3:21b–22. We cannot keep God's holy law because we are prisoners of sin. God's law shows us how impossible it is for us to become right with God ourselves. It leads us to Jesus so that we will trust Him to do everything for us that needs to be done. Then we can be forgiven and declared right with God. **Read Galatians 3:24.**

WEDNESDAY

God created us for the wonderful purpose of knowing, loving, and glorifying Him. Because of sin, all of us are born God's enemies. So another serious problem for us is that we cannot know the very One we were created to know. We are cut off from Him and cannot be what we were made to be. Living to have fun or living to get rich or living to be famous or even living to love others is not enough for us.

We have been created for something much bigger than any of these. We have been created to know and love God. One benefit of our effective calling is that we are made able to know God. But God is so good to us that the way we can know Him now is not just as creatures knowing their Creator. Those who have been redeemed by Jesus Christ know God as their Father. What a wonderful thing! Even though we sinned against our Creator, making ourselves His enemies, He redeems us and makes us not only His servants—He adopts us as His children! God's solution to our problem of not being able to know Him is to adopt us. **Read 1 John 3:1.**

THURSDAY

There is still another problem we have because of sin: we are unable to please or to obey God. God created us with the ability to obey Him. Adam could choose to do good or to do evil. Once Adam sinned, though, he lost the ability to do anything that pleases God. People can still do things that other people count as good, but they do these things to please others or to feel good about themselves. True righteousness, done only for God, is impossible for those who have not been effectively called.

God's solution to this problem of ours is sanctification. The Holy Spirit changes the hearts of those whom He effectively calls so that they can desire and do what pleases God. The Bible calls this changed heart a "new self." Being given a new self that desires holiness is one part of sanctification. At the same time, God's people still have sin left inside from their old way of life. The Bible promises us that until we go to heaven, we will have to fight the sin left inside of us. When we safely arrive in heaven, there will no longer be any sin left inside to trouble us. In the meantime, the Bible tells us to use those things God has provided to help us grow. If we do, God promises that the Holy Spirit will cause us to become more and more like Jesus, even while we are still in this life. Growing in Christlikeness is the other part of sanctification. **Read 2 Corinthians 3:18.**

FRIDAY

Sometimes people talk as if going to heaven when we die is the main reason to believe in Jesus. The Bible tells us that heaven will certainly be wonderful, more wonderful than anything that we could imagine. But as this question and answer point out, the benefits of believing Jesus begin in *this* life, not just after we die.

Because people are sinful inside and because Satan works hard to keep people distracted, non-Christians keep busy with jobs and fun. They do not often stop to realize how miserable they are without Christ. Those who do not enjoy the benefit of justification (being declared righteous by God) have a tremendous load of guilt to carry around all the time. If they are honest with themselves, they know that they have done many things to hurt themselves and others and to offend God. They cannot undo any of those things and they cannot be forgiven apart from Christ.

Someone who does not enjoy the benefit of adoption has no relationship at all with God. This is a very lonely way to live, because all of the wonderful friends and family in the world cannot make up for the relationship with God that we were created to have. Those who do not enjoy the benefit of sanctification (God making us able to grow constantly in holiness) can never obey God and live as they were created to live. In *this* life, the benefits of being effectively called give joy, peace, and fullness to life that a non-Christian cannot know. **Read Psalm 16:11.**

SATURDAY

There are two men in the Bible named Saul. If we compare them, we can see what a difference the benefits of effective calling make. The Old Testament Saul was a king. He lived in a palace and he could have anything he wanted. When he gave orders, people obeyed. The New Testament Saul became the apostle Paul. He lived a life of hardship and suffering, often going without the basic things we need for everyday life. He was beaten, stoned, put in prison, and chased out of towns by people who did not like him.

Which Saul would we naturally expect to be the most satisfied and content? King Saul, of course. However, that was not the case. The Holy Spirit had effectively called the New Testament Saul. This Saul had been justified, and he rejoiced because his sins had been forgiven. He had been adopted by God the Father, and he knew that, however many enemies he had, he was God's son and God would always love him. This Saul had been sanctified and was able to spend his life serving God and becoming like Jesus.

King Saul, on the other hand, was an angry, bitter man who had no peace at all. Demons would even come and trouble his mind. He lived much of his life in rebellion against God and died knowing that God was his enemy and that he had no hope at all. Those of us who have received the benefits of effective calling should certainly not consider ourselves better than others because we had nothing to do with saving ourselves; God did it all. But how very grateful we should be that God has rescued us and freely given us all these benefits. **Read Ephesians 2:12–13.**

Q.33. WHAT IS JUSTIFICATION?

A. ✍ *Justification is the act of God's free grace by which He pardons all our sins and accepts us as righteous in His sight. He does so only because He counts the righteousness of Christ as ours. Justification is received by faith alone.*

MONDAY

Read Romans 3:22–24. It is very important for man to be righteous in the sight of God. No one can appear before God without perfect righteousness. These verses tell us that we receive the only righteousness God accepts when we trust Christ to provide it for us. None of us provide our own righteousness before God. Justification (God pardoning our sins and accepting us as righteous) is an act of God's free grace. That means we cannot earn it for ourselves. Anything God gives us by His grace is something we did not deserve, but something that He simply chose to give us.

When God justifies us, He does not ignore our sin. He never says, "Oh, well, that's okay," about sin. God is always holy and just, so He always punishes all sin. God can justify us because Jesus was punished in our place for our sin. Because of Jesus' death in our place, God can justify us and still be perfectly just in always punishing sin. **Read Romans 3:25–26.**

TUESDAY

Justification has two important parts. The first one is the pardoning of all the sin we have committed. The Bible tells us that, whenever we sin, we sin against God. Even when our sins hurt other people, it is God against whom we sin. He created us and gave us the laws by which we are to live. Before God, every one of us is like a criminal standing before a judge in a courtroom with a long, long list of crimes we have committed. When God pardons our sin, He does not undo all the wrong we have done. He does not say that we have not sinned. To pardon our sin is to no longer hold it against us. We no longer have to pay for it. We will not have to suffer the punishment our crimes against God deserve. God has pardoned our sins because Jesus has taken every last bit of punishment our sins deserved. Nothing remains for us to pay. **Read Psalm 32:1–2.**

WEDNESDAY

Even if God has pardoned our sins, there is something we need to be right with God. We need to be righteous. God would not be pleased with someone simply because that person had done nothing wrong. Only the person who has done *all* of the righteous acts God commands, without ever failing once, pleases God. We can never be righteous with the perfect righteousness that God requires.

The second important part of justification is God accepting us as righteous in His sight. We have not done what God required, but we have put our faith in His Son. God credits or counts the righteousness of Jesus to us as though we had lived the life of perfect obedience that He lived. **Read Romans 4:3–5.**

THURSDAY

How can God accept us as righteous in His sight when we are not righteous at all? "He does so only because He counts the righteousness of Christ as ours." Imagine that you need a great deal of money for something important. However, not only do you not *have* a great deal of money; you are deeply in debt. Along comes your friend who has worked hard for years to build a big savings account in the bank. He feels sorry for you and offers to pay your bills. Now you are no longer in debt. This is something like Jesus paying for our sin by His death on the cross. Now we no longer owe God anything for all our sins against Him.

However, just because your friend paid your debt does not mean that you have solved your problem. You still need a great deal of money and you have absolutely none. So now your friend does something else for you. He has your name added to his bank account so that now you can use all his money. This is something like Jesus living a life of perfect obedience to God in our place. He is the One who is righteous. He is the One who did the obeying, but all His righteousness is credited to us. God counts the righteousness of Christ as ours. **Read 2 Corinthians 5:21.**

FRIDAY

We receive the justification that God gives us by faith alone. Many people believe they must do certain things to be right with God—go to church, help poor people, do good deeds. Others would say they believe in Jesus but they must *also* do certain things. Faith in Jesus *plus* their own good deeds make them right with God. The Bible clearly teaches that all we need to do to be justified is to receive by faith what God gives us. He has pardoned all our sin, and He has declared us righteous with the perfect righteousness of His own Son. We can add nothing to what Jesus has done. We simply accept by faith that He has indeed done it. No one can brag about how good he or she is. All of us receive justification by faith alone and not by any goodness or obedience of our own to God's law. **Read Romans 3:27–28.**

SATURDAY

Read Zechariah 3:1–5. This passage describes the vision of Zechariah, an Old Testament prophet. The vision is a picture of what God does for His people when He justifies them. This Joshua is not the same one that led an army against Jericho. This Joshua was a high priest in Israel. This means that he represented the people of God. In Zechariah's vision, he saw Joshua dressed in filthy clothes.

This is a picture of us, God's people, in our sin. In the vision, the angel of the Lord had the filthy clothes removed from Joshua, saying, "See, I have taken away your sin." In the Old Testament, whenever "the angel of the Lord" appears, it is always the Son of God before He took on a human body. So it is the Lord Jesus Christ who takes away the sin of His people. But that was not all that the angel of the Lord did for Joshua. He also dressed him in clean, rich clothing. Jesus not only takes away the sin of His people, He gives them His very own righteousness as well.

A. ✑ *Adoption is the act of God's free grace by which we become His sons with all the rights and privileges of being His.*

MONDAY

Before man sinned, he belonged to God. After the Fall, man still belonged to God, but God was angry with him. The only relationship that sinful man can have with God is one of fear. Whenever God effectively calls a person, the relationship changes. God adopts that person as His child. All whom God has effectively called have God as their Father. (Many people like to talk about God as the Father of *all* human beings, but the Bible teaches that only those who have believed in Jesus Christ can call God Father.) **Read 1 John 3:1–2.** God is very gracious *not* to punish us as we deserve. He is gracious to justify us and to save us from our sins. Even more than that, His love for us is so great that He even adopts us as His children and becomes our Father!

TUESDAY

It is wonderful to be able to say we are God's children and He is our Father. In addition, we also have rights and privileges as children of God. For one thing, we no longer have to be afraid of God. Certainly we should always have the fear of God spoken of in the Bible, a fear that causes us to show reverence and take care not to sin. But we no longer have to be terrified of God. We do not have to fear that He will stop loving us or will punish us if we sin. There are good human fathers and bad human fathers. God is like the very best of human fathers, but even better. **Read Romans 8:15.** These verses say we call God "Abba." "Abba" was the word for

"Daddy" in New Testament times. God's children have the closest and most loving relationship possible with their Father, God.

WEDNESDAY

We no longer need to be afraid of punishment for our sin. That does *not* mean that God will allow us to sin without doing anything about it. A good parent will not allow children to continue being naughty without doing something to stop them. Good parents discipline naughty or foolish children to train them to behave wisely and well. God is the best Father there is. Of course, He disciplines His children when they need it.

Sometimes, we do wrong and suffer for it later. That is one way God disciplines us. Sometimes we have not done anything that is sinful, but we go through something difficult. God uses that difficult thing to better train us to be what He wants us to be. That is His discipline, also. We do not usually think of the hard things we face as privileges, but for God's children, they are. One of the privileges that we have as God's children is the privilege of knowing that our Father will not allow us to do whatever we please. Instead, He will discipline us so we will grow into wise and mature Christians. **Read Hebrews 12:5–10.**

THURSDAY

One of the privileges a child of good parents has is that his parents provide for him. Good parents make sure that their children have everything they need. God is the best Father. He has promised to care for His children and to provide for them.

Children have the right of sharing in everything their parents own. We call this the right of inheritance. If parents die and they have not left a will saying that something different should be done, their children automatically inherit or receive everything that belonged to the parents. Of course, our Father God will never die. But He calls us His heirs, or the ones who will inherit what belongs to Him. Jesus is God's true Son, begotten and not adopted. He always obeyed His Father and is called God's heir. Now that God has adopted us into His family, we are co-heirs with Jesus. The glory and all the spiritual blessings that belong to Jesus, He will one day share with us. **Read Romans 8:16–17.**

FRIDAY

Being the adopted children of God is a wonderful thing, with many rich privileges. Whenever we have privileges, we usually have responsibilities as well. Children of God have responsibilities. One responsibility we have is that of becoming what God wants us to become. When He made us His children, it was not so that we could simply sit back and enjoy our privileges as His children. **Read Romans 8:28–29.** These verses tell us that God has chosen and called us to be His children for a purpose that we all become more and more like His only begotten Son, Jesus.

SATURDAY

One specific way in which the Bible tells us that children of God should be like Jesus is in love. The Bible says that if we say we are God's children, we will love His other children as well. We will not just love the ones we find easy to love. Because God is our Father and theirs, we will love all those who belong to the family of God. The Bible even says that if there are Christians whom we hate (or do not love), we lie when we call ourselves children of God.

Another specific way in which we are to be like Jesus is in righteous living. God hates sin. No child of His will practice sin. That does not mean that God's children are perfect. However, when they *do* sin, they will repent of it and try hard not to do it again. It is the person who continues to *practice* sin and refuses to stop, whom the Bible says is not really one of God's children. **Read 1 John 3:10.**

Q.35.

WHAT IS SANCTIFICATION?

A. ✒ *Sanctification is the work of God's free grace by which our whole person is made new in the image of God, and we are made more and more able to become dead to sin and alive to righteousness.*

MONDAY

Read 1 Corinthians 6:11. One of the things God does in us and for us when He saves us is to sanctify us. To sanctify means two things. First, it means to set aside for something special. God paid for us with the blood of His own Son. We belong to Him and He has a purpose for us. He wants us to be holy, as He is holy. He wants us to become like His Son, the Lord Jesus Christ. So the first meaning of sanctification is being set aside by God to be holy. This is something that God does once for all when He saves us.

To sanctify also means to change a person, little by little, until he or she actually *becomes* holy. When God sanctifies us, He sets us apart to be holy and then begins to work in our sinful hearts to change us. We will grow less and less sinful and more and more holy. God's work of sanctification continues throughout a believer's life. It is never finished in this life. No one on this earth ever becomes perfect. The older believers become, the more like Jesus they should grow. When we go to heaven, God will finish the work of sanctification He has begun in us. In heaven, we will never sin but will always obey God perfectly.

TUESDAY

God created man in His own image. In many ways, we can still see the image of God in man. But at the same time, all people are now born in the sinful image of Adam. In sanctification, God makes

116

us new again in His image. Sin is not completely gone from our hearts. But now we have a new self who wants to do what pleases God. That new self will grow stronger and stronger while the sin that remains becomes weaker and weaker. This is sanctification. Everything about us is made new and grows in Christlikeness—our desires, our thoughts, our attitudes.

Sometimes, it seems like we never will be Christlike. We find it so hard to break sinful habits. New Christlike habits are so hard to develop. However, sanctification is God's work. He always finishes what He begins. We can be sure that God will keep working in us until He has completed our sanctification and we are holy and blameless. **Read 1 Thessalonians 5:23–24.**

WEDNESDAY

Because sin remains, even inside Christians, we find that we often want to do wrong. Because God has made us His children, we have a Christlike character that wants to do what pleases God. All the rest of our lives, the sin inside us and our new Christlike nature will fight one another. Sometimes we will want very badly to do wrong and it will take a great deal of strength to resist doing it.

Sin always fights for its own way. Whenever we give in and sin, we find that we do not enjoy it as we thought we would. That is because our new self wants to please God and cannot be at peace when we sin. As God works in us to sanctify us, the sin inside us with all its habits and desires will gradually weaken. Our new holy character will grow stronger and new Christlike attitudes will become ours. **Read Ephesians 4:22–24.**

THURSDAY

Like justification and adoption, sanctification is something *God* does. We could try as hard as we could to get rid of sin on our own and we would never be able to do so. We could work hard every day at trying to be like Jesus, but if God did not sanctify us it would be no use at all. The work of sanctification is given to God the Holy Spirit. When God effectively calls a person, the Holy Spirit comes to live inside that person. He always works in each believer, causing that person to love and desire Christ and to want to please Him by being like Him.

Read 2 Corinthians 3:18. The Bible tells us that we can see when we are letting the Holy Spirit have His way in our lives by looking at our attitudes. When we show love, joy, peace, patience, kindness, goodness, faithfulness, gentleness, and self-control, we are living by the Holy Spirit and not by our old sinful desires (Gal. 5:22–23).

FRIDAY

Although God is the One who does the work of sanctification in the believer, that does not mean that we sit back and do nothing. God requires us to cooperate with the Holy Spirit in our sanctification. We must work hard every day at breaking sinful habits and refusing to have sinful attitudes. Every day we must seek to follow Jesus' example and to try to please Him. That is why the New Testament is so full of instructions to God's people about how to live, how to be holy, and how to love God and others.

God has given us means that we are to use to grow in sanctification. Reading the Bible, praying, listening to the preaching of God's Word and worshiping with others at church are all things that God tells us to do to grow in sanctification. We should work hard at doing what God has called us to do, but we never have to feel discouraged because we do not change as quickly as we would like. We know that sanctification is God's work. He will continue to work in us until He has made us perfect at last. **Read Philippians 2:12–13.**

SATURDAY

Over and over again every day, we will want to sin—and we will want it badly. Perhaps someone has done something that has made us angry and we feel like *acting* angry! Maybe we know something about someone and we desperately want to tell someone else, although we know that we should not say it. There may be something we think we would enjoy doing even though we think it is wrong. It is difficult to resist doing these sinful things when we feel so strongly that we just *have* to do them. Not doing the sin we feel like doing is so hard that the Bible speaks of it as "putting to death" our sinful desires. We must die to ourselves by not doing the sin we feel like doing if we want to grow in sanctification. Over and over again, we will have to tell ourselves "No" when we are tempted to sin. **Read Colossians 3:5.**

The Bible tells us that our minds play an important part in our sanctification. God changes our character by changing how we think about things. He changes how we think about things by His Word. We must study God's Word every day to fill our minds with what it says. We will act like Jesus when we have learned to think like Jesus. **Read Romans 12:2.**

Q.36.
WHAT BENEFITS IN THIS LIFE GO WITH OR COME FROM JUSTIFICATION, ADOPTION, AND SANCTIFICATION?

A. ✥ *The benefits that in this life go with or come from justification, adoption, and sanctification are: the assurance of God's love, peace of conscience, joy in the Holy Spirit, and growing and persevering in grace to the end of our lives.*

MONDAY

God is good to all His creatures. God's special love, however, is only for His people. Sin turns all human beings into God's enemies, with whom He is angry. God's people are just as sinful as anyone else, but God has chosen to love them. He does not love them because they are good or because they are lovable. He loves them just because He is love and has chosen to love them.

Because God loves His people, He has given His Son to die in their place so that He can forgive their sins. Because God loves His people, He justifies them—counts them as righteous—since His Son has lived a life of perfect righteousness in their place. The prophet Jeremiah describes God's love for His people. **Read Jeremiah 31:3.** God's love for His people is an everlasting love. If you are God's adopted, justified child, you can be sure that God loves you with a love that had no beginning and will have no end—no matter what!

TUESDAY

Sometimes God's children may *feel* like God does not love them. Perhaps they have done something wrong and even after asking

God to forgive them, they feel like God could not possibly love them any longer. Or perhaps their circumstances have become very difficult. Terrible things have happened to them and it seems to them that, if God loved them, He would not let such things happen to them. Sometimes people just feel discouraged and find it hard to believe that God loves them.

Even in times like these, we have the assurance of God's love. How can this be? It is because our assurance is not a feeling we have inside. Our assurance is what God Himself has said. God never lies. He never changes. When He promises that He will love His children always, no matter what, we know that He will. When we do not *feel* assurance of His love, we go to His Word and look again at His promises. Because He has said that He will always love His children, we are sure that He will always love us. **Read Romans 8:35–39,** making a list of the things that cannot separate us from the love of God.

WEDNESDAY

God created man with a conscience. Conscience is the awareness of right and wrong. The Bible tells us that even people who have never seen a Bible or heard about the true God feel guilty sometimes. This is because they know that they have done wrong. When man sinned, his conscience became fallen. It no longer worked as well as it was intended to work. Now we find it easy to excuse the wrong things we do. The mark of someone who is very far from God and who is deeply trapped in sin is that his conscience hardly ever troubles him. He can do the most evil things and never feel badly about them at all.

When the Holy Spirit begins to work in a person's heart to effectively call that person to faith in Christ, He makes the person's conscience very sensitive. The person begins to see the many ways he has sinned against God and is troubled about it. Once the person puts his faith in Christ, his conscience has peace. That is because he knows that Jesus took the punishment he deserved. He knows that God has forgiven him and has cleansed him of his sin.

Does this mean that a child of God can sin and never feel guilty for it? Not at all. The true child of God will have a more sensitive conscience than anyone else. Whenever he sins, he will be very sorry that he has done something to offend his Father, God. Because he is a child of God, he will know what to do about a guilty conscience. He confesses his sin to God and knows that God will forgive him because of Jesus. Then his conscience is at peace again. **Read Hebrews 10:22.**

THURSDAY

As God's children, we have assurance of His love and we have peace of conscience. We also have joy in the Holy Spirit. Joy in the Holy Spirit is different from happiness. Happiness comes and goes and depends on what happens around us. Believers can have joy in the Holy Spirit all the time. It comes from knowing Jesus and knowing what He has done for us.

No matter what happens around him, the child of God knows that Jesus died for him. He knows God is working in his life and in the world to accomplish His wonderful plans. No matter what the child of God does *not* have that he wishes he had, he knows that he has Jesus now and will have heaven later. The Holy Spirit continually reminds us of Jesus' love for us and of all that He has given us, causing us to rejoice no matter what our circumstances. This is why, when Paul and Silas were in jail with their feet in stocks and their backs sore from having been beaten, they still sang praises. **Read 1 Peter 1:8.**

FRIDAY

Children start life very small (about the size of a pencil dot!) and grow rapidly. Children of God grow too. All through this life, God's children grow. They grow in love, in knowledge of God and of His Word, and in patience. They grow to be like Jesus. This is what we mean by growing in grace. God's Spirit works in His children, causing them to grow into what He wants them to be. As we grow older, our bodies slow down and weaken. Once perfect eyes need glasses. Ears that heard perfectly need hearing aids. Strong bodies are not so strong anymore. The apostle Paul wrote about this. Paul added that Christians can be encouraged because, even while their outer body gets older and weaker, on the inside they are being renewed day by day. They are growing in grace every day. **Read 2 Corinthians 4:16.**

SATURDAY

Not only do God's children enjoy the benefit of growing in grace, they also enjoy the benefit of persevering in grace to the end of their lives. This means that, no matter what temptations they face, they will never turn away from God or stop trusting in Christ for their salvation. Is that because God's children are so strong or good or holy? No, they will persevere in grace—they will continue to trust and obey Jesus—their whole life because God will make sure that they do.

Read John 10:27–29. Jesus speaks of His people as His sheep. He says that no one can snatch them out of His hand. God the Father also holds His people in His hand. Those of us who have put our faith in Jesus Christ to save us from sin know that we will continue to have faith in Him all the way to heaven. God Himself has promised to keep us.

Q.37. WHAT BENEFITS DO BELIEVERS RECEIVE FROM CHRIST WHEN THEY DIE?

A. 🖋 *When believers die, their souls are made perfectly holy and immediately pass into glory. Their bodies, which are still united to Christ, rest in the grave until the resurrection.*

MONDAY

When someone we love dies, it makes us sad. When we love people, we want to be with them. Death separates us from people we love so that we can no longer be with them or talk to them. Death was not a part of what God originally made. Sometimes you will hear people say that death is just a natural part of life on this earth. That really is not true. Death is *un*natural. People die because sin came into the world. If Adam and Eve had never sinned, no one would ever die. People do not like death and dying. We all see death as an enemy. God does not like death either. It comes from sin. God made everything perfect. Sin and death come from man. They add an ugliness to God's creation that was not there when He created it. **Read Romans 5:12.**

TUESDAY

The Bible tells us that everyone ever born will die someday—unless they are still living when Jesus comes back for His people (Heb. 9:27). What happens when a person dies?

Each of us is made up of two parts. We each have a body and a soul. Our body, of course, is the part of us that people can see, hear, and touch. With our bodies, we see, hear, and touch the world around us. Our soul is the part of us that people cannot see, hear, or touch, but that is real and important just the same. Your soul is the part of you that thinks and that loves and hates. Your soul contains your personality and your personality makes you unlike anybody else in the world. Without your soul, your body could not go on living. A body without a soul cannot think or feel or breathe or do anything at all.

When a person dies, the soul and body are separated. The body still looks like it always did, but the soul inside is not there anymore. Where does that soul go? A wonderful benefit of being one of God's people is that, when we die, our souls "pass immediately into glory." That means that, right away, without having to wait for anything, we go straight to heaven. Why is that called "passing into glory"? Because in heaven, we will get to be with Jesus. We will see Him as He is now, in all His glory. He will welcome us and we will live with Him forever. Those of us who believe in and love the Lord Jesus are very close to Him here in this life and He is always with us. When our souls go to be with Him in heaven, though, we will be much closer to Him than we are now. **Read Philippians 1:21, 23** to see what the apostle Paul looked forward to about dying.

WEDNESDAY

Going to be with Jesus is a wonderful benefit of belonging to Him! When people are very young, they have a hard time believing that being in heaven with Jesus is better than being here on earth with family and friends. That is normal. But the longer we live and the better we get to know Jesus, the more we look forward to living with Him forever in a way that is much closer than anything we experience here on earth.

There is another wonderful benefit that Jesus gives His people when they die. He makes them perfectly holy right away. Here on this earth, we sin every day. We wish we did not, but we do. The more we grow to know and love Jesus, the more unhappy we feel when we sin and do what we know He does not like. Imagine living with Him in heaven and sinning against Him as much as we do here! Fortunately, we do not have to worry about that. When our souls leave our bodies at death and go to be with Jesus, they are "made perfectly holy." We will never do another thing or say another word or think another thought that displeases Jesus! What a wonderful benefit that is! **Read 1 John 3:2.**

THURSDAY

Death separates the soul from the body. When one of God's children dies, the soul goes immediately to be with Jesus, where it is perfectly holy forever. But what about the body? Some people speak as though only the soul matters and the body does not. That is not what God says. God made each of us to be a body and a soul. Our bodies matter to God too.

When we become united with Christ, it is our soul *and* our body that are united with Him. The Lord Jesus Christ has the same body now that He had when He lived on earth. It has been "glorified," which means that it can do things that human bodies here on earth cannot do, but it is the same body. Jesus' body even has the scars from the nail and spear wounds when He was crucified. It is God's will that we have our bodies in heaven, too, as Jesus does. When someone dies, his soul leaves his body, and his body will not stay alive. His friends lovingly wash and dress his body and then bury his body in the ground. God's people especially show respect for the body because they know that the body is important to God.

God has promised to raise from the dead the bodies of all who believe in Jesus. He will do this when Jesus comes again. Even believers who died hundreds of years ago will rise from the dead and have their own bodies back again. They will be better, "glorified" bodies that can never get sick or become old. The believer's soul, which has been with Jesus ever since that person died, will be reunited with her or his body when Jesus raises it from the dead. **Read 1 Corinthians 15:42–44.**

FRIDAY

It is a wonderful thing to think about going to heaven to live with Jesus. It is also wonderful to know that although our bodies will die someday (unless Jesus returns first), He will raise them again and we will have them as perfect bodies in heaven forever. But it is very important to pay attention to what this question says about *who* will receive these benefits. These benefits are for *believers*.

What is a believer? A believer believes what God has said about him—that he is a sinner with whom God is angry. He believes what God has said about Jesus Christ—that He is the Son of God and the only One who can save a sinner from the punishment he deserves. Everyone wants to think that he will go to heaven when he dies. Everyone hopes he will be happy in heaven forever. The Bible tells us that heaven and eternal life are only for believers. Only those who have put their faith in Jesus to save them from God's anger and make them right with God will go to heaven when they die. The rest will have to face God and His anger at their sin all alone. **Read John 3:36.**

SATURDAY

Does thinking about death scare you? Are you afraid of dying? All through history, ever since Adam and Eve sinned, people have feared dying. Death is the enemy that all people fear the most. But those of us who have believed in the Lord Jesus have nothing to fear. There are two things about death that especially frighten people. One is not knowing what will happen to us after we die. The other frightening thing would be having to meet a great and holy God all by ourselves.

But Jesus has put an end to our fears. We do not need to wonder what will happen to us. Jesus has already gone through death and is alive again. He will go with each of us through death as well. We do not have to fear meeting God alone. When Jesus died, He took all of the anger God had toward the sins of His people on Himself. We who believe in Him will never have to face God's anger. Jesus will keep our souls, making sure that they never die, and He will raise our bodies to live forever in heaven with Him. **Read Revelation 1:17–18.**

Q.38.

WHAT BENEFITS DO BELIEVERS RECEIVE FROM CHRIST AT THE RESURRECTION?

A. *At the resurrection, believers, raised in glory, will be publicly recognized and declared not guilty on the day of judgment and will be made completely happy in the full enjoyment of God forever.*

MONDAY

This question asks what believers will receive from Christ at the resurrection. What is the resurrection? The Bible teaches us that, one day, God will bring this sinful world to an end. God will destroy His enemies and Jesus Christ alone will rule. At the time that this world ends and Jesus' reign begins, there will be a resurrection of all the people who have ever died. This will be a joyous time for believers. The Lord Jesus will bring their dead bodies back to life. He will make their bodies better bodies than they had been on earth because He will glorify them.

We do not know all that it means to have a glorified body, but we do know that our glorified bodies will never get sick or old or hurt. Even believers who died hundreds of years ago or believers who had been badly burned or damaged in accidents will receive their bodies back again, raised from the dead, perfectly restored and glorified. We know this will happen because Jesus has promised it. A resurrected, glorified body is one of the benefits believers will receive from Christ. **Read John 6:39–40.**

TUESDAY

The end of this sinful world and the resurrection of the dead will take place when Jesus returns. But what about those believers who have *not* died? What about those who are still alive when Jesus returns? **Read 1 Thessalonians 4:16–17.** The dead in Christ will rise from their graves. Then, those who are still living, will rise up to meet the Lord in the air.

What will happen to the *bodies* of those believers who are still alive when the Lord returns? Since they were not raised from the dead, will they be glorified bodies too? The Bible teaches that the bodies of believers who are still living will be changed in an instant (1 Cor. 15:51–52), so that these believers too will have glorified bodies that will live forever with no sickness, pain, or death.

WEDNESDAY

Have you ever been a member of a group to which you were proud to belong? Have you ever been glad that people knew that a certain person was *your* dad or *your* friend? If you are a believer, the Bible tells us that when Jesus returns, He will let everyone know that you belong to Him. This is one of the benefits believers will receive from Christ at the resurrection. Here in this life, God's enemies make fun of and even hurt those who say they belong to Jesus. Sometimes, that makes it hard for us to let others know that we follow Him. At the resurrection, *everyone* will see how much better it is to belong to Jesus. Of all who loved and obeyed Him during their lifetimes, He will say, before the Father and the angels, "This person belongs to me." **Read Matthew 10:32–33.**

THURSDAY

What about those who are not believers? What will happen to them at the resurrection? The Bible teaches that everyone who has ever lived will come before God to be judged. Everything people did, said, or thought in this life will be out in the open. God will judge each person according to what he or she has done. If the judge were a human comparing us to other human beings, some of us would look bad and others of us would look better.

But God is the perfect Judge. He only judges the person "good" who has never broken even one of His commands and has obeyed all His Word perfectly. Do you think anyone is *that* good? Anyone who has failed to keep even one of God's commands is guilty before Him and deserves His punishment. Jesus took the guilt and the punishment for all who have believed in Him. Because He took the punishment in their place, they will never have to face God's anger.

The Bible says that the names of believers are written in the Book of Life. They are sinners, but because they have put their trust in Jesus to save them from their sin, God will declare them "Not guilty" on the day of judgment. This is another of the benefits that believers will receive from Christ at the resurrection. **Read Revelation 20:12–15.**

FRIDAY

Do you have a special person with whom you really enjoy spending time? For children, it may be a best friend or a grandparent. For an adult, it may be a husband or wife. When we spend time with a special person, it does not seem to matter much what we do or where we go; just *being* with that person is what we enjoy. As we grow to know God better and better, He becomes to us the most special person we know. Some people go to church, read their Bibles, or pray because they feel that they have to do those things. People who know God well do those things because they enjoy them. The better we know God, the more we enjoy Him.

Those of us who know and love God believe that the best benefit we will receive from Christ at the resurrection is this one: "we will be made completely happy in the enjoyment of God." We will be able to know and enjoy God much more fully than we can know or enjoy Him here on this earth. We will no longer have sinful desires for anything other than God, so all our happiness will be in Him alone. On this earth, with all of its sin and sadness, no one is ever completely happy; in heaven, we will be completely happy and our happiness will be in God where it belongs. **Read Revelation 21:3–4.**

SATURDAY

The benefits that Christ gives His people will last forever. The glorified bodies of believers will be healthy and whole forever. They will be reunited with their souls, which will be perfectly holy and free from sin forever. They will always be with the Lord and will enjoy His presence forever. **Read Revelation 22:3–5.**

Q.39. WHAT DOES GOD REQUIRE OF MAN?

A. God requires man to obey His revealed will.

MONDAY

Read Psalm 95:1–6. Verse 6 of this psalm reminds us that God made us. Verse 3 tells us that God is the greatest King of all. Because God made us, we belong to Him and He is our King. We should see ourselves as His servants, ready to do whatever He commands. This question and answer say that God requires us to obey Him. He can do that for He is the King and we belong to Him.

TUESDAY

Kings expect their people to obey them. What if there were a king who would punish his people when they failed to obey him, but who never told anyone what he wanted or what his rules were? If you lived in his country, you would always be afraid that you were going to do something to make him angry without knowing it.

God is a good and gracious King. He makes very clear to us what He requires of us. To reveal something is to make known what could not possibly have been known otherwise. We would never have known God's will if He had not graciously revealed it. God has not told us everything there is to know. There are many things about which we may wonder, but God has not chosen to reveal those things to us. He has revealed to us, though, what He requires of us. **Read Deuteronomy 29:29.** God reveals His will to us so we may obey it.

WEDNESDAY

Our King expects us to obey Him. He reveals His will, not so that we will know it or so that we will know facts about God. He reveals

His will so that we will obey it. Sometimes, when we are very familiar with something, it is easy to think that we are doing it because we
know it. **Read James 1:22–25.**

THURSDAY

Sometimes, teachers grade more easily on hard tests. The
teacher will look at the best paper in the class and find that even
that student missed a few questions. So, the teacher will lower the
standards a little so everyone gets a higher grade. Some people talk
about God as though He were like that. People say things like,
"Well, nobody's perfect. God knows that I do the best I can. He understands when I mess up."

This is not what the Bible teaches. God is perfectly holy. He requires us to obey His holy law perfectly. Question 39 says that God requires man to *obey* His will. He does not require us to *try* to obey it or
to obey part of it. God requires man to obey every law He ever gave,
perfectly, without ever failing once. God promises to judge everyone.
He will punish those who have done evil. He will reward any who have
done good—as long as they have obeyed perfectly, always, without
ever failing. This is what God requires and He will not accept anything
less. When we understand this, we see how much we need a Savior—
Someone who would be punished in our place and who would live a
life of perfect obedience to God in our place. **Read Romans 2:9–13.**

FRIDAY

God has forgiven all the sins of those who believe in Jesus. He
will never punish them because Jesus took the punishment they deserved. Can believers, then, do whatever they want and live however
they please? Not at all. God is still holy and still requires holiness.
God's people depend on Jesus to make them right with God because
they could never have been good enough on their own. But they also
work hard to live lives that please God. **Read 1 Peter 1:14–17.**

SATURDAY

God rules as King over all mankind because He made us all. He
requires all people to obey Him. Those of us who have believed in

Jesus as our Savior have Jesus as our King. If He is our King, we will obey Him. **Read Matthew 7:21–23.** Jesus said there are people who say He is their Lord and who keep busy working for Him—but they do not obey what He has told them to do. These people will never enter heaven. Just saying we are Christians does not make us Christians. Working for Jesus does not make us Christians. Christians are those who believe in Jesus as their Savior and Lord. True Christians will obey Him and do what He says. **Read the familiar story in Matthew 7:24–27.** Notice that the wise man is the one who hears Jesus' words and *puts them into practice.*

Q.40.

WHAT RULES DID GOD FIRST REVEAL FOR MAN TO OBEY?

A. ✑ *The rules He first revealed were the moral law.*

MONDAY

Because God is man's Creator and King, He makes the rules by which man must live. These rules are called the moral law. They tell us how to behave toward God and toward others. God does not want us to obey on the outside only, but in our hearts as well. He not only requires us to do His will; He requires us to love and desire His will as well.

God gave the Ten Commandments to His people at Mount Sinai. He revealed more and more of His will over the centuries and had people write it down as Scripture. Even before there were any written rules, God had revealed to man His moral law. In fact, even people living today who have never seen or heard of a Bible have God's moral law. God reveals the moral law to us in our hearts.

God made man in His image. Part of being made in the image of God means that we have an awareness of right and wrong. Animals and other creatures have no conscience. They do just what their instincts tell them to do. Man is different. God created man with a conscience. Man knows when he is following God's rules and when he is not. Because of the Fall, every part of man is sinful, including his conscience. Now our consciences become hardened because we ignore them and choose to sin in spite of them. Even then, we know right from wrong and have no excuse for disobeying the rules of our King and Creator. **Read Romans 2:14–15.** Where does this verse say that the requirements of the law are written for those who have never had the law?

TUESDAY

God gave Moses many laws to pass on to His people, the Israelites. Some of those laws were a part of the moral law. Others were a part of what we call the ceremonial law. The ceremonial law was made up of rules about things such as how to offer sacrifices, what the priests should wear, and what to do inside the Tabernacle. These were all things that were pictures of what Jesus would do for us once He came. Now that He has come, God no longer requires His people to keep all the rules of the ceremonial law. The moral law is different. God requires all people everywhere to keep it all the time. No matter who a person is, no matter when he lived in history, and no matter what is his country, his Creator-King requires him to obey the moral law. **Read Matthew 5:17–19.**

WEDNESDAY

Everything God gives is good. The moral law is one of God's good gifts to man. The moral law does several important things for us. It shows us what God is like. God is holy. He hates evil and loves righteousness. By creating us in His image and placing within us a conscience that tells us when we are doing right and when we are doing wrong, God shows us what He is like. By requiring righteousness and holiness from us God demonstrates His own righteousness and holiness. **Read Leviticus 20:7–8.**

THURSDAY

The moral law does another important thing for us. It shows us what God requires of us. Since God created and designed us, He knows what is best for us. The best thing for us is to do what God, our Creator, says we are to do. God could have made us and then simply left us here on earth. We would not have known His purpose for us. We would not have known what to do to please Him. By creating us with a conscience and giving us His Word, God revealed to us how to live the best lives possible. God revealed to us how to be right with Him, our Maker. People do not have to wonder what to do to please God. We do not have to wonder how we should live. God has revealed those things to us through His moral law. **Read Micah 6:8.**

FRIDAY

The moral law does one other important thing for us. It shows us how sinful we are. It causes us to see our danger and our need for a Savior. If God had not revealed His moral law to us in Scripture and if we never felt bad when we do wrong, we would think we were fairly good people. After all, all kinds of people behave much more badly than we do. God does not allow us to think like that. He reveals His perfectly holy moral law that, as sinners, we can never keep.

When we feel guilty for the wrong that we do and when we compare our lives with what God asks of us in the Bible, we see that we can never please God by ourselves. We can never do all that He asks of us. This is when we realize that we are wicked and guilty before God and we can do nothing about it. All we can expect from Him is anger and punishment. Then, when we learn that God has provided a Savior in Jesus, we realize how much we need Him. Without God's moral law, we would not turn to Jesus to be saved because we would not know we needed to be saved. **Read Romans 3:20.**

SATURDAY

There is yet another thing the moral law does for us, but it only does this for the person who has already trusted in Jesus to make him right with God. You might think that this person does not need to bother with the moral law anymore. After all, thanks to Jesus, his sins have been forgiven. Jesus has completely fulfilled all the requirements of the moral law in his place. God has declared him righteous. The moral law causes the believer to see how much he owes to Jesus.

The better we know what God requires, the more we realize how impossible it would have been for us to do it. Then we begin to understand how much Jesus has done for us. The moral law makes us grateful for the Savior God has provided. It also shows us what we can do to prove our thankfulness to Jesus. We can live in a way that pleases God, obeying the moral law. We will fail, of course, but we will always want to please God and we will continually grow in holiness because of our gratitude to Him. **Read Colossians 1:10.**

Q.41. WHERE IS THE MORAL LAW SUMMARIZED?

A. *The moral law is summarized in the ten commandments.*

MONDAY

God created man with a conscience. Our conscience lets us know when we obey God and when we sin against Him. But because we are sinful, we cannot always trust our consciences. Sometimes we fail to feel badly when we do wrong. Sometimes we feel guilty when we do what is right. God, in His goodness, has given us His moral law in a form that can never be wrong. He has given us the Holy Scriptures, which are His own words written down so that they cannot be forgotten or changed.

God did not give us the whole Bible all at once. One of the first parts of the Scripture that God gave is the Ten Commandments. **Read Exodus 34:27–28.** The Ten Commandments are the summary of all God's revealed will for us. A summary gives the most important parts of something in as short a form as possible. The Ten Commandments tell us all that God requires of us in just a few words. The rest of the instructions and commands of Scripture explain the Ten Commandments, helping us to see more fully what God meant when He gave them.

TUESDAY

When the Ten Commandments tell us we are not to do something, we must not do that thing or anything like it. We are to do the *opposite*. For instance, one of the Ten Commandments tells us that we must not murder anyone. Not only should we not kill an innocent person, we must not harm someone at all in any way. More than that, we must not *say* anything that would harm another. Even inside our hearts we are not to wish harm to another. Instead of all these things, we are to love and do what is best for others. Because the Ten Commandments are a summary of God's moral law, all those things are included in the commandment: "You shall not murder." **Read Matthew 5:21–22.**

WEDNESDAY

God is very serious about His law. He does not give us the moral law as wise advice on how to live a good and happy life. God *requires* that we obey His moral law. Like a general in the army or like the king of a country, God gives commands and expects us to obey them. When God first gave the Ten Commandments, He gave them to the Israelites whom He had chosen to be His people over all the other nations on earth. The Bible tells us the story of God giving the Israelites the Ten Commandments. God told His people that He would meet with them on Mount Sinai.

A meeting with an important person requires special behavior. If you went to meet the president of the United States, you would not wear your old work clothes, chomp on bubble gum, or put your feet up on his couch. A meeting with God is much more important than meeting with any ordinary person. The Israelites had to do certain things to get ready. They had to keep certain rules of behavior when they met with God. **Read Exodus 19:10–13.**

THURSDAY

When the time came for the Israelites to meet with God, they gathered at the bottom of Mount Sinai. **Read Exodus 19:16–19 and Exodus 20:18–19.** Although God does not want us to be afraid of Him the way we would be afraid of an evil monster, He does want us to fear Him. **Read Exodus 20:20.** We will be careful not to sin against God when we fear Him in the right way.

FRIDAY

God had special rules of behavior for the Israelites when they met with Him because He wanted them to understand how great and holy He is and what respect He deserves. When God came down on the mountain, He came with thunder, lightning, fire, smoke, an earthquake, and a very loud trumpet that terrified the Israelites. God wanted them to realize that they must obey Him and take seriously the laws He was giving them. God does not allow any of His rules to be broken. Even if a person were to obey God's moral law carefully *almost* all the time, God would still be angry about the times that person disobeyed. Obeying sometimes is not good enough for God. **Read James 2:10.**

SATURDAY

We cannot possibly keep all of God's laws all the time. God is angry and punishes sinners when even one law is broken. How can we hope to ever please Him? Our only hope is to trust Christ to obey the law perfectly for us. **Read Romans 10:4.** If we believe and trust Christ to meet all God's requirements for us, does that mean that we no longer have to worry about keeping God's moral law? Not at all. Now we are God's children and want to be like Him. We want to show Him how much we love Him. **Read John 14:15.**

Q.42. WHAT IS THE ESSENCE OF THE TEN COMMANDMENTS?

A. ✍ *The essence of the ten commandments is to love the Lord our God with all our heart, with all our soul, with all our strength, and with all our mind, and to love everyone else as we love ourselves.*

MONDAY

Have you ever memorized the Ten Commandments? If you have, repeat them now. If you have not, here they are (in short form): (1) Have no god but God, (2) Make no idols, (3) Do not misuse the name of God, (4) Keep the Sabbath Day holy, (5) Honor your father and mother, (6) Do not murder, (7) Do not commit adultery, (8) Do not steal, (9) Do not give false witness, (10) Do not covet.

Once, someone asked Jesus which of the commandments was the greatest. Jesus' answer may have surprised him. **Read it in Matthew 22:37–39.** Jesus said that the greatest commandment is to love God with all that you are. He said the second greatest commandment is to love your neighbor as you love yourself. Can you see either of these two commandments in this list of ten? Although we do not find these two commandments in the Ten Commandments, these two sum up all of the ten. That is why Jesus said these are the two greatest commandments. **Read Matthew 22:40.**

TUESDAY

Look at the Ten Commandments as they were listed on Monday. Some of them tell us how to love God. Others tell us how to love other people. The first four talk more about loving God. The answers Jesus gave to the question, "Which is the greatest commandment?" are found in the Old Testament Scriptures. **Read**

Deuteronomy 6:4–7, looking for the first answer Jesus gave. Loving God with all we have and all we are sums up the first of the commandments.

We will worship only God and will not create idols of any kind if we truly love God. We will reverence God's name and will not use it as a swear word or use it lightly when we truly love God. Keeping the Sabbath Day as a special day to worship and learn about God will be just what we want to do when we love God. If we could love God perfectly, we would never break any of these first four commandments. Even the other six commandments, which deal more with our relationships with other people, would never be broken if we loved God perfectly. Since He has made man in His image, any time we sin against another human being, we sin first against God who created him.

WEDNESDAY

Read Leviticus 19:11–18, watching for the second commandment Jesus said was important, "Love your neighbor as yourself." We often hear people telling us how important it is to love yourself. The Bible never tells us to love ourselves. It tells us to love other people as much as we already love ourselves. We always take care to get what we need for ourselves. God wants us to be just as careful to help meet others' needs. We go out of our way to keep from hurting ourselves. When we love others as we love ourselves, we will carefully protect them from being hurt.

Whenever we make a mistake, we have plenty of good reasons why it happened. If we love others as we love ourselves, we will not become angry with them when they make mistakes. We will look for the reasons they make mistakes and forgive them, just as we would do for ourselves. We always look out for ourselves. We do not have to learn this. God commands us to look out for others in the same way that we always look out for ourselves.

THURSDAY

Whenever we love others as we love ourselves, we will be careful to do nothing that harms them. The last six of the Ten Commandments forbid us from doing things that would hurt others: do not murder, do not commit adultery, do not steal, do not lie, do not covet. If we love only ourselves, we may do some of these things. If we love others as we love ourselves, we will not do any of these things because we do not want to hurt them. **Read Romans 13:8–10.**

FRIDAY

When we love others as we love ourselves, we will not only take care not to hurt them, we will look for things we can do to help them. Do you like it when someone encourages you by telling you that you do something well? Other people like that, too. You can show someone love by encouraging them as you would like to be encouraged. Do you like it when someone does something kind for you or gives you a thoughtful gift? Others like that, too. You can show love to others by doing an act of kindness or giving a gift like you would like to receive. If you are actively looking for loving things to do for others, you are fulfilling the law. **Read Matthew 7:12.**

SATURDAY

Read John 15:12–14. These are Jesus' words to His disciples. What command does He give them in verse 12? What did Jesus do to show His love for His people? What does Jesus say we must do to show that we are His friends? If we love God with all of our heart, our mind, our soul, and our strength, we will be keeping the moral law as it is summed up in the Ten Commandments.

Q.43. WHAT INTRODUCES THE TEN COMMANDMENTS?

A. ✍ These words introduce the ten commandments: *I am the Lord your God, who brought you out of Egypt, out of the land of slavery.*

MONDAY

God is the King of the universe. When He gives a command, He requires us to obey it. God is the Creator of all that is. When He tells any of His creatures to do something, they must do it. God gave man the moral law and He requires that we obey it. He owes us no explanations. Sometimes when parents or teachers tell a child to do something, the child responds with "Why?" We have no right to ask God why we must obey His law.

Since God is good and gracious, He *does* give us reasons for obedience. God created us able to think and understand and so He explains to us *why* we should obey. The Ten Commandments summarize the moral law God requires us to obey. Before giving the Ten Commandments, God gave His people a reason to obey them. Turn to **Exodus 20,** the story of God first giving the Ten Commandments, and read the reason God gave for His people's obedience. It is found in *the second verse.*

TUESDAY

God had done a great thing for the nation of Israel. They had been slaves in Egypt, where the Egyptians had treated them cruelly. God had convinced the Egyptians to let the Israelites go free. God had done this by sending ten different plagues on the country of Egypt. Their crops were destroyed, their cattle were killed, one terrible thing after another happened. Finally, the oldest boy in every Egyptian family died. At last the Egyptians were convinced that God would not leave them alone until they let the Israelites go free. The Israelites left Egypt rejoicing that God had so powerfully acted on their behalf.

Then the Egyptians changed their minds. They came after the unarmed and helpless Israelites with soldiers and chariots. They chased the terrified Israelites to the very edge of the Red Sea. There God did a wonderful thing to save the Israelites. He divided the sea so that the water stood up like walls on each side, with a dry path leading right through the middle. The Israelites crossed the sea on dry land. When the Egyptians tried to follow, God caused the water to come crashing back down where it had been and the entire Egyptian army drowned.

From that day on, the Israelites always looked back with rejoicing on the salvation God had accomplished for them. He had delivered them from slavery. He had saved them from enemies too strong for them to fight. God had done this with a mighty display of power. This salvation marked the beginning of a special relationship that Israel would have with God. **Read Exodus 15:1–2.**

WEDNESDAY

God saved the Israelites because He wanted them for His own people. Of all the nations in the world, He made a covenant only with them. This means that He entered into an agreement with them. He made promises to do special things for them and required certain things of them. Very soon after God delivered the Israelites from Egypt, He gave them the Ten Commandments. God gave the law at Mount Sinai, also called Horeb. In **Deuteronomy 5,** Moses reminded the Israelites of the Ten Commandments God gave them. He said that when God gave the law, "our God made a covenant with us." **Read Deuteronomy 5:1–6.**

THURSDAY

The book of Deuteronomy is a sermon Moses preached just before the Israelites entered the Promised Land and just before he died. In this book, Moses reminded the Israelites of all that God had done for them. He urged them to be faithful to do all that God had told them to do in His law. **Read Deuteronomy 4:5–8.** Moses said that if the Israelites would keep God's laws carefully, other nations would say of Israel, "Surely this nation is a wise and understanding people." He said no nation had God near it like Israel did. Having God's law would make Israel great.

FRIDAY

God did amazing and powerful things for the nation of Israel in the Old Testament. He saved them in a mighty way, delivered them from their enemies, and gave them great blessings. God has done much greater things for His people today. He has saved us in a mighty way from sin and from His wrath at our sin. He has delivered us from our enemies, sin, Satan, and death. God has given us great blessings by adopting us as His children, giving us His Holy Spirit to live inside us, and giving us the gift of eternal life.

If the Old Testament people of God had good reason to obey the moral law He gave, surely those of us who are His people now have much more reason to serve God in obedience. God gave the Israelites a leader, Moses, to save them, but He has given us His own Son, Jesus, who died to save us. The Lord wanted the Israelites to live in obedience to Him because of all He had done for them. How much more should we give our lives to obeying what God has told us He wants us to do? **Read 2 Corinthians 5:14–15.**

SATURDAY

On Thursday, we read in Deuteronomy that the Israelites were special because God was near to them, much nearer than He was to any other nation. God is not only near to His people whom He has saved through Christ, He actually lives *in* them by His Holy Spirit. God required His people in the Old Testament to be holy, because He lived among them. How much more does He require *us* to be holy, since He lives *in* us? God promised to be the Israelites' God, so He expected them to obey Him and live lives worthy of Him. He has promised to be our Father and expects us to keep ourselves from sin and obey Him faithfully. **Read 2 Corinthians 6:16–7:1.**

Q.44.

WHAT DOES THE INTRODUCTION TO THE TEN COMMANDMENTS TEACH US?

A. ✑ *The introduction to the ten commandments teaches us that, because God is Lord and is our God and redeemer, we must keep all His commandments.*

MONDAY

Why should we obey God? The short introduction to the Ten Commandments implies three reasons. These reasons were good reasons for the Israelites, to whom God originally gave the Ten Commandments. They are even better reasons for those of us who are the people of God today.

The first reason for obeying God is that God created us. The one who makes a thing owns it. God made the universe. It all belongs to Him. God made us. Every human being belongs to God and must obey Him. When He gives us commands, we must obey Him because we belong to Him. It is His right to command us. God's people obey Him because He is their Creator. **Read Psalm 100:2–3.**

TUESDAY

The second reason the Israelites were to obey God's law was that He had made a covenant with them, an agreement to be their God and to have them for His people. In this covenant, God promised the Israelites that He would set them apart from all the other nations in the world. They alone would be special to Him and honored by Him. He would love them and care for them above all other nations. The Israelites' part of the covenant was keeping God's commands. God is holy. He could only have a close relationship with a holy nation. God's people in the Old Testament were to obey God's commandments because He was their God and they were His people. **Read Deuteronomy 26:16–19.**

WEDNESDAY

The second reason that God's people today must obey His commands is that He has made a covenant with us too. When Jesus Christ came, God made a new covenant with His people. This covenant is much better than the one He had with the nation of Israel in the Old Testament. People from all nations can take part in this new covenant. Under the new covenant, we have a special relationship with God not by perfectly keeping every rule, but by faith in what Jesus has done for us. Under the new covenant, God gives us new hearts so we can obey Him. He makes us not just His people, as wonderful as that is, but He adopts us as His own children.

The Israelites had a wonderful privilege in being the people of God, and they were to be holy because He was holy. We have a much more wonderful privilege. We are the children of God and we are to *look* like God's children by living holy, obedient lives. **Read 1 Peter 1:14–17.** As God's people under the new covenant, we are to obey God's commandments because He is our God and we are His people.

THURSDAY

The third reason that the Israelites were to obey God was to thank Him for all He had done for them. He had redeemed or rescued them from Egypt where the Egyptians had treated them cruelly as slaves. He took them safely through the wilderness, providing for their every need along the way. God gave them the land He had promised to give them, driving out larger and stronger nations so that they could have it. He settled them securely in the land and made of them a great, strong, and wealthy nation, the only nation in the world who knew Him as their God.

Israel had all these reasons to be grateful to God, their Redeemer. Wanting to please the One who had been so loving and so good to them should have been plenty of reason to obey His commands. **Read Deuteronomy 7:7–11.** The Israelites were to obey God's commandments because He was their Redeemer and had accomplished so much for them.

FRIDAY

The third reason God's people today should obey God is that they have so much for which to thank Him. He has done so much more for us than He did for the Israelites in the Old Testament. He has rescued us from Satan's hold on us. God has redeemed us by forgiving our sins because of Jesus' death on the cross. He has set us free from the fear of death, promising that we will live forever in heaven with Him. He has given us His Holy Spirit to live inside us, enabling us to please Him.

God has given us these wonderful gifts. It cost Him a great deal to purchase them for us. He bought them at the price of the death of His own Son. How much we owe God! How eager we should be to show our love and gratitude by faithful obedience to what He has said He wants from us. As God's people today, we should obey God's commandments because He is our Redeemer and we are to live for Him. **Read Titus 2:11–14.**

SATURDAY

God is our Creator. We obey Him because we belong to Him. If we are Christians, God is our God and we obey Him because He is holy and wants holy people. God is our Redeemer, the One who has rescued us from sin, Satan, and death. We obey Him because we are so grateful for all He has done for us. God saves His people so they can obey Him. He saves us to be holy. Right before Jesus went back to heaven, He gave His followers a task. **Read Matthew 28:19–20.** Jesus told His followers to make disciples of people from all nations. What did He say they were to teach these disciples?

Q.45. WHAT IS THE FIRST COMMANDMENT?

A. ✐ The first commandment is: *You shall have no other gods before me.*

MONDAY

Read the first commandment in Exodus 20:3. There is only one God. Nothing and no one in the universe is like God. He alone deserves our worship. But because we are sinful and rebellious, we make other gods for ourselves. So the very first commandment God gave tells us plainly not to have other gods.

When God first gave this command to the Israelites, all the nations around them worshiped idols. These idols were statues that could be seen and touched but could do nothing at all. God had warned the Israelites not to be like the nations around them. Now we might laugh at people who prayed to statues as though the statues could hear and answer, but people today have idols as well. Whatever is most important to a person is that person's god. If the most important thing to someone is anything other than the true God, that person has an idol. Each day this week we will look at a different kind of idol. Some of them are obviously idols. Some of them are harder to see.

TUESDAY

God had promised to meet with His people, the Israelites, on Mount Sinai. He was going to give to them His law. He told the people to spend several days preparing to meet with Him. When the day finally came, they heard the voice of God. They saw the mountain shaking and smoking because God had come down to it. The people were frightened and begged Moses to go talk to God himself and then come back and tell them what He had said. So Moses did.

Moses went up on the mountain where he met with God and received instructions from Him. Moses stayed on the mountain forty days and nights. **Read Exodus 32:1–4** to see what the Israelites did while they waited.

When Moses came down and saw what they had done, he was furious. He threw down the stone tablets on which were written the Ten Commandments God had given him and shattered them. God was angry also and commanded Moses to have men go through Israel's camp with swords killing people. Three thousand people died that day. God threatened to abandon the Israelites, but Moses prayed for them, pleading with God to glorify Himself by showing patience and forgiveness. God answered Moses' prayer.

WEDNESDAY

All through the Old Testament, God's people struggled with idol worship. In spite of all God's commands to worship Him and Him alone, the Israelites kept wanting what the nations around them had. All the other nations had many gods, not just one. The other nations could see their gods. Of course, their gods were only statues and could do absolutely nothing at all. But, over and over, the Israelites tried to be like the neighboring countries, attempting to worship God *and* idols. Finally, God sent strong and cruel nations to destroy Israel's cities and carry the people away captive. This cured them of their idol-worship. Once they were allowed to return to their country and rebuild their cities, they never again worshiped idols—at least not idols that were statues.

But sinful people always make idols for themselves, even when they do not actually build statues to worship. One story tells of a faithful Jewish man who worked hard at obeying God's commands who would never have dreamed of praying to a statue. Yet he certainly had an idol. **Read his story in Matthew 19:16–22.** What was this man's idol?

THURSDAY

Another story in the New Testament tells about a man and his wife. They belonged to the early church. They were generous, giving a large amount of their money to help poorer people in the church. However, they lied. The apostle Peter said their lie was to God Himself. They had an idol that caused them to do this. The story will not specifically tell you what was more important to them than God, but you can know from reading it. **Read Acts 5:1–11.** What do you think their idol was? It was not money, or they would not have given so much of their money away. It was their reputations that mattered so much to them. They wanted people in the church to think they were even more generous and more committed to Christ than they were, so they lied to make them think that.

FRIDAY

Read Philippians 3:18–19. In these verses, the apostle Paul describes those who are enemies of God. What does he say is their god? Of course, this does not mean that they pray to their stomachs! It is a way of saying that satisfying their appetites matters more to them than anything else. To many people, being comfortable and having a good time are the most important things in the world. They spend every minute trying to find more and better ways to enjoy pleasure. They try to avoid things that are hard or that require discipline or work. Such people want to have fun and feel good all the time. Does that sound familiar to you? It should! This idol of comfort and pleasure is probably the number one idol in America.

SATURDAY

Read Colossians 3:5. There is another common idol in America. The Bible teaches us to be content with what we have. All that we have is God's gracious gift to us. If there are things He has not given us, it is not because He could not give them but because, in His wisdom, He has chosen not to give them now. When we complain because we do not have them or when we neglect the things that are most important in order to get more "stuff" for ourselves, we have a god other than God.

Q.46. WHAT DOES THE FIRST COMMANDMENT REQUIRE?

A. ✒ *The first commandment requires us to know and recognize God as the only true God and our God, and to worship and glorify Him accordingly.*

MONDAY

Do you remember the very first question and answer of this catechism? "What is the primary purpose of man?" "The primary purpose of man is to glorify God and to enjoy Him forever." God designed us to know Him, to enjoy Him, and to glorify Him. This first commandment tells us to have no gods but God. This is not at all an unreasonable command. It simply commands us to do what God created us to do. Because we were designed to enjoy and to glorify God, we will be the most satisfied and the most joyful when we *are* enjoying and glorifying God. So this first commandment requires us to do that which will make us the happiest.

Many people choose to serve other gods. They live to make money and have nice things or they live to have power or to have pleasure. They think they are doing what will make them happy, but they will finally discover that these things cannot satisfy them. God did not create people for these things. He created us to know Him. **Read Jeremiah 9:23–24.**

TUESDAY

The first commandment requires us to recognize God as the only true God. People worship many different things in the place of the one true God. In Old Testament times, people worshiped statues instead of God. Today, there are religious people of all kinds who worship something they call "God," but it is not the true God who has told us what He is like in the Bible. Instead, these people worship a god they have made up in their own imaginations.

Sometimes even people who call themselves Christians do this. Instead of studying the Bible to see what God is like, they form an opinion of what they *like to think* God is like and worship that. Other people put things and pleasure in the place of God, giving all their time and attention to these things. In this first commandment, God requires all people to recognize Him alone as the only true God. **Read Isaiah 43:10–12.**

WEDNESDAY

God requires His people not only to know and recognize Him as the only true God. He also requires us to know and recognize Him as *our* God. He is to be more important to us than anything else. Of course, most people would say that God means more to them than anything else, because they know they are *supposed* to say that. If God is truly more important to us than anything else, our lives will show it. We will do things that help us get to know our God better. We will spend time seeking Him through prayer and in His Word. We will feel that we *must* have God and nothing else will do in His place.

Read Psalm 63:1–4. David says that God is *his* God. He wants God as badly as a man in the desert would want a drink of water. If we know and recognize God as *our* God, we will seek Him earnestly.

THURSDAY

If God is the only true God and if He is our God, then we must worship Him. That is what the first commandment, "You shall have no other gods before me," requires. The English word for worship comes from the word "worth." When we worship something, we declare that it has great worth. Worship is more than just praising God now and then when we pray. It is more than just singing hymns and praise songs when we come to church.

To worship God is to declare to all the world around us how much He is worth. We do that by living our whole lives for Him. When all day every day we seek to get closer to our Lord, we live lives of worship. When everyone who knows us can see that the most important thing in the world to us is knowing God, we are worshiping Him. We are saying to the whole world, "Look how much God is worth! I would give up everything else so I could have Him." **Read** Paul's words of worship in **Philippians 3:7–8.**

FRIDAY

If we recognize God as the only true God, we understand that He created all things to give Him glory. That includes us. If we know God as *our* God, we are so thankful for all He is to us that we want to please Him. The first commandment requires us to glorify God, to live for God's glory. **Read 1 Corinthians 10:31.** Even things as necessary and as ordinary as eating and drinking are to be done for God's glory. How do we do something for the glory of God? We glorify God when we do everything to the very best of our ability. We glorify God when we are careful not to do what would be sin, and when we do all things, not from selfish motives, but so that God will be honored.

SATURDAY

People have many different ideas about God. Of course, they cannot all be true because they do not all agree. And yet, if you listen to people talk or if you read books or magazines, people talk as if *all* the opinions about God are true—even the ones that are direct opposites of each other! People will say it does not matter what we believe as long as we believe what we think is best. They say that it is wrong to tell someone that what he or she believes about God is false. That might hurt that person's feelings. When it comes to those who have no interest in God at all, people will say we have no right to tell them they are wrong for ignoring God.

But God Himself commands us to have no gods but Him. He does not *suggest* it or tell them that this commandment is just for those who want to obey. God *requires* that all people worship Him and worship Him alone. He promises to destroy those who refuse to obey His command. **Read Psalm 50:22–23.**

Q.47. WHAT DOES THE FIRST COMMANDMENT FORBID?

A. ❧ *The first commandment forbids denying God or not worshiping and glorifying Him as the true God and our God. It also forbids giving worship and glory, which He alone deserves, to anyone or anything else.*

MONDAY

When something is forbidden, it is not allowed. Each of the Ten Commandments *requires* certain things (says they must be done) and *forbids* other things (says those things are not allowed). The commandment to have no other gods before God forbids several things.

First, God forbids people to deny Him. To deny God is to say that He does not exist. A person who says there is no God is called an atheist. Atheists often claim that they do not believe in God because no one can prove there is one. This makes them sound scientific and smart. God has something else to say about the person who denies Him. What does God call the atheist? **Read Psalm 14:1** to see.

TUESDAY

Some people, like atheists, deny that there is any god at all. Many more people *say* there is a God and even claim to believe in Jesus, but they *live* as though there were no God. Many people go to church on Sunday but live the rest of the week without considering at all what God would want from them. They do not look into God's Word to see what He requires. They do not spend time in prayer, seeking His help to obey Him. These people live as they want to live. To watch them, you would never know that they had ever heard of God.

When our lives are no different from the lives of our neighbors, when we spend no more time in prayer or in reading the Bible than non-Christians do, we deny God by our lives. God describes such

155

people in many places in His Word and promises to judge them. **Read Isaiah 29:13.**

WEDNESDAY

The first commandment forbids denying God, or saying with our mouths or by our lives that He does not exist. It also forbids us to not worship Him. In other words, we are not allowed to *not* worship God. Most people see worship as something they can choose to do when it is convenient for them. Many people never go to church at all. Even among people who *do* go to church, if they wake up tired and would rather go back to sleep or if they have somewhere to go or something to do on Sunday morning they will choose to do that rather than attend worship. Most of us seem to think there is nothing wrong with that. Church is something people can attend when they would like to, but they are free to choose. That is not what God says in His Word. Many places in Scripture command us to come together regularly with God's people to worship God and learn from His Word. Worship is not a choice. God commands us to worship Him and forbids us to *not* worship Him. **Read Hebrews 10:25.**

THURSDAY

The commandment, "You shall have no other gods before Me," makes it a sin to not give God the worship and glory that He deserves. **Read 1 Chronicles 16:23–29.** This passage says glory is due to God's name. When something is due someone, it is owed to that person. When my library book is due, I have to give it back to the library. The book belongs to the library and I owe it to them. When I get a bill for something I bought, it says on the bill, "Payment due." That means I owe a certain amount of money and must pay it. Glory and worship are due to God. We, His creatures, owe worship and glory to Him. As the answer to this catechism question says, God alone deserves worship and glory for He is the only true God.

FRIDAY

The first commandment forbids denying God. It forbids failing to give God the glory and the worship that we owe Him as the one true God and our God. And it forbids giving worship or glory to anything or anyone else. God designed us to worship. We are different from all other creatures on earth because we can know God and because we have a built-in need to worship. Of course, God intended us to worship *Him,* the only One worthy of worship. Because people are sinful, they choose to disobey God and not worship Him. Since they are designed to worship, if they do not worship God, they always find something else to worship and glorify instead.

The apostle Paul taught that all people know there is a God because they can see what He has made and because they have a conscience. What does Paul say people failed to do? **Read Romans 1:21. Read verses 22–23** to see what they exchanged for the glory of God. **Read verse 25.** What did people exchange the truth of God for? What did they worship and serve instead of the Creator?

SATURDAY

We all know it is wrong to bow down and pray to an idol or to the moon or to another human being. We may believe we are keeping this first commandment because we do not do any of those things. To be sure that we are keeping the first commandment, "You shall have no other gods before Me," there is a question we must ask ourselves. Does anything keep me from worshiping God and from glorifying Him the way I should?

For instance, a student might worry that the kids in his class will not think much of him if he lets them see that he is interested in the Bible or if he shows the kind of respect for the teacher that he should. So, without really appearing rebellious, he does not respond as quickly to the teacher as he should and he does not let anyone see him with a Bible. The opinions of other people are a god to him before the true God. Another person may know she should spend time reading her Bible and praying, but she keeps too busy. Day after day goes by and she just never finds the time for prayer or for God's Word. She is making her own convenience and her likes and dislikes a god before the true God.

When Joshua led the Israelites into the Promised Land, he challenged them to choose either to wholeheartedly serve the one true

God or to serve the gods of the people around them. **Read Joshua 24:14–18.** We face the same challenge. All around us, people have made gods of themselves, of good times, of having things. Will we serve these gods first, giving the true God what we have left over? Or will we obey the commandment of God and have no other gods *but* Him?

Q.48.

WHAT ARE WE SPECIFICALLY TAUGHT IN THE FIRST COMMANDMENT BY THE WORDS *BEFORE ME*?

A. *The words* before me *in the first commandment teach us that God, Who sees everything, notices and is very offended by the sin of having any other god.*

MONDAY

Although God does not have eyes like we do, He sees better than we can. God sees all places and all at the same time. God can do this because He is omnipresent, or able to be in all places at all times. The Bible tells us that God sees every tiny bird that falls from the sky. It says that He sees little children before they are born, while they are still inside their mothers. There is nothing hidden from God. He sees everything that happens. God even sees inside people's hearts so that He knows what they are thinking. No sin can be hidden from God's sight. If a person makes something other than God to be his or her god, the true God knows it. When someone refuses to worship and serve Him, God knows it.

Sometimes a person goes to church and lives a good life, but he only does it so he will look good to others. He really has no interest in God at all; he is just pretending to worship Him. He may fool everyone else, but God knows that such a person is not keeping the first commandment. **Read Psalm 44:20–21.**

TUESDAY

God always notices the sin of having another god. It does not matter who it is that worships something other than God. God is offended, or made angry, by anyone worshiping something instead of

Him. It does not matter where people live who worship another god. The true God will notice.

The Bible tells of the Philistines, idol-worshipers who prayed to a statue named Dagon. Because the Israelites had been disobedient to God, the Philistines were able to beat them in battle. The Philistines gave praise and honor for this to their idol, Dagon. They had captured the Ark of the Covenant from the Israelites. This was the special box in which the stone tablets with the Ten Commandments were kept. To show how much greater their idol, Dagon, was than the true God, the Philistines put the ark of the covenant in their temple to Dagon, as though God were the prisoner of an idol. **Read 1 Samuel** to see what happened. That was not all. The people of the city themselves developed painful sores and some of them died. Even though the Philistines were not *God's* people, God was offended that they would honor their idol before Him. Their failure to give glory to Him made Him angry and He punished them.

WEDNESDAY

God is offended by those who fail to worship Him. The Bible tells us that He is a jealous God. Sometimes people are jealous in sinful ways and for sinful reasons. If we are jealous because we do not want to share or because we want the best things for ourselves, our jealousy is wrong. There are times when jealousy is right. A man might be jealous of his wife. He does not want anyone else to treat her like a wife, because he is her only husband. It would be wrong for someone to act like a husband toward *his* wife.

When the people He made treat something else like it is God, God is jealous. He alone is God. He created people to worship Him. Nothing else is worthy of worship. It is wrong for people to worship something other than God. It is harmful to those who do it. These are some of the reasons why God is so offended by people who fail to worship Him. When God is jealous, it is never sinful. **Read Isaiah 42:8.**

THURSDAY

The book of Acts tells us about the first Christians. They lived among people who worshiped many gods. These people even worshiped their rulers—ordinary men—as though they were gods.

Surely these rulers knew they were only men and not gods! Maybe after hearing over and over that they were gods, they would begin to believe it. Maybe they never believed it, but they liked people to believe it so they could have honor and the people would obey them. A story in Acts tells of a king named Herod. He fought against the true God by trying to keep the apostles from preaching the Word of God. He did this by killing the apostle James and planning to kill the apostle Peter. God sent an angel, who set Peter free from the prison where he was being held. King Herod looked like a fool when he sent his soldiers to get Peter to have him killed, but Peter was not there! Herod had no idea where he was and he never found him.

As for King Herod, he had a meeting with some people who were trying to get something from him. They flattered him by praising him and calling him a god. **Read what happened in Acts 12:21–24.** Herod died an unpleasant death because he accepted the praise only God deserved. Meanwhile, God's Word, which he had tried to stop, continued to increase and spread.

FRIDAY

Do people today ever accept praise and honor from people, almost as though they were gods? Do people today ever act as though they do not have to obey God's rules because they are great and famous? God has not changed. He feels just the same about people today who honor and worship other people and about people who receive such honor as He did in the story of King Herod.

Read Ephesians 5:5–6. This passage tells us that a covetous person is an idolater. A covetous person wants more than what God has given. This person has no part in God's kingdom. God's wrath will come on her or him. God's wrath is His holy, powerful, and terrible anger. God is very offended at those who have anything or anyone else as a god. Although He waits patiently for them to repent, His wrath will finally fall on them. The Bible tells us that "it is a terrible thing to fall into the hands of the living God" (Heb. 10:31).

SATURDAY

Today people believe that we show kindness and love by accepting everyone's opinion about whom to worship. People can worship whomever they want to worship. Or they can simply not worship at all. No one way is better than any other. That is what people today say about worship, but God disagrees. When any person fails to worship God, that person sins. God warned the Israelites that once they were comfortably settled in the Promised Land, they would be tempted to forget Him. If they forgot Him and worshiped other gods, He promised to destroy them. **Read Deuteronomy 6:10–15.**

Q.49. WHAT IS THE SECOND COMMANDMENT?

A. ✍ The second commandment is: *You shall not make for yourself an idol in the form of anything in heaven above or on the earth beneath or in the waters below. You shall not bow down to them or worship them; for I, the Lord your God, am a jealous God, punishing the children for the sin of the fathers to the third and fourth generation of those who hate Me, but showing love to a thousand [generations] of those who love me and keep My commandments.*

MONDAY

The second commandment, telling us not to make idols or to bow down to idols, sounds like the first commandment, where God said to have no gods before Him. The difference is this: in the first commandment, God tells us *what* to worship. We are to worship the true and living God and Him alone. The second commandment tells us *how* to worship. We are not to use statues or idols in our worship of God, nor do any other thing in our worship that would displease Him.

In the Bible, God tells us how He wants us to worship Him. We may not worship Him any way we choose. We must follow the guidelines He has given us. Do you remember the story of the Israelites making and worshiping a golden calf while Moses was up on the mountain receiving the Ten Commandments? This was a serious sin that made God angry. **Read Exodus 32:4–6.** Aaron told the people there would be a festival the next day. He said it would be a festival for the Lord. At that festival, the people sacrificed to the golden calf. They had a wild and disorderly celebration, and they did sinful things. Yet they called it a "festival to the Lord." They claimed to worship the true God. Yet they tried to worship Him with an idol and by doing things that displeased Him. God is angry when people worship something other than Him. He is also angry when people worship Him in ways that go against what He has commanded.

TUESDAY

When we come together as God's people, the most important part of our worship is reading His Word and listening as it is preached and taught. The apostle Paul wrote a letter to Timothy, a young pastor. The letter tells Timothy what things matter most in a worship service. Paul told Timothy to devote himself as a pastor to doing certain things. To devote yourself to something is to make it your number one priority. If you are devoted to something, you will make sure it gets done even if you do not have time for anything else. **Read 1 Timothy 4:13.**

The reading, preaching, and teaching of Scripture is the church's first responsibility when God's people come together to worship. The church must keep God's Word central by reading it together and by preaching and teaching from it. In this way, God's people protect themselves from worshiping a god they have made up in their own minds. They keep seeing what God says about Himself in His Word. In this way, too, God's people protect themselves from worshiping God in ways that displease Him. They are always looking in God's Word to find what *is* pleasing to Him.

WEDNESDAY

In the same letter to the young pastor, Timothy, the apostle Paul wrote of another important thing we should do as a part of our worship. **Read 1 Timothy 2:1** to see what it is. The Bible tells us that God hears and answers our prayers when we pray according to His will. This is another good reason for the church to keep God's Word central in its worship service. We can only pray according to God's will when we *know* His will by reading about it in the Bible.

In a letter to the church of the Colossians, Paul spoke about something else God has given us to do in our worship. He said we should sing psalms, hymns, and spiritual songs to God. **Read Colossians 3:16.** We want God's Word to "dwell in us richly" when we sing.

Many people enjoy music. Sometimes we enjoy the music of a song so much that we do not pay attention to the words. The words of a song must agree with God's Word or we must not worship Him with it. When you sing in worship, always listen to what you are singing. If the words say something about God that the Bible does not teach, do not use that song to worship. If the song praises God in a way that agrees with Scripture, sing it sincerely and offer it as your worship to God.

THURSDAY

Two other important parts of Christian worship are baptism and the Lord's Supper. A person is baptized to show that he or she is joined to Christ and becoming a member of the people of God. A person does this publicly, before the rest of God's people. A baptism is very serious, but it is also a time of great celebration. The Lord's Supper is also very serious, because the people of God gather to remember that Jesus died. It, too, is a time of celebration because we remember that Jesus died for us so that our sins have been forgiven. We do both of these special acts of worship because the Lord Jesus commanded us to. **Read Matthew 28:19 and 1 Corinthians 11:23–26.**

FRIDAY

God tells us to worship no god but God. He tells us to be careful to worship Him only in the ways He tells us to. God does not offer suggestions. He commands us. This commandment has a threat attached to it. God warns us that He is a jealous God and that there are consequences for disobeying Him. Here He says that He will punish the sin of those who hate Him, even in their children and grandchildren. That is one of the horrible things about sin. It hurts many more people than just the one who commits it. A person passes on a sinful lifestyle to children and to grandchildren.

Ahab was a king of Israel in Old Testament times, but he was wicked and an idol-worshiper. When God's prophet told Ahab God would judge his household because of his wickedness, he repented. Still, sin always has consequences. **Read 1 Kings 21:25–29.** When would God bring disaster?

SATURDAY

This second commandment also has a promise attached to it. God promises to show love to those who love Him and keep His commandments. Not only that, but God will bless the children and the grandchildren of those who love Him as well. As a child, attending worship may seem hard to do. Public prayer seems long. You may find the sermons hard to understand. The music may not be the kind you enjoy. Sometimes you wish you could stay home on Sunday morning instead of coming to the worship service.

But as you come with your parents week after week, you learn to worship the true and only God. As you watch them worship and as you worship with them, you learn to worship God as He wants us to worship Him. You learn to worship through the reading and preaching of His Word, through singing and prayer, through watching a baptism, and through observing or taking part in the Lord's Supper. If your parents worship God as He commands, there will be blessing for you as their child. Take advantage of having such parents and learn from them to love and worship God for yourself. Learn to worship Him because you want to worship Him and not because someone makes you go to church. **Read Psalm 103:17–18.**

Q.50. WHAT DOES THE SECOND COMMANDMENT REQUIRE?

A. ✑ *The second commandment requires us to receive, respectfully perform, and preserve completely and purely all the regulations for religion and worship that God has established in His word.*

MONDAY

When God led the Israelites out of Egypt, He gave them His law. We can divide the law God gave into three kinds of law. The civil law gave rules specifically for the Old Testament nation of Israel. The moral law tells God's people how to behave. Even now, thousands of years after God gave it and even now that Jesus Christ has come, God still requires His people to keep the moral law. The other kind of law is the ceremonial law. The ceremonial law contains long lists of rules about things like how to offer sacrifices, what kind of sacrifice to offer, and what priests should wear. The ceremonial law was to be a picture of what Jesus would do when He came. He would be the greatest priest, bringing His people right into God's presence. He would be the perfect sacrifice to take away sin forever. All the details of the ceremonial law were simply pictures of Jesus.

Now that Jesus has come, we no longer need the pictures. We know the *true* priest and the *true* sacrifice God has provided. **Read Hebrews 10:1, 10.** The parts of the Bible that tell about the ceremonial law still give us good pictures of what Jesus did. So we should still read them, but we no longer have to keep that part of the law. The moral law, however, is still for us to obey. This is just as true for us who live after Jesus came as it was for those who were alive when it was written.

TUESDAY

Once a woman asked Jesus how to worship God. She wondered where to worship. She was concerned with the ceremonial part of the law. Jesus' answer made it clear that, now that He had come, the ceremonial part of the law did not matter. Worship itself, however, would still be important. It would be so important to God that He would *seek* people to worship Him correctly. Those who worshiped Him correctly, said Jesus, would worship Him in spirit and in truth.

If we want to worship God in a way that He accepts, we must worship Him according to the truth of what He has told us in His Word, not according to our own ideas. Jesus said that God's worshipers *must* worship Him in spirit and in truth. To worship God as *we* think best and not as God tells us to worship is to not worship God at all. **Read John 4:23–24.**

WEDNESDAY

God has established in His Word regulations (or rules) for religion and worship. He wants us to worship Him and He wants us to do certain things when we worship Him. God requires His people to gather regularly to worship. When they do that, He requires them to read His Word together and to listen as His Word is preached. He wants them to sing His praises. He wants them to pray together. God also requires His people to remember the Lord's death for them through the Lord's Supper and to be baptized into the church. Those who truly belong to the Lord will receive these requirements of His. They will gladly participate in these things. Those who belong to God will *want* to be with the Lord's people on the Lord's Day. They will want to sing His praise and hear His Word taught, even if they do not always understand everything. If you always find going to church on Sundays unpleasant, you need to ask yourself if you are truly one of God's people. **Read Psalm 122:1.**

THURSDAY

God wants us to "respectfully perform" the requirements He has given us for worship. That means that we not only do what God requires when we worship, but we do it with respect for Him. We owe to God much greater respect than we owe to parents or to others in authority. The respect we owe to God is so special that it has a special name: *reverence*. We are to show reverence for God. Reverence means a respect so great that it is actually a kind of fear. It is a fear of doing anything that would offend God.

When we worship reverently, we will be serious about our worship. A reverent worshiper does not talk or laugh or play during worship. He does not let his mind wander to all sorts of other things. A reverent worshiper participates as fully as possible in the worship service. People today like to think of God as a "Big Buddy." People who forget how much greater God is than we are will not be reverent in their worship. Although Jesus came to make us God's children, He still requires us to worship God with reverence. **Read Psalm 5:7.**

FRIDAY

God requires His people to "preserve completely and purely" the regulations He has given for worship. That means that we must take care to always worship as God has commanded us to worship. As time goes by, people can become careless and forget what God has commanded. They may stop doing things God has said they are to do and begin to add things to their worship that God does not want. The New Testament tells pastors and church leaders to preach and teach what God has commanded. It also warns that people— even in churches—will want to believe their own ideas and will not like hearing what God says is true.

Some churches say they worship God but they do things in their worship God has not commanded in His Word. People can let things they enjoy doing replace things God has commanded, such as listening to His Word. Always remember that the purpose of worship is not to have fun, but to obey and honor God. We must be careful to worship God as He requires us to do in His Word. **Read 2 Timothy 4:1–3.**

SATURDAY

Nadab and Abihu were priests who decided to worship God in their own way instead of according to the regulations He had given them for worship. Priests had the job of offering incense to the Lord. Incense is a kind of powder that smells good when it is burned. Part of the worship of God in the Old Testament was burning incense as an offering to Him. God had given Moses very exact instructions on how to mix the incense. The priests could only use a certain kind of incense in worship. Nadab and Abihu offered incense other than what God had said to offer. **Read Leviticus 10:1–3.**

God insists that those who worship Him treat Him as holy. He wants to be worshiped with reverence. He insists that people who come to worship Him honor Him as He deserves to be honored. This includes worshiping Him according to *His* instructions and not according to human opinions.

WHAT DOES THE SECOND COMMANDMENT FORBID?

A. 〰 *The second commandment forbids our worshiping God with images or in any other way not established in His word.*

MONDAY

God has commanded His people to worship Him and He has told them the things that He wants them to do in worship. God's people are not to imitate those who are *not* God's people when they worship. Back in Old Testament times, when God first gave the Ten Commandments to the Israelites, the temptation they had to guard against was the worship of statues. All of the nations around them, who were not God's people, worshiped idols they could see. Over and over again, the Israelites wanted to be like the people around them and they would try to use idols in the worship of the true God.

That is why the second commandment so clearly forbids making idols and using them in worship. Not only were God's people not to worship statues of *other* gods; they were not to make statues of the *true* God to use in worship. God is Spirit. He has no body that can be seen. He does not want His people to make something they can see and then say that it is God or that it looks like God. **Read Deuteronomy 4:15–18.**

TUESDAY

Read Acts 17:29. People in modern-day America do not make gods out of gold or wood or stone and bow down to them. God's people today will not be tempted to make statues and say, "This is God." Today, people make false gods in their imaginations. They build idols out of ideas. Most people believe there is a God. But people have many different ideas of what God is like. If the ideas do not agree with what God says He is like in His Word, they are wrong ideas. When people have wrong ideas of God, the god they believe in is a false god, or an idol.

Sometimes, people listen to what someone else says about God and believe it without checking it out in the Bible. You should never trust your own opinion of what God is like. Nor should you trust the opinions of other people. There is only one way to be sure that you are worshiping the true God and not an idea of God that someone has made up. You must make sure that what you believe about God comes from the Bible. To do that, you must get to know the Bible well. If you know only part of the Bible, you cannot have a true idea of God. God has revealed Himself to us in His Word. We can worship Him as He commands us to only if we know the Bible.

WEDNESDAY

Why was it so important to God that His people not make statues or pictures of Him? Why is it so important to God that His people find out what He is like from Scripture instead of imagining what He is like? God is very great. No one could make a statue or a picture of God that would show how great He is. No one could make up a god in his mind as great as the true God. Statues, pictures, or opinions only take away from the greatness of God.

Read Psalm 97:1–2. What do these verses say surround God? **Now read 1 Timothy 6:15–16.** Where do these verses say God dwells? Why would one verse say God is surrounded with thick darkness while another verse says He lives in light so bright you could not come near it? Both verses give us a picture of how very great and beyond our understanding God is. He is so far beyond our understanding that it is as though He were in a blinding light. He is so hard for us to understand that it is like He is in thick darkness. God is great beyond any pictures or statues we can make. He is great beyond anything we can imagine. We are to get our ideas of what He is like from what He has told us in His Word alone.

THURSDAY

The second commandment forbids our worshiping God with images that we have made either with our hands or with our minds. The Israelites got into trouble by adding to the worship of God things that

He had not established. They did it the first time when they set out to worship the God who had brought them out of Egypt and created a golden calf to represent Him. They did it over and over again later by trying to add the worship of idols to the worship of God.

We can also understand this commandment to mean that we must not add *anything* to the worship of God that He Himself has not established. The apostle Paul wrote to the Colossian Christians about people who were telling them that their worship of God had to include eating some things and not eating other things. They were making up rules for worship about making certain days special. **Read Colossians 2:16, 20–22.** Paul said these rules were based on human commands and teachings.

Like having their own ideas about God, people also have many opinions about how to worship. Sometimes they push aside the things that matter most to God to make room for things based only on people's ideas. Again, it is important to know the Bible well to know if we are worshiping God the way *people* think is best or the way *God* requires.

FRIDAY

Jesus spoke to some people who had pushed aside God's commands to do what they wanted to do instead. God commands grown children to honor their elderly parents and help provide for the things they need. The people to whom Jesus spoke had made up their own rules and traditions about what to do with their money. They chose to follow those rules instead of God's. Jesus told these people they were breaking God's command for the sake of traditions made up by human beings. **Read Matthew 15:3, 8–9.**

Things often happen in worship services today that God has not commanded in His Word. At the same time, worship services do not include things God requires us to do when we come together to worship. Why is that? Churches have set aside what *God* commands to do things *people* think would be better. Jesus says such worship is vain. It has no value. It does not honor God.

SATURDAY

Unfortunately, sometimes people who claim to be God's people teach ideas of God that cannot be found in Scripture. There are preachers and authors of books who either do not know the Bible very well or do not care what it says. They say things about God that are the opposite of what the Bible teaches. They do things in worship that do not honor God. Remember that just because something is said by a preacher or is written in a book, that does not make it true. We must check everything against what the Bible teaches. When we find someone teaching what is not true about God, we should not listen to that person at all. **Read Deuteronomy 13:1–4.**

Q.52. WHAT ARE THE REASONS FOR THE SECOND COMMANDMENT?

A. *The reasons for the second commandment are that God totally rules over us, that we belong to Him, and that He is eager to be worshiped correctly.*

MONDAY

God totally rules over all He has created, which means He totally rules over us. Kings have the right to command their subjects to approach them in the way that they desire. How much more does God, the King of all, have the right to tell His subjects how He wants them to worship! Beyond that, we who are God's people through faith in the Lord Jesus Christ have committed ourselves to serving Him forever as our Lord and Master. We are to be eager to serve Him. We should be glad that He has told us how to worship Him so that we can do as He wills. **Read Psalm 145:1–3, 10–13a.**

TUESDAY

Because God made all things, all things belong to Him. That includes us. Because God bought His people for Himself with the blood of His Son, we *doubly* belong to Him. We belong to Him because He made us and because He bought us for Himself. God has the right to do as He pleases with us, His creatures. When He tells us how to come to Him in worship, we are to obey Him. **Read Psalm 95:1–7a.**

WEDNESDAY

The reasons for the second commandment are that God totally rules over us, that we belong to Him, and that He is eager to be correctly worshiped. God is eager to be worshiped because He is worthy of worship and because the highest good for man is to worship God. God is eager to be worshiped *correctly* because worship that is other than what He has commanded harms man and insults God. As the Israelites prepared to enter the land God had promised them, God told them that He would make them able to drive out the people who had been living there. This was because those people served other gods. Their worship of idols was extremely offensive to God. He warned the Israelites that, when they entered the Promised Land, they must destroy all the idols and places of worship these people had used. They must not leave anything that might tempt them to worship the true God incorrectly. **Read Exodus 34:13–14.**

THURSDAY

The end of this second commandment tells us that God punishes the sin of those who hate Him. This shows us how strongly God feels about those who try to worship Him in ways that are different from what He has required. He considers such worship sinful and sees those who worship Him in this way as those who hate Him. In many churches, those things that God requires in our worship have been replaced with things that people enjoy. People in such churches may believe they worship God, but they really show a kind of hatred for God. They reject those things in worship that He has commanded.

The prophet Malachi wrote God's message to His people during a time when their worship was sloppy and not according to God's command. Instead of bringing Him their best animals as offerings, the people brought sick, unhealthy ones. God said this was evidence of their lack of respect for Him. He said He would rather have no worship at all than worship that showed His people's lack of reverence and obedience. **Read Malachi 1:6–11.**

FRIDAY

The final words of this commandment say that God shows love to those who love Him and keep His commandments. We show our love for Him by *wanting* to know what He wants so that we can do it. Those who truly love God will eagerly search His Word to know what kind of worship He wants so that they can give it to Him. They will not make up their own kind of worship. They will not do what they want to do in a worship service, ignoring what God wants them to do. We show our love for God by knowing and obeying His commands. Jesus said the same thing in **John 14:21.**

SATURDAY

God promises to bless the children of those who obey His commandments. Specifically, this commandment promises blessing for the children of people who worship Him as He requires. You may have friends who go to church on Sunday and do things that seem more fun than what you do at your church. That may be because the people there have traded what God requires for what people find enjoyable. You may have friends who do not go to church at all but stay home to sleep in or to watch television on Sunday mornings. But if you have parents who are developing in you a habit of worshiping God regularly in the ways that He requires, you should be thankful. God promises blessing to you because of your parents' faithfulness. If you continue to worship Him faithfully yourself, you will be even more blessed and *your* children will be blessed after you as well. **Read Deuteronomy 5:29.**

Q.53. WHAT IS THE THIRD COMMANDMENT?

A. ✍ The third commandment is: *You shall not misuse the name of the Lord your God, for the Lord will not hold anyone guiltless who misuses his name.*

MONDAY

When we introduce ourselves to another and tell that person our name, it is because we want to have a relationship with that person. We see people every day who never say a word to us. We may see other people who greet us politely but whom we really do not know. But when someone stops us, introduces himself to us and tells us his name, we know that he wants to have a closer relationship with us than he has had before.

God has done something wonderful for us. He has told us His name! We could never have known much at all about God and we certainly would not have known His name if He had not told us. But God *has* spoken to us in His Word. He has told us His name because He wants us to know Him. He wants to have a relationship with us. God is so great that one name would not begin to tell us all about Him. So, in the Bible, God uses many names, each of them showing us a little something more of how wonderful He is.

When God called Moses to lead the Israelites out of slavery in Egypt, Moses worried that people would want to know who had sent him. "What shall I tell them Your name is?" he said to God. **Read God's answer in Exodus 3:14–15.**

TUESDAY

As Moses obeyed the Lord and served Him by leading His people, he grew to know God better and better. The more Moses knew about God, the more he wanted to know about Him. One day, Moses asked God to show him His glory. God replied that no man could see Him and live. So God told Moses that He would put him in a hollowed-out spot in a rock, where he would be protected. Then God, would cause all His glory to pass by Moses. At the same time, God said, He would proclaim, or tell, His name to Moses.

So God placed Moses in the hollowed-out spot in the rock and passed by him as He had said He would. **Read Exodus 34:5–7.** God had said He was going to proclaim His *name* to Moses. Instead, He told Him all these things about what He is like. God's name stands for all that He is. God told Moses that He is compassionate and gracious. He is patient, forgiving, loving, and faithful. He is holy and He punishes sin. All these things about God are summed up in His name.

This is why we must treat God's name with special honor and reverence. It stands for all that God is. To speak God's name disrespectfully is to show disrespect to God Himself.

WEDNESDAY

Read Psalm 8:1. All that God does brings praise and honor to His name. This psalm tells of the wonder of God's work of creation. Throughout the whole universe, we see something of the majesty of God's name because we see how wonderful all that He has made is. God's works on behalf of His people in the Old Testament showed to all who saw them that God's name is great and glorious. The most wonderful work God has done is that of providing salvation for His people through His Son. We should praise the name of our great God for giving us salvation.

Often people think that God's main reason for doing all that He has done is for *our* sake. God loves His people and He does things for them because of His love. God's first reason for all that He does is to bring glory and honor to His own name. God often told the Israelites that He did what He did for them, not because they were any better than anyone else, but for the sake of His great name. God's people in the Old Testament often asked Him for forgiveness or for protection, not because they deserved it, but for His name's sake. **Read Psalm 115:1.**

THURSDAY

God's name is greater than any other name. God's name stands for all He is. God does all the amazing things He does in order to gain glory and praise for His name. He requires us to honor His name and to treat it with respect. Those of us who love Him will be glad to give praise to God's great name. **Read Psalm 113:1–4.**

FRIDAY

Read Luke 11:1–4. Jesus' disciples asked Him to teach them how to pray. If prayer is talking with God, Jesus knows all there is to know about it. Jesus, who is God the Son, has been alive forever. From all eternity, He has loved and communicated with God the Father. Because He is God, Jesus knows the mind of the Father. He knows how we should pray in a way that is pleasing to God. The very first thing Jesus said we should ask for in prayer is this: "Hallowed be Thy name." Usually, when we pray, the first thing we think to ask for is whatever it is that we need the most at the moment. Jesus taught us that the very first thing we should ask for is that God's name would be hallowed or honored as it deserves.

SATURDAY

All that God says about His own name He says about the name of the Lord Jesus Christ as well. Jesus is God the Son, and God the Father wants Jesus' name to be honored as well as His own. Besides that, because Jesus became man and died for the sins of God's people, God the Father wants His Son to have even greater honor. **Read Philippians 2:8–11.** The name of Jesus is included in this commandment to not misuse God's name. All the reverence, honor, and respect we show the name of God must be shown to the name of the Lord Jesus Christ as well.

Q.54.   WHAT DOES THE THIRD COMMANDMENT REQUIRE?

A. *The third commandment requires the holy and reverent use of God's names, titles, qualities, regulations, word, and works.*

MONDAY

The first of the Ten Commandments tells us *what* to worship: God, and God alone. The second commandment tells us what to do and what to use *when* we worship. We must not worship with idols or with other things God has not required but with those things He has commanded. This third commandment also focuses our attention on the worship of God. This commandment tells us what *attitude* to have when we worship. Especially in our worship, but any time at all that we use the name of God, we must be careful to be very respectful. The respect we are to have for God is a respect so great that it has a special name: *reverence.* We are to be reverent when we speak about God and when we speak to God. That is because He is so much greater and higher than we are. **Read Psalm 99:1–5.**

TUESDAY

In an earlier question and answer, we learned that the Ten Commandments summarize the moral law. They are a short form of all the laws God has given man to obey. The questions and answers in the catechism about the Ten Commandments show us that it would not be enough to obey only the exact words of the commandments and nothing more. For instance, if we kept this third commandment by not misusing the name "God" and still we make fun of God's Word, we would not really be keeping the third commandment. So the catechism's answer to this question of what the third commandment requires includes more than the reverent use of the word "God." This answer says that God also requires us to reverently use all His names, titles, qualities, regulations, Word, and works. These are all the things by which God reveals Himself to us.

God has many names and titles in Scripture. Both His names and His titles help us see who He is. God has revealed to us in Scripture what He is like. He has told us of certain qualities He has, such as holiness, goodness, justice, and power. God has given us regulations or guidelines for coming to Him and for growing in Christlikeness. Those regulations help us to know Him better when we use them. God has also revealed Himself to us in His Word, the Bible. God shows us what He is like in His works, too, or in the things He does. We see what God is like when we study His creation, His everyday care for all His creatures, and the salvation He has accomplished for us. **Read Psalm 138:1–2.**

WEDNESDAY

God has many different names in Scripture. That is because no one word can cover all that God is to His people. Can you think of some of the names for God in the Bible? In addition to His names, He also has titles such as "Creator" and "Preserver of men" and "King of kings and Lord of lords." Whenever we speak *of* or *to* God, we should be careful to use the names and titles Scripture uses. To say "someone up there likes me," or to speak of God as the "man upstairs" does not show Him the proper respect. God has shown us in Scripture what He is like. He has shown us many of His qualities. God has revealed His names, titles, and qualities to us so that we would know Him. He wants us to study these things in Scripture and to think often of them. We should let these things God has revealed to us cause us to grow in love for Him. As we think of God's names, titles, and qualities, we should learn to fear Him and to delight in Him. **Read Psalm 145:1–5.**

THURSDAY

God has provided us with things that will cause us to grow to know Him better and to live as He wants us to when we use them. If we want to keep this third commandment, we will treat these things with reverence. We will faithfully use what God has provided for our growth. God has given us prayer as one way to help us grow in Christ. We are to be faithful to pray and, when we pray, we are to be reverent in our prayers. God has provided us with other Christians in the church. He wants us to meet with them regularly to hear God's Word read and preached and to worship Him with them. God has provided us with baptism and the Lord's Supper, which also cause us to know Him better and to grow more like Jesus.

It is easy to neglect these regulations God has given us. Sometimes we keep so busy that we find it hard to make time to pray or to be in church. But God requires us to use these things He has given us. We treat these regulations from God reverently when we use them, taking care to use them as God tells us to use them. The early Christians give us an example of people faithfully and reverently using what God had provided for their growth. **Read Acts 2:42–47.**

FRIDAY

If we want to honor God's name, we will honor His Word in which He has revealed it to us. Our attitude in worship honors God when we use His Word and use it reverently. The Bible is a wonderful treasure—a whole book in which God tells us what He is like, what He does for us, and what He wants of us! It is foolish to have a Bible and hardly ever use it! We should study God's Word every day, eager to know all we can of it. Of course, it is not enough just to know and study God's Word. We do not treat it with reverence unless we read it as the command of our King and look for His will in it so that we can eagerly obey it.

King Josiah is an example of someone who had this kind of reverence for God's Word. Long before he became king, the Israelites had begun to worship idols. They had used the Temple of God less and less until it had become dirty and run down. King Josiah had workmen clean and repair it. As they worked, they came upon a scroll. The scroll contained the law of God. The Israelites had ignored God for so long that this was the only copy of God's Word around—and it had been lost for years! King Josiah had someone read God's Word to him. As he listened, he realized how disobedient his people had been all this time. He recognized the law for what it was—the Word of God that is to be obeyed.

Read 2 Chronicles 34:19–21, 31 to see how he responded to what God said in His Word.

SATURDAY

God makes Himself known to us by His works or the wonderful things that He does. One of God's works is creation. All of God's creation shows that God is great. We are to honor Him for what He has made, letting the wonder of what we see in creation remind us of our wonderful God. God's works in providence show God to us as well. Every day He cares for His people, giving them what they need and arranging everything that comes into their lives for their good and for His glory.

As we watch God work out His plans through all that happens, we should praise Him for what He does and trust Him. God's greatest work is His work of salvation. He reveals Himself best of all by providing salvation for His people. We must accept the salvation He provides and live lives of obedience out of gratitude for what God has done. We make reverent use of God's works of creation, providence, and salvation by letting these things draw us to praise and love our God better. **Read Revelation 15:3b–4.**

Q.55. WHAT DOES THE THIRD COMMANDMENT FORBID?

A. ❧ *The third commandment forbids our treating as unholy or abusing anything God uses to make Himself known.*

MONDAY

We saw in the last question and answer that, when God commands us not to misuse His name, He is concerned with our attitude toward Him. The third commandment covers more than just our attitude toward God's name. It also requires a reverent attitude toward everything God uses to make Himself known. We saw in the last question and answer that God makes Himself known to us through all these things: His names, titles, and attributes, His regulations for coming to Him and for growing in godliness, His Word, and His works.

This third commandment requires us to use all these things to grow in our knowledge of God and in our obedience to Him. It requires us not only to use these things, but to use them *with reverence.* At the same time, of course, there are things this commandment forbids. We are forbidden to show irreverence, or disrespect, to any of the things God has given to make Himself known to us. God forbids us to treat these things as though they were ordinary things. We must treat them as holy. We may not abuse these things or fail to use them as God intended them to be used. God insists that we honor Him as He ought to be honored. **Read Malachi 2:2.**

TUESDAY

God is high and lifted up. He is much greater than we are. God's name stands for all He is, so His name must be treated as high and holy. People often use God's name as a common expression in everyday language. This is blasphemy. It is an insult to God. As the

Israelites traveled from Egypt to the Promised Land, two men got into a fight. You know how it is when you are angry. You say things you normally might not say. One of the men used God's name as a curse word. Someone reported this to Moses. Moses had the man locked up until God would show them what to do with the man who had misused God's name in this way. To see what God said to do with the man, **read Leviticus 24:13–16, 23.**

Whenever we read a story like this in the Bible, we need to remember that it shows us what God is like, how God feels toward the one who misuses His name, and how God will judge that person. God does not change. He feels the same way today about the one who uses His name as a curse word, or as an everyday expression, or who speaks of God lightly. We are to treat all of God's titles and all of God's attributes reverently as well. **Read 2 Kings 19:22.**

WEDNESDAY

God has given us regulations that will help us to know Him and to grow in Christlikeness when we use them as He intended us to use them. This commandment forbids us to misuse any of these things. We misuse God's regulations or ordinances when we do any of the following. During a worship service, we might laugh or whisper or sleep or slouch rudely in our seats. When we do these things, we fail to show reverence for the regulations God has given us. If, during prayer or worship or the reading of God's Word, we let our minds wander to things other than God, we misuse God's regulations and do not treat them as if they were holy.

Another way of misusing God's regulations is by doing them on the outside only, while, inside, our hearts are not God's at all. Sometimes, people do all the things that true Christians would do, but they only do them so that people will notice and think they are good. In their hearts, they have no true love for God and are not interested in Him at all. All these ways of misusing God's regulations show a lack of reverence for Him. **Read Psalm 50:16–17.**

THURSDAY

We are to use God's Word and use it reverently. Sometimes, children who have grown up in Christian families, attending Christian churches, behave as though they are tired of God's Word. Instead of bringing their Bibles with them to use them in a Sunday school class, they do not even want to use one the teacher lends them. They excuse themselves by saying things like, "I already know this." Such children show disrespect for God's Word.

People also misuse God's Word by using verses from it to teach things it really does not teach. These people use one or two verses, instead of using *all* of God's Word. They make those verses say things God never intended His Word to say. The apostle Peter wrote about Paul's epistles, which are a part of the Word of God. He spoke about people who were making Paul's letters say things they did not really say. **Read** what he said about such people in **2 Peter 3:16.**

People also misuse God's Word when they call their own opinions "the word of the Lord." People will say things like, "The Lord told me to do that," or "God spoke to me." They are really talking about a feeling or an opinion they have had. God has told us everything He has to say to us in the Bible. He does not speak in any other way. **Read Jeremiah 23:34–36.**

FRIDAY

God has given us His works as one more way that He makes Himself known to us. We are to let creation remind us of the greatness of the Creator. Many people today say that all of the creation put together *is* God. We must not misuse God's work of creation in this way.

God works every day in providence. He gives us good things for which we should thank Him and He gives us difficult things through which we learn to trust Him better. We misuse God's work of providence when we take our blessings for granted and let them draw us *away* from God. **Read Hosea 13:6,** where God complains about His people's ingratitude for His gifts. We also misuse God's work of providence when we become bitter about hard things in our lives, instead of seeing them as God's correction or as ways to help us grow. **Read Jeremiah 5:3.**

SATURDAY

God's greatest work is His work of salvation. We honor God when we accept His salvation, trusting Christ to save us and living for Him as our Lord. One way to misuse God's name is to call ourselves by it when we really are not His and do not live for Him. Many people say they are Christians or God's children, but they live so that anyone can see they do not know Him. The only people God allows to call themselves by His name are those who live for Him and are becoming like Him. **Read Matthew 7:21–23.**

Q.56. WHAT IS THE REASON FOR THE THIRD COMMANDMENT?

A. ❧ *The reason for the third commandment is that the Lord our God will not allow those who break this commandment to escape His righteous judgment, although they may escape punishment from men.*

MONDAY

God has been good to us. His name is very important to Him. He wants it always to receive the honor it deserves. He has given His name to us as the name we can call on to be saved. God tells us that He punishes sin severely. Then He tells us that He Himself will save us from that punishment, if we will call on Him to save us. **Read Romans 10:12–13.** God not only tells us what His name is, He tells us His name so we can call on it for the salvation from sin we need.

TUESDAY

Every human being should recognize how good God has been in telling us His name. This is especially true since He has told it to us so we can use it to call on Him to be saved. All of us should be very thankful to God for making His name known. We should want to treat His name with respect. Yet many people do not treat God or His name with any respect at all. Many people misuse God's name and few people mind when that happens. God is even so good that He sends troubles to get the attention of those who misuse His name. He sends these things to cause people to repent and honor Him. Often people refuse to repent and they dishonor God's name even more. **Read Revelation 16:8–9.** The longer these people refuse to repent, the more God stores up judgment for them.

WEDNESDAY

God is good to have told us His name so we could call on it to be saved. Another way in which He uses His name with us is also very gracious. All whom He saves, He allows to be called by His name. Names for believers such as "the people of God" or "children of God" or "Christians" are ways in which we are called by the name of God. It is a tremendous privilege to be called by God's name. **Read Deuteronomy 28:9–10.**

THURSDAY

It is good of God to allow His people to be called by His name. They must remember, though, that He requires them to honor it. It is a privilege to be called by God's name, but it is also a great responsibility. If we claim to be the people of God, we must act like it. If we say we follow the Lord Jesus Christ, we must take care to honor Him by obeying His commands. When we say that God has made us His children, we should live so that God's name receives glory from our lives and attitudes. Anyone who claims to be one of God's people and yet ignores what God says in His Word shows that he or she was never really one of God's people. No matter how much someone claims to love God, disobedience to God's commands shows that a person really hates Him. God will judge such a person for dishonoring His name. **Read 2 Timothy 2:19.**

FRIDAY

We should honor God's name out of gratitude that He has told it to us. God's people should honor God's name because He has made it known to them as the name they can call on to be saved. We must also honor God's name because He promises to severely punish those who do not honor it. Disrespect for God's name is common. No one seems to care that God's name is used as a swear word or that God's Word is not honored or obeyed. God cares. He will punish the misuse of His name and the failure to obey Him. **Read Deuteronomy 28:58–59.**

SATURDAY

When we respect and show reverence for God and for His name, God does not owe us anything because we have done that. Yet God is so good that He promises to reward us for doing what we simply ought to have done in the first place. He promises to reward us for reverencing His name. He promises to count us among those who love Him when we honor His name. God promises to bless us, our children, and our grandchildren—"to a thousand generations." Although now He waits patiently for people to repent, the day will come when He will punish those who show disrespect for Him and for His name, just as He has promised. **Read Revelation 11:16–18.**

Q.57. WHAT IS THE FOURTH COMMANDMENT?

A. 🐾 The fourth commandment is: *Remember the Sabbath day by keeping it holy. Six days you shall labor and do all your work, but the seventh day is a Sabbath to the Lord your God. On it you shall not do any work, neither you, nor your son or daughter, nor your manservant or maidservant, nor your animals, nor the alien within your gates. For in six days the Lord made the heavens and the earth, the sea, and all that is in them, but he rested on the seventh day. Therefore the Lord blessed the Sabbath day and made it holy.*

MONDAY

Read Genesis 2:1–3. God created all that is from nothing. He created it all in six days. On the seventh day, God rested from all His work. God was not tired. God is Spirit and has no body. He cannot get tired. Yet God chose to make the seventh day a special day of rest and peace. This day was to be a special day for man to stop his usual work and spend the entire day resting and enjoying God.

TUESDAY

Many years after God had created all things, God called the Jews to be His special people and He gave them His law. One of the laws He gave them was this commandment we are learning now. The Jews were to be careful to set aside one day in seven as a day to rest from their work. God's Old Testament people had other Sabbaths as well. They were to work on their farms for six years, but on the seventh year they were to give the land a Sabbath rest.

During the seventh year, they were not to plant any crops or work the land at all.

Every fiftieth year was to be a special Sabbath as well. It was called the Year of Jubilee. People who had become so poor that they had sold their land were to receive their land back again at the Year of Jubilee. In the same way, people who had become so poor that they had sold themselves to be servants were to be set free on that fiftieth year (Lev. 25). **Read Exodus 31:12.** All these Sabbaths were pictures of the Lord Jesus who would give His people rest from all the ceremonies and sacrifices they had to keep until He came.

WEDNESDAY

When Jesus was on earth, He often made the Pharisees angry. (Pharisees were people who were very concerned with keeping many rules.) One thing that made them angry was that Jesus was not as careful about what He did on the Sabbath as they thought He should be. He would heal people on the Sabbath and once He allowed His hungry disciples to pick and eat grain on the Sabbath. What does Jesus call Himself in **Matthew 12:8**? Jesus is the fulfillment of the Sabbath. The Sabbath was a picture of the rest that He would give to His people. He would perfectly keep the law of God for them, as they could never do it for themselves. They would no longer have to offer many sacrifices, over and over, all offered exactly right. All the sacrifices and ceremonies and special days were pictures of what the Savior would be to His people.

THURSDAY

God did all the wonderful work of creation and rested on the seventh day of the week. So the Old Testament people of God kept the seventh day as a special day of worship and rest. The Lord Jesus Christ did all of His wonderful work of saving His people and then rose from the dead on the first day of the week. So the people of God now keep the first day as a special day of worship and rest. **Read Acts 20:7.** This verse gives an example of God's people meeting on the first day of the week. They met to take the Lord's Supper and to listen to Paul preach.

FRIDAY

Read Colossians 2:16–17. Special celebrations and Sabbath Days were a shadow of the things to come. They were pictures of Jesus. Jesus is the One who gives us perfect rest and the Sabbath is a picture of Him. Some people believe that, since Jesus has come, we are no longer required to keep the Sabbath. Other people say that, since keeping the Sabbath is one of the Ten Commandments, it is a part of the moral law and people today are still required to honor it.

SATURDAY

True Christians who want to know and obey God's Word do not always agree with each other. Whether Christians must honor the Sabbath Day in the same way that Old Testament believers did is one of those areas where Christians disagree. **Romans 14:5–6a, 22** gives us some guidelines on how to handle our differences.

Q.58.   WHAT DOES THE FOURTH COMMANDMENT REQUIRE?

A. ✑ *The fourth commandment requires us to set apart to God the times He has established in His word—specifically one whole day in seven as a holy Sabbath to Him.*

MONDAY

A Sabbath is a rest. At the time of creation, on the first Sabbath, God *rested* from all His work of creating. This fourth commandment called God's people to honor the Sabbath by *resting* from all their everyday work. Old Testament laws required people to give the land a Sabbath. Every seven years, the land was to *rest* and no farming was to be done. What was the purpose of all this resting? It is good for human beings to set aside regular times of rest from their work. It is also good for farm land to have times of being unused.

But God's first reason for all that He does is not man's good, but God's own glory. The Sabbath was to remind all God's people that they need rest. God was calling them to share in His own rest. He was reminding them that true rest and peace are in Him alone. Setting aside for God one day in seven and doing no ordinary work that day would remind God's people of these things. **Read Psalm 62:1, 5.**

TUESDAY

God's people find true rest in Him alone. Rest is one of many blessings that God gives to His people. All of the blessings God gives to His people, including rest, come to us through the Savior God provided, Jesus. Old Testament believers celebrated the Sabbath and looked ahead to the rest God would give them when the Messiah came.

In the story *Pilgrim's Progress,* Christian has a large and heavy burden on his back that he cannot remove. He carries it so long and it is so heavy that he finds he can think of nothing but finding rest from this terrible burden. He sets off on a journey to find rest and he finally finds it at the cross. As he comes to the cross, the burden falls off his back all by itself and rolls away. Christian never sees it again.

Jesus gives God's people rest from the burden of sin. He gives them rest from the impossible task of trying to earn God's favor. Jesus gives them rest from the many sacrifices and ceremonies they were required to do before the Messiah came. The Sabbath was a picture of the perfect rest Jesus gives. **Read Matthew 11:27–29.**

WEDNESDAY

The Sabbath is a picture of the rest believers have in Jesus. When we come to Jesus in faith, trusting Him to give us rest from keeping the law and from the burden of our sin, we do what the Sabbath pictured. We rest from our works. We no longer try to earn God's favor by what we do. **Read Hebrews 4:8–11.**

THURSDAY

What do we do to enjoy the perfect rest that God gives in Jesus? When we hear the gospel, we believe it. It is that simple. The gospel is the good news that, although we had always been God's enemies because He hates our sin, God has made a way for us to become His friends. God gave His Son to die in our place, taking the punishment for all our sin. His Son lived more than thirty years on this earth, never sinning once, but always perfectly keeping God's law. This is what God requires of us, but we cannot do it. When Jesus obeyed God's law, He did it in our place. He paid for our sins for us and He kept God's law for us. There is nothing left for us to do. That is the gospel.

What God commands us to do now is to believe the gospel. If we believe the gospel, we agree with God that we are sinners who deserve His anger and we can do nothing to change that. When we believe the gospel, we believe that Jesus has done all that needs to be done to take away our sin and to make us God's friends instead of

His enemies. Faith in the gospel is how we come to enjoy the rest provided by God and pictured in the Sabbath. **Read Hebrews 4:1–3a.**

FRIDAY

God gave this commandment about keeping the Sabbath to His people in the Old Testament, the Israelites. For some, it was a reminder of the perfect rest from sin and from trying to earn God's favor that God would provide. These were the people who believed God's promises and trusted Him to keep them. They did not know about Jesus. They did not understand that all God's promises would be fulfilled in Him. But they believed that God would keep His promises and would meet all their needs. These Israelites believed that God would give them rest.

Other Israelites were part of the people of God because they had been born Israelites, but they were not really God's people. These Israelites had not put their faith in God and in His promises. Their lack of faith in God showed in their behavior. These Israelites rebelled against God and His commands over and over. God gave them many opportunities to repent and to believe in Him, but they did not use them. The time came when God was no longer willing to be patient with them. He became angry with them and said this: "So I declared on oath in my anger, 'They shall never enter My rest'" (Heb. 3:11). **Read Hebrews 3:16–19.**

SATURDAY

If the Sabbath pictures the perfect rest we have in Jesus, now that He has come, can we do whatever we want to do on Sundays? Does it no longer matter if Christians work on Sunday? Are we free to skip church so we can do what *we* want to do, instead of spending the day in the worship of God? Because of what Christ has done for us, we do not keep the Sabbath to make ourselves right with God. As children of God, we'll want to keep the Sabbath because we love Him so much. We want to thank Him for giving us all He has given in His Son, the Lord Jesus Christ. When we really understand what God has done for us, it will make us eager to spend a day each week learning about and praising Him. **Read Titus 3:4–8.**

Q.59. WHICH DAY OF THE WEEK HAS GOD DESIGNATED AS THE SABBATH?

A. *From the beginning of the world until the resurrection of Christ God established the seventh day of the week as the Sabbath. From that time until the end of the world the first day of the week is the Christian Sabbath.*

MONDAY

The Sabbath was a picture of the rest we would have in Christ. From the time of creation until the Savior came, people looked ahead to the rest the Lord Jesus would give them. The Sabbath Day was at the *end* of the week. All week long, God's people looked *forward* to the Sabbath, just as, all through Old Testament times, they looked forward to Christ's coming. Now Christ has come and we look *back* on what He has done for us. Now our Sabbath *begins* our week. **Read Exodus 31:12–13, 17.**

TUESDAY

God made it clear to the Israelites that He wanted them to take the Sabbath seriously. The punishment for breaking the Sabbath was death! As the Israelites traveled on their way to the land God had promised them, they needed food to eat. So God provided manna for them. Manna was little pieces of white bread that tasted like wafers made with honey. God caused this manna to fall from the sky for the Israelites. Every morning, when they got up, the manna covered the ground and they only had to go out and pick it up. God told them to only gather as much as they would need for their families for one day. If they gathered more than one day's worth, the manna would have worms in it by the next day. However, He told them not to gather it on the Sabbath Day. On the day before the

Sabbath, what did Moses tell the people about having food for the next day? **Read Exodus 16:23–30.**

WEDNESDAY

The Sabbath on the seventh day of the week was important to the Jews because it was important to God. Why was it changed to the first day of the week? In Old Testament times, the Sabbath celebrated the end of God's work of creation. On the seventh day, God finished His work of creating and He rested. The day of rest and worship in our time celebrates the end of God's work of redemption. On the first day of the week, the Lord Jesus Christ rose from the dead. He had finished His work of paying the penalty for the sins of His people. **Read** about this most important event in **Luke 24:1–8.** On this same day, the first day of the week, Jesus first appeared to His disciples after rising from the dead. **Read John 20:19–20.**

THURSDAY

When Jesus appeared to His disciples in the evening on the day that He rose from the dead, one of His disciples was not with the others. This disciple was Thomas. When the others told Thomas that they had seen Jesus, Thomas thought that was too good to be true. He refused to believe it until he saw Jesus with his own eyes. Thomas told the other disciples, unless he could touch the scars in Jesus' hands from the nails and feel the hole in His side from the soldier's spear, he would not believe that Jesus had risen from the dead. **Read John 20:26–29.** Jesus appeared to Thomas and spoke with him a week after He had appeared to the other disciples. It was Sunday again.

FRIDAY

The resurrection of Jesus is a very important event to Christians. Without it, there would be no Christianity. If Jesus had not risen from the dead, nothing else that He did would matter. Jesus' resurrection is the proof that Jesus is truly God, so that His death has enough value to pay for the sins of His people. Because the resurrection is so important, because it was such a great victory for Jesus, and because it took place on the first day of the week, the early Christians began to call the first day of the week "the Lord's Day." We see an example of this where the apostle John explains how he came to write the book of Revelation. **Read it in Revelation 1:9–11.**

SATURDAY

The Lord's Day or the first day of the week was a special day to the early Christians. On it, they met together to pray, listen to the apostles' teaching, give offerings of money to God, and celebrate the Lord's Supper. This is how the first day of the week became the day that Christians set aside for worship and rest. **Read Acts 20:7 and 1 Corinthians 16:1–2.**

Q.60. HOW DO WE KEEP THE SABBATH HOLY?

A. ✍ *We keep the Sabbath holy by resting the whole day from worldly affairs or recreations, even ones that are lawful on other days. Except for necessary works or acts of mercy we should spend all our time publicly and privately worshipping God.*

MONDAY

We stay home from work or school on Sunday so that we have more time free to read God's Word and to worship Him. A wise use of the extra time we have on Sundays would be to use it to learn about or to worship God. Of course, some kinds of work *have* to be done, even if it is the Lord's Day. These are works that are absolutely necessary and acts of mercy.

Works that are absolutely necessary are works we could not have done earlier and cannot put off until later. They must be done this very day. An example is the work of caring for small children or the work of preparing and cleaning up after a meal for the family. On the way to church, a tire on the family car may blow out. Changing the tire would be a necessary work. Things like homework or yardwork are not necessary works because they could have been done the day before. What necessary work was done in **Matthew 12:1–8?**

TUESDAY

The other kind of work that should be done even on the Lord's Day is work that is an act of mercy. When someone needs something that cannot wait, whoever helps that person still honors the Sabbath. When Christian doctors, nurses, fire fighters, and police officers go to their regular jobs on Sunday, they go there so they can be available to do acts of mercy. Their job is helping people that need help right away. What act of mercy was done on the Sabbath in **Luke 13:10–16?**

WEDNESDAY

Since we have no school or work on Sunday morning, we could stay home and stay in bed. If we choose to do that, though, we fail to use the Lord's Day to honor God. When we take the whole day off from our ordinary, everyday work, it should be so that we can spend it in worshiping God and learning about Him. You may sometimes hear, "I don't have to go to church to worship God," and this is true. But most of the time, if people choose to stay home from church on Sundays, they end up doing things they want to do rather than spending the time in the worship of God. Besides, God requires that we gather with His people for public worship. **Read Isaiah 58:13–14.**

THURSDAY

Another reason for going to church on the Lord's Day is that those of us who belong to God belong to His people. In both the Old and New Testaments, God deals with His people as a group. He wants each of us who know Him to participate in that group and not try to get along as Christians all by ourselves. The Bible does not let us think only of "God and me," but calls us to think of "God *and His people* and me." We honor and obey God when we gather with God's people, praise and worship Him together, and learn from His Word together. **Acts 20:7** describes the early church gathering together on the first day of the week, or Sunday. What two things that we often do in our worship services does this verse describe them doing?

FRIDAY

God's people gather on the Lord's Day to listen to His Word, to celebrate the Lord's Supper, and to worship Him together. **Read 1 Corinthians 16:1–2.** The apostle Paul told the Corinthian church to set aside offering money on the first day of the week. We worship God when we bring an offering of money. Our offering shows that all we have is God's gift to us, for which we are thankful. It shows that we trust Him to give us what we need. We can give away some of our money without worrying that we will not have all we need. Giving our offering shows that we want all we have and are to be used for God's glory and not for ourselves. Christians who have any money at all, even if it is just a small allowance, should be giving some part of it regularly to God. This is an important part of our worship and of our honoring God.

SATURDAY

The psalms were written as songs to be used by God's people in their worship and when they pray. Many psalms have headings. Some tell us what was going on that caused the writer of the psalm to write this particular one. Other headings tell us how the psalm was to be performed musically. Some headings tell us when the psalm was to be used. **Psalm 92** has a heading that tells us when it was to be used. It is "a psalm. A song. For the Sabbath day." Read it today in preparation for worshiping God tomorrow.

Q.61. WHAT DOES THE FOURTH COMMANDMENT FORBID?

A. ✍ *The fourth commandment forbids failing to do or carelessly doing what we are supposed to do. It also forbids treating the day as unholy by loafing, by doing anything in itself sinful, or by unnecessary thinking, talking about, or working on our worldly affairs or recreations.*

MONDAY

We honor the Lord's Day when we set it aside as a day for being with God's people. We keep it a special day to worship God and to hear His Word. But we must not only honor the Lord's *Day* by doing these things, we must honor *the Lord* by the *way* we do these things. Some people attend worship out of habit or because someone makes them attend. Such people go to church grudgingly, wishing they did not have to go. They would rather stay home. All the time they are in the worship service, they think about what they will do later. They watch the clock all through the service, and if it goes past the time to end, they feel irritated. The Old Testament prophet Amos had an angry message from God for the people of Israel. The Israelites were doing what made God angry. In the first half of **Amos 8:5,** read something they were saying that made God angry.

TUESDAY

We fail to rightly honor God on the Lord's Day when we are careless about our worship. We can be careless about our worship in several ways. Often, people come into the worship service late. Imagine receiving an invitation to a meeting with someone important and showing up late! Coming to worship God is at least as important as meeting with an important human being. Yet Christians seem to feel quite free to walk in to church late.

Imagine being in a meeting with someone important—the president of the United States, for instance—and not paying attention to what he said. People often fail to pay attention in a worship service. When people sit in church, letting their minds wander during the sermon or when they sing the words of hymns without paying attention to them, they are being careless about honoring God.

The prophet Malachi wrote down God's message to His people. He complained about their carelessness in worshiping Him. In the case of the Israelites, they brought sick or damaged animals for offerings to God. God was offended because they should have brought Him their best. "Would you give a damaged gift to your governor?" he asked them. If such a gift would insult a human leader, would it not dishonor God? We no longer bring animal sacrifices as a part of our worship, but the principle is still true. God's people should bring their best to God—their best worship, their best attention. We should be careful, not careless, as we come to worship our great God. **Read Malachi 1:6–8.**

WEDNESDAY

When we come to a worship service to hear God's Word proclaimed, we should come with our hearts prepared. It is not enough to simply come. Nor is it enough to simply listen to the sermon. Because it is God's Word that is being preached, we must listen carefully. We are to listen humbly, willing to change in order to do what God's Word says to do. We should come listening for something that we can obey from what we hear that morning. God tells us what attitude He wants us to have toward His word. **Read Isaiah 66:1–2.** It is a good idea to spend some time before coming to the worship service, either on Sunday morning or on Saturday night, praying. Ask God to prepare you to listen and to obey what you will hear in His Word.

THURSDAY

A true Christian wants to honor God every day, not just on Sundays. He understands how much God has done for Him in the Lord Jesus Christ, so he does not worry about giving too much of his time to God. He will set aside one day in seven as a special day of worship, but he will live the other six days for God as well. The true child of

God is thankful for all Jesus has done for him. He will look for ways to show his thankfulness. He wants every day to belong to the Lord. **Read 2 Corinthians 5:14–15.**

FRIDAY

God's people want to spend time in His word and in prayer. When the Holy Spirit causes a person to be born again, He puts a love for those things into that person's heart. Before a person is a believer, he has no interest in church or in reading the Bible or in praying to the true God. When the Holy Spirit changes a person's heart, he has a new love for those things. He will not grow bored with those things because they help him get to know God better. He will eagerly do these things every day, not only on Sundays. **Read Psalm 119:147–148, 164.**

SATURDAY

"Worldly affairs" are those things we need to think about and spend time on in order to be responsible. For a child, these might be chores or homework. An adult's "worldly affairs" would include the things he must take care of for his job. It is *not* necessary, however, to do these things on the Lord's Day. If we are careful to plan ahead, not leaving things until the last minute, we can take care of all our responsibilities on Monday through Saturday, leaving Sunday free to concentrate on the things of the Lord. Our recreation too—the things we do for fun and for relaxation—can be planned so that Sunday is free for worship, study, and fellowship with God's people. **Read Ephesians 5:15–20.**

Q.62. WHAT ARE THE REASONS FOR THE FOURTH COMMANDMENT?

A. *The reasons for the fourth commandment are these: God allows us six days of the week to take care of our own affairs; He claims the seventh day as His own; He set the example; and He blesses the Sabbath.*

MONDAY

When God asks us to give Him something, He is gracious in what He allows us to keep for our own use. In the Old Testament, God asked His people to give Him 10 percent of all their money. That meant that from every ten pieces of money they had, they were to give God one. That left nine for them to use as they thought best. In the same way, by commanding us to set aside one day in seven for the worship of God, God graciously allows us to keep six for our own work. The work we have to do on our ordinary days is a gift from God. He planned for man to have work to keep him busy with something enjoyable and profitable. We learn about God as we work in the world He made. God leaves us six days of the week for the work we have to do. **Read Genesis 2:8–10, 15.**

TUESDAY

The fourth commandment asks us to give only one day in seven to God. One day in seven is not very much to give to God when you consider what we owe Him. We owe Him all we have and all we are because He made us in the first place. He planned how many days each of us would have in our lives. He planned what would happen to each of us on each of those days. Our whole life is a gift from God. Each day of our lives is a gift from God. He has given us so many days in which to know and love Him. To give God one day in seven is not much to give Him in return. **Read Psalm 139:15–16.**

WEDNESDAY

Christians who understand all that God has done for them will be eager to set aside time to honor God. Christians have more to be thankful for than anyone else has. God has given life to every human being. He has given *eternal* life to His people.

The Christian's life belongs to God, not only because God created us and gave us life in the first place; the Christian's life belongs to God because God bought it for Himself. God gave what was most valuable to Him so that we could be free from sin and belong to God. **Read 1 Peter 1:17–19.** The Christian understands that every day of her or his whole life belongs to the Lord and should honor God.

THURSDAY

One reason for keeping the fourth commandment is that God allows us six days of the week to do the work He has given us and claims only one for Himself. Another reason is the example that God Himself set when He had finished His work of creation. The Bible tells us that God rested on the seventh day, because He had finished His work. The Lord Jesus Christ, too, when He was on earth, honored the Sabbath. **Read Luke 4:16** to see a custom or habit of Jesus.

FRIDAY

Another reason for remembering the Lord's Day is that God blessed the Sabbath. On the first Sabbath, when God rested from His work of creation, the Bible tells us that "God blessed the seventh day and made it holy." Because God made us to honor and glorify Him, we are at our best and happiest when we *do* honor and glorify Him. When we honor Him by setting aside a day for His worship, we do what is best for *us*. God will bless *us* when we rightly use the Lord's Day to learn of God and to worship Him. We will grow in love for God as we spend time with Him. We will be blessed by learning what He says in His Word. When we love the Lord and celebrate Him on His Day, we will find that it brings us joy as well. **Read Isaiah 56:6–7.**

SATURDAY

When we set aside one day a week to spend thinking about, talking to, and learning of God, we are blessed. The more we learn about God from His Word, the more we will see how wonderful He is and the more we will love Him. The more time we spend in prayer and praise to God, the better we will know Him and the more we will rejoice in how wonderful He is. As God's people spend Sunday doing the things that will cause them to grow in the knowledge of God, they will be blessed. They will be always finding more to love and rejoice about in God. In this way, the Sabbath is a blessing to God's people. **Read Isaiah 58:13–14.**

Q.63. WHAT IS THE FIFTH COMMANDMENT?

A. ✐ The fifth commandment is: *Honor your father and your mother, so that you may live long in the land the Lord your God is giving you.*

MONDAY

Remember that the Ten Commandments *summarize* the moral law. A summary leaves out the details and gives only main points. That is why when we learn each of these Ten Commandments, we are not to think that we only have to do *exactly* what it says and nothing more. We also have to keep all the laws that each particular commandment summarizes or stands for. As we study this commandment about honoring our parents, we are going to see that it is a summary of how God wants us to behave toward all kinds of people, not just our parents. **Read Romans 13:6–10.**

TUESDAY

The first authority we have over us is our parents' authority. As we grow, we find other kinds of authority we must honor as well. All human beings are required first of all to fear God. He is the Creator and the King of all things and we owe Him complete respect and obedience. In all areas of life, God has established authorities we must honor. God gives certain people the task of providing for and protecting others. Parents provide for and protect their children. Husbands provide for and protect their wives. Kings or other rulers provide for and protect their citizens, and pastors and elders provide for and protect their churches.

These people cannot do the tasks God has given them to do if they must constantly argue with those who are under their care about what is best. So God has given them authority. The people under them are to respect them and obey them. People in authority are not always right. But, unless they command us to disobey God, we must respect and obey them. When we fail to show respect for authority, we show disrespect for God, who put certain people in positions of authority. **Read Romans 13:1–2.**

WEDNESDAY

God has established authority in the family. The husband is over the wife. He is to provide for her, protect her, and do all he can to help her grow in Christlikeness and use the gifts God has given her. The wife is to submit to the husband. She is to respect his authority and to do what she knows he wants done, even if she would rather do something else. Parents are over children. Parents are to provide all that their children need to grow up with healthy bodies, minds, and spirits. They are to protect them and train them. Children must respect the authority of parents and obey them immediately. **Read Colossians 3:18–21.**

THURSDAY

God has established authority in other areas besides the home. God has established governments so justice will be done. He has established kings, presidents, and governors to punish those who do what is evil and to protect those who abide by the law. We may not always agree with everything a president or a governor does, but we must always treat them with respect. We must obey the laws they make, unless those laws require us to disobey what God has told us in His Word. **Read 1 Peter 2:13–14, 17.**

God has also established authority in His church. Elders and pastors provide the teaching Christians need. They protect the church from false teachers. Pastors and elders encourage God's people to follow Christ and they warn them when they sin. Christians are to submit to the decisions of the elders and pastors of their churches. They are to obey them and follow their teaching. **Read Hebrews 13:17.**

FRIDAY

God wants us to respect those who are in authority over us, or those who are above us. He also calls us to show the proper respect to those who are below us and those who are equal to us. By "below us," we do not mean that some people are not as good as we are. People who are below other people are those who are under their care and protection. We say that wives are below husbands. This does not mean that wives are less valuable or less gifted or less intelligent than their husbands. It simply means that they are beneath their husbands' authority. Citizens are below their rulers. People who work for someone are below the boss. Younger people are below older people. Children are below their parents. This commandment tells us to treat those below us as God wants us to treat them. People in authority may not misuse that authority. They are to be faithful to carry out all the responsibilities God has given them for the people who are below them. **Read 1 Timothy 5:8 and Ephesians 6:4.**

SATURDAY

This commandment calls us to honor our parents. That implies respecting all authority over us and includes treating those below us as God wants us to. But this commandment also tells us how we are to treat those who are not in authority over us and are not below us. These are our equals. They are the people near us in age who are not our teachers or bosses or elders or rulers. We are to treat them with respect because they are made in the image of God and we are to love them. **Read Romans 12:10 and Philippians 2:3–4.**

Q.64.

WHAT DOES THE FIFTH COMMANDMENT REQUIRE?

A. ✑ *The fifth commandment requires us to respect and treat others, whether above, below, or equal to us, as their position or our relationship to them demands.*

MONDAY

Since the Ten Commandments summarize all the moral law God has given, this commandment tells us how to treat people of all kinds. Because the commandment specifically deals with the relationship of children to their parents, we will spend several days looking at what God has to say about how children should treat their parents. God's Word tells children about several duties they have toward their parents. One duty is that of paying careful attention to what their parents teach them. Children are born knowing nothing at all. They depend completely on their parents to teach them what they need to know. As children listen to their parents, they learn to talk. They watch them and learn to walk.

The most important things children can learn from their parents are the truths found in God's Word. God requires Christian parents to teach their children who He is and what He requires of them. Parents must teach children what God values and how to live for His glory. God requires children to listen attentively to their parents' teaching and remember what they are told. They should treasure the teaching of Christian parents and let it guide them their entire lives. **Read Proverbs 6:20–23.**

TUESDAY

Another duty of children toward their parents is that of obeying their parents. They may learn so well what their parents want them to know that they could say it back perfectly, but they must do more. They must go on to obey that teaching. Often children know and remember what parents have taught them to do, but when their parents are not with them, they disobey their parents' teaching. This commandment requires children to do what their parents have told them to do, even when their parents are not present.

Besides obeying the *teaching* of their parents, children are to obey the *word* of their parents. As soon as a parent gives a child a command, the child should obey. He should not wait to see if the parent will make him do it. He should not ask "Why?" or argue. The child is to obey immediately, just as he would if it were God who had told him what to do. After all, God has given each child his parents and God requires us to respect their authority. **Read Ephesians 6:1.** In the same way, when a teacher or a babysitter is responsible for a child while his parents are not there, the child must obey and respect the teacher or babysitter just as he would his own parents.

WEDNESDAY

Sometimes parents have the unpleasant task of disciplining their children. Maybe they cannot let them have something because they know it would not be good for them. Maybe the child has done something wrong and must suffer the consequences, such as being grounded or getting a spanking. Parents would prefer *not* to do these things. Faithful, loving parents will discipline their children because they know that if their children always get their own way and are never corrected, they will be selfish, ungodly adults. It is the parents' responsibility to discipline their children when they need it. It is the responsibility of children to accept their parents' discipline and learn from it.

Discipline is not pleasant for anyone. But a wise son or daughter realizes that discipline is for his or her own good. Wise children are thankful for parents who will correct them when they need it. Wise children learn from being disciplined. Foolish children refuse to learn when they are disciplined. They laugh about it and continue to do the same wrong things so they need to be disciplined over and over again. **Read Proverbs 12:1 and Proverbs 13:1.**

THURSDAY

Children are not only to respect their parents while they are children; grown children also have responsibilities to their parents. Children never become so old that they may stop honoring their parents. They are to continue to show their parents respect as long as they live. Once children are grown, their parents do not tell them what to do the way they did when the children were little. Even so, grown children will honor their parents by asking them for their advice and considering it carefully.

Even when people are adults, their parents have still lived longer than they have and have had more experience. The advice of parents is always valuable, no matter how old the child is. Grown children also honor their parents by speaking to them and about them with respect. They can also show respect for their parents by taking care of them when they are old and need help. Older people may need help with money when they can no longer work. Grown children who honor parents ask for and listen to their advice, speak of them with respect, and help them when they are older and need help. **Read Proverbs 23:22.**

FRIDAY

We have studied several of the duties that children have toward their parents. These are: listening to their teaching, obeying them, accepting and learning from their discipline, and honoring them when they are older. Children will do all these things when they have a right attitude toward their parents. The right attitude to have toward parents is an attitude of respect. Children who respect their parents are afraid to displease them. This is not a fear of getting caught and of punishment. It is a sincere desire to do what would please the parent and to keep from doing what would make the parent unhappy. Of course, both parents and children are sinners. Sometimes parents sin and do things that make it hard for children to respect them. Sometimes children sin and do not feel like showing respect for their parents. This commandment calls us to always respect our parents, no matter how we feel. **Read Leviticus 19:3.**

SATURDAY

In some countries, older people receive a great deal of respect. In those places, the older a person is, the more he or she is respected for his or her wisdom. In our country, older people do not receive much respect. Younger people receive more respect because they are stronger or prettier. In our country, people value physical attractiveness and strength more than wisdom! These values are not God's values. God commands us to show respect to people who are older than we are. **Read 1 Peter 5:5 and Leviticus 19:32.** Do you show respect to adults, even adults you do not know? Do you greet them, let them go ahead of you, hold doors open for them, and other things that would show respect? Or do you ignore them or, worse, make fun of them or cause problems for them? If an adult who is not your parent tells you to do something (or to stop doing something), do you respond with respect? These things are more and more unusual in our society, but they are things that God requires of us.

A. ❧ *The fifth commandment forbids being disrespectful to or not treating others as their position or relationship to us demands.*

MONDAY

The Bible teaches children how to treat their parents. It tells them what they should not do as well as what they should do. As children are commanded to honor their parents, so they are forbidden to *dishonor* them. They must not show disrespect in any way. Unfortunately, we see all around us children of all ages who demonstrate disrespect for their parents. Such attitudes have become so ordinary that we hardly notice them when we see them. God considers disrespect toward parents as something very serious. God gave the Israelites twelve curses to pronounce as soon as they entered the Promised Land. These were curses for people who would do any of twelve very wrong things. The curses were for things like killing innocent people or worshiping idols. One of the curses was for anyone who would treat his parents with disrespect. **Read it in Deuteronomy 27:16.**

TUESDAY

What are the ways in which children could dishonor their parents? One obvious way is by trying to hit or kick or hurt a parent. Sometimes, grown or nearly grown children will become angry with parents and hit them. Sometimes even very small children will become angry about not getting what they want and will hit or kick at their parents. Because God has placed parents in authority over children, to attack a parent is like attacking and trying to fight with God. **Read** what God's law for the Israelite nation said should happen to such a disrespectful child in **Exodus 21:15.** Another way of attacking parents and desiring their hurt is cursing them, or saying that you want something terrible to happen to them. The same punishment was to happen to children who cursed their parents. **Read Exodus 21:17.**

WEDNESDAY

I hope that no one reading this has ever hit his or her parents or cursed them. But there are other ways of showing disrespect to parents that we might think are not so bad, things all children do sometimes. But Scripture teaches us that these are also forbidden and are also serious in God's eyes. Because children are sinners (like everyone else), children sometimes fail to obey their parents. This is sin, not only against parents but against God as well. Some children enjoy sneaking away to do things they know their parents would not let them do. They carefully plan how to disobey and get away with it. This is even worse than a single act of disobedience. This is an attitude in which a child thinks he knows better than his parents and their rules. The child with this attitude "scorns obedience." He thinks he is too smart and too grown up to have to obey.

Another disrespectful attitude toward parents is a mocking attitude. A child who mocks his parents shows disrespect to them when he is around his friends. He makes fun of his parents, letting his friends know that his parents say and do stupid things, and that he is not like them. He speaks to them in a sharp voice when anyone is near and tries never to be seen with them. This is a mocking attitude. **Read** what the Bible has to say about the child who mocks his parents or who scorns obedience to them in **Proverbs 30:17.**

THURSDAY

Children are forbidden to dishonor their parents by attacking them physically, by cursing them, by refusing to obey them, or by mocking or making fun of them. Children also dishonor their parents when they refuse to learn from their teaching. Almost all parents want the best for their children. They teach them what they believe they should know. Children do not always see why their parents' teaching is so important, yet they should believe that their parents are wiser than they are. They need to be diligent to learn what their parents teach them. Especially when children have Christian parents who will teach them the truth of God's Word, they should work hard at learning what their parents want them to know.

Unfortunately, sometimes the children who hear God's Word often become bored with it. This is a sinful attitude. Children who turn away from their parents' Christian teaching when they grow up sin in two ways. They sin by choosing to do things that are wrong. They also sin because God has given them the gift of Christian teaching, a gift many children do not have, and they refuse to use this gift. **Read Proverbs 4:1–5.**

FRIDAY

Sometimes grown children find ways to use their parents to get what they want. They refuse to get jobs even though they are healthy and grown. They continue to expect their parents to provide for them. Grown children may also become selfish, forgetting all their parents have done for them and being unwilling to help them with the things they need. As parents grow older, they cannot always work as much as they used to or they may not be able to work at all. They may not have enough money for the things they need. Older people may need help doing things, because they do not have good health. Using parents for selfish reasons and refusing to help older parents when they need help dishonor parents. These things are also forbidden by God. **Read Proverbs 19:26.**

SATURDAY

God gave the Israelites ceremonial laws, having to do with sacrifices, priests, and washings. He gave them moral laws, which are true for all people in all times and in all places. God also gave the Israelites civil laws, laws just for the Old Testament kingdom of Israel. We no longer follow these civil laws. However, when we read the civil laws God had for Israel, we see some of the things that are important to God. There was a civil law that required punishment for a child who continued to be rebellious and wicked, in spite of his parents' teaching and discipline. Although God no longer requires us to do what this law said to do, it does show us how serious a sin rebellion is in God's eyes. **Read the law in Deuteronomy 21:18–21.**

Q.66. WHAT IS THE REASON FOR THE FIFTH COMMANDMENT?

A. ✥ *The reason for the fifth commandment is the promise of long life and prosperity, if these glorify God and are for the good of those who obey this commandment.*

MONDAY

As in several of the other commandments, God gives us a reason for obeying this one. Of course, we should always obey any of God's commandments just because God says so. But because God is good to us, He often gives us reasons for what He commands. He shows us what will happen if we obey Him and what will happen if we do not. God first gave this commandment to the Israelites as they were about to enter the Promised Land.

The reason God gave them for keeping this commandment to honor their parents was "so that you may live long in the land the Lord your God is giving you." God had promised His people that they would live in peace in the land He gave them *as long as they obeyed Him.* If they stopped obeying Him and following His commandments, God would bring enemies against them who would carry them away to other countries. An important part of living as God's people was obeying this commandment for children to honor parents.

The catechism uses the fifth commandment as it is written in Exodus 20:12, where the promise is that the people will live long in the land God will give them. The same commandment is repeated in **Deuteronomy 5:16.** Read it to see what is added to the promise there.

TUESDAY

God first gave the fifth commandment to the Israelites. He promised they would live long in the Promised Land if they kept it.

God's people no longer live in one special country. Does that mean this promise is no longer good? No, the apostle Paul repeated the promise in the New Testament, when God's people lived in many different countries. **Read it in Ephesians 6:1–3.** This promise does not mean that the only people who die young are those who failed to honor their parents. Usually, those who honor parents and follow their advice will stay healthier and live longer than those who ignore what their parents tell them.

Sometimes, though, God is glorified more by one of His people dying young than He would be by that person dying when he is older. When this happens, we can trust that God knows and is doing what is best. The answer to this question says God gives those who honor their parents long life and prosperity, *"if* these glorify God and are for the good of those who obey this commandment."

WEDNESDAY

God tells us to keep this commandment so that it will go well with us and we will enjoy long life on the earth. The book of Proverbs shows us some ways this happens. **Read Proverbs 1:8–9.** A garland on your head or a chain or necklace on your neck makes you more attractive. Does this mean you will be better-looking if you honor your parents? No, but you *will* be more attractive. When we honor our parents by paying attention to their instruction, we will have character qualities that make us more attractive to others and that please God. When our character is Christlike and we live to please God, things *will* go well with us and we will enjoy life.

THURSDAY

Read Proverbs 3:1–2. These verses promise us long life and prosperity when we remember the teaching of godly parents and keep their commandments in our hearts. Again, we will probably live longer on this earth if we live wisely, as our parents have taught us. But even if our lives on earth are *not* long, we will live forever in heaven if we have kept the teaching of Christian parents. They will have taught us to put our faith in Jesus Christ and to follow Him. Keeping our parents' teaching brings us prosperity. That does not mean that obedient children will be millionaires! We probably *will* have more money if we listen to the wise counsel our parents give us about work, saving, and spending. But we will certainly be rich in the things that matter most, in the things of God, if we keep the teaching our Christian parents have given us.

FRIDAY

Read Proverbs 4:20–22. These verses tell us to pay attention to our parents' teaching. You often see children or teenagers who interrupt their parents, saying things like, "I know, I know." They need to listen and pay attention, not act like they know it all, as though there were nothing they could learn from their parents. These verses say our parents' teaching will be life and health to us. Parents guide children into doing what is good for their bodies, like getting enough sleep and eating the right kinds of foods. Parents warn children about drugs or other things that could hurt their bodies. Godly parents give us teaching that keeps us healthy in other ways as well. Advice from parents about friends will usually keep children healthier and happier if they follow it. Parents are wise enough to recognize when someone is not good for their children. And again, if we have parents who teach us to love and follow the Lord, we will be healthy spiritually, which is the most important of all.

SATURDAY

Read Proverbs 6:20–23. When we honor our parents by taking their teaching seriously, their teaching guides us throughout our lives. It protects us from things that would harm us if we did not know to stay away from them. The teaching of godly parents is like a light or a lamp. A light enables us to see clearly so we choose rightly and so we will know what to do. We must honor our parents when they correct and discipline us too, even though these things are not pleasant. These verses remind us that the correction and discipline of godly parents are the way of life for their children. These are just some of the ways in which honoring our parents causes things to go well with us and helps us to enjoy long life on the earth.

Q.67. WHAT IS THE SIXTH COMMANDMENT?

A. ✍ The sixth commandment is: *You shall not murder.*

MONDAY

After the flood, when Noah and his family began life on earth all over again, God gave Noah a command for all mankind. God said that if anyone shed a person's blood, his own blood was to be shed. Why did God say that? It was not just because hurting people is unkind. **Read Genesis 9:6** to see why people may not kill or hurt other people. It is because people have been made in the image of God. To attack people is to attack God who made them in His image. Killing an animal or a bird or a fish is different. These creatures belong to God and we should treat them with compassion and glorify Him in how we use them. But it is not wrong to catch and kill a fish to eat or to put a sick dog to sleep. It *is* wrong to kill a human being because human beings bear the image of God. To hurt or kill a human being is not only cruel, it is insulting to God.

TUESDAY

There are times when killing a human being does not break God's commandment to not murder. One of these times is when it is a case of self-defense. **Read Exodus 22:2.** In this passage, a person is defending his house and property and kills the robber in the process. By God's law, the person being robbed was not at fault for killing the robber. Another exception to this commandment would be wartime. Often war is a form of self-defense. Or it is a means of preventing other nations from doing cruel and greedy things to a smaller country. Fighting in a war and killing someone if it is necessary does not break the sixth commandment.

WEDNESDAY

Read Numbers 35:30. Another exception to the commandment not to kill is capital punishment. Today many people believe that capital punishment should never be allowed. Capital punishment is punishing a murderer by putting her or him to death. In the Bible, God not only allows capital punishment, He requires it. Killing a person is an attack on God who made man in His image. God requires that, when a person has murdered another person, the murderer is to be punished by being put to death. The one who puts the murderer to death does not break God's commandment.

THURSDAY

Not only are we forbidden to kill other people, this commandment forbids us to kill ourselves. Suicide is just as wrong as murder. Usually, a person thinks about killing himself because life seems too hard. Something very sad has happened to him or he has to live without someone or something that he feels he has to have. He would rather stop living than to live in the circumstances he has, so he chooses to kill himself. When a person chooses to kill himself, he chooses *not* to accept what God has chosen for him. Since God controls all things, He has chosen each person's circumstances. When we have to suffer, we are to trust God is doing what is best for us. We are to trust Him to give us what we need to get us through the suffering. Choosing suicide is rebellion against God. It is telling Him, "No! I will *not* accept what You have given me and I do *not* trust You to do what is best for me!" To see a godly attitude in suffering, **read 1 Peter 4:19.**

FRIDAY

When you read the sixth commandment, you may think, "What an easy commandment to keep! I would never kill anyone!" But we have to remember that the Ten Commandments summarize all God's moral law. When we think about this commandment to not murder, we have to think of all that it summarizes. Murder is an act that begins with an angry thought. The anger grows into an attitude of hatred that results in a murder. If you have ever felt hatred to-

ward another person or even had an angry thought toward someone, you have taken the first step toward murder. **Read 1 John
3:11–12, 15.**

SATURDAY

The sixth commandment does not just forbid murder. It tells us
how to treat human beings. It tells us what not to do and, as we think
about all it means, it helps us see what we should do in our relationships with people. This commandment is not only a call not to kill; it
is a call to love. There is another catechism (the Heidelberg Catechism) that also teaches about this commandment. That catechism
says: "In forbidding murder, God teaches us that He abhors [or
hates] its very root, namely: envy, hatred, anger, and desire of re-
venge; and that in His sight all these are hidden murder. . . . In con-
demning envy, hatred, and anger, God requires us to love our
neighbor as ourselves, to show patience, peace, meekness, mercy,
and kindness toward him, and to prevent his hurt as much as possible; also, to do good even unto our enemies." **Read Romans 13:9–10.**

Q.68. WHAT DOES THE SIXTH COMMANDMENT REQUIRE?

A. 〜 *The sixth commandment requires making every lawful effort to preserve one's own life and the lives of others.*

MONDAY

God values human life, so we must value it too. God wants us to preserve and protect human life. However, we are not to try so hard to protect human life that we do what is not lawful and sin against God. Many Americans do not see anything wrong with abortion, or killing babies before they are born. Abortion is wrong because it kills a tiny human being. People who believe God's Word should work hard to end abortion in their country.

Sometimes, though, people have killed others over the issue of abortion. This should not happen. Killing an unborn baby is wrong. Killing people who believe in abortion is just as wrong. God has established governments and has given them the job of punishing wrongdoers, such as people who perform abortions. **Read 1 Peter 2:13–14.** Ordinary people may not punish wrongdoers. That is for governments to do. We are not to preserve life by doing what is not lawful.

TUESDAY

Down through the centuries, God's people have been killed for *being* God's people. God has many enemies and those enemies have always tried to turn His people away from Him. Christians have often had to choose either to say they would no longer follow Christ or die. For a Christian to save his or her life by denying Christ is not lawful. **Read Matthew 10:32–33, 39.** In every way that *is* lawful, we must preserve our lives and take care of our bodies, keeping them healthy and well. Eating nutritious foods and getting enough sleep and exercise are not only wise ideas. They show obedience to God's commandment to preserve life and not kill.

WEDNESDAY

We might feel pleased with ourselves for obeying this commandment to not murder because we have never killed anyone. This commandment goes beyond that, though. It requires us to make every lawful effort to preserve life. If we could provide things that would keep people from dying, we must love them enough to give them those things. If we do not, we are at least partly responsible if they die because they did not have what they needed. God is not satisfied if we simply do not kill people. God requires us to show love and compassion by sharing with those who are in need. **Read 1 John 3:17–18.**

THURSDAY

Read Luke 10:25–37. Jesus told an expert in the law that all he had to do to earn eternal life was to love God with all his heart, soul, mind, and strength and love his neighbor as he loved himself. Jesus wanted him to see how impossible it is to do that. But the expert in the law actually thought he could do it! He wanted to justify himself. He wanted to prove he was righteous, so he asked, "Who is my neighbor?" Jesus told this story to show him that every time we see a need that we can meet, God's law requires us to meet it.

FRIDAY

God's people should want to be holy. They should want to do the things that help them to grow in holiness, things like reading their Bible, praying, and worshiping God with other believers. It is possible, though, for God's people to be so concerned about their own growth in holiness that they have no time or energy left to care about others. God's people should gather to encourage each other to grow in Christlikeness. But it is possible for them to spend so much time with each other that they have no time or desire to show love or share the gospel with those who do not know Jesus.

This commandment calls us to care about others, not just our own Christian lives and our Christian friends. It calls us to be concerned enough about others that we will do something about it. In the book of Isaiah, God complains about His people doing plenty of religious activities but failing to demonstrate love to people in need. He tells them what they must do if they really want to grow in holiness. **Read Isaiah 58:3–10.**

SATURDAY

The sixth commandment requires us to show love to all people, because all people are made in the image of God. God does not require us just to love those who love us or those who are easy to love. We must love every human being. God does not even allow us to hate evil people, who fight against God. God may convert them so they become His children instead of His enemies. If He does not do that, He will judge them when He is ready. Meanwhile, we must forgive them when they do what hurts us and show love to them. **Read Romans 12:17–21.**

Q.69. WHAT DOES THE SIXTH COMMANDMENT FORBID?

A. ✍ *The sixth commandment forbids taking one's own life or the lives of others unjustly or doing anything that leads to suicide or murder.*

MONDAY

When the sixth commandment forbids murder, it does not forbid the act only. It also forbids the attitudes that lead to murder. God is absolutely holy. He hates sin in any form. The sin of hating another in your heart and holding a grudge against that person rather than forgiving is, in God's eyes, another way of breaking the sixth commandment. **Read Leviticus 19:16–18.** Jesus told us that anger toward someone or name-calling makes us guilty before God (Matt. 5:21–22).

TUESDAY

Murder is an *act* that God forbids. Hatred and holding grudges are *attitudes* that God forbids. Hatred for someone usually begins with anger over something the person has done that we did not like. This kind of anger is self-centered and therefore sinful. Today, people teach that we must be sure to feel enough anger when someone wrongs us and we should express it freely. If we do not, these people tell us, we will not be healthy. People who have been hurt are encouraged to keep thinking and talking about what it was that hurt them and to keep feeling the anger again.

The Bible teaches exactly the opposite. When people hurt us (and they will), we must forgive them and go on with our lives. The 37th psalm speaks of wicked people who hurt others. Even with people like these, this psalm tells us, we should trust God to take care of us and to do what is right in judging them. The psalm tells us several times not to "fret" over what people do that is wrong. To fret over something is to continue to think about it and to continue to let it bother you. When we fret over what someone has done to hurt us, we nurture our anger and cause it to grow. It will quickly turn into hatred. God condemns both anger and hatred, not just murder. **Read Psalm 37:7–9.**

WEDNESDAY

"Sticks and stones may break my bones, but words can never hurt me." Sometimes people say this to try to comfort someone who has been hurt by the unkind words of another. No matter how old you are, you probably realize that this little saying is not true. No doubt at least once in your life someone has said something to you that hurt you very badly. God's Word does not agree with this saying about words not being able to hurt. **Read Proverbs 12:18.** We could murder someone with a sword and so break the commandment not to murder. But we could also pierce someone with our words and break the commandment that way. Sometimes a person who hates another might lie about him on purpose or call him names intended to hurt him.

The words in this verse are "reckless words," words not meant to be mean, but words that were just not careful. Perhaps we did not mean to hurt someone by joking in a way that hurt him. Maybe we did not intend to hurt him by passing on what we have heard about him that he would not want others to know. It is easy to be reckless with our words. We say whatever we feel like saying without thinking about the harm we could do. We might be more careful with our words if we would consider that what we say can be a form of "hidden murder" by how it hurts another.

THURSDAY

Not only does this commandment forbid the attitudes of hatred and anger because they are the beginnings of murder, it also forbids the attitude of indifference. To be indifferent is to be unconcerned, to not care. There are many people who need food or shelter and who have no money to buy what they need. Their needs are so great that they will die if someone does not help them. When we are aware of people like this and when we have enough money that we could help them, this commandment forbids us to be indifferent. It forbids us being unconcerned and ignoring such people. Job said that whenever he knew of someone in need, he helped him because he knew that if he did not help him, he would be sinning against God. **Read Job 31:16–23.**

FRIDAY

Sometimes we think that as long as we do not hurt anyone we please God. God requires more of us than just *not* doing what might be considered wrong. God requires that we keep busy all the time doing what is right. When He commands us not to murder, He also commands us not to do other things that would hurt someone. When He commands us not to do what would *hurt* others, He also commands us to do what would help others. Jesus taught that one of the ways we can recognize the people who belong to Him is that they are busy doing things to meet the needs of others. He also said that when we do that, it is just as though *He* had a need we are meeting. **Read Matthew 25:31–46.**

SATURDAY

This sixth commandment tells us not to kill or hate, not to be angry or hold grudges, and not to say or do anything that would hurt another in any way. It calls us to forgive, to be kind and compassionate, to share what we have, and to keep busy doing what is good for others. If we did what comes naturally to us, we would try hard to keep this commandment, but only with our friends and with those who love us. When it comes to our enemies or to the people who have done things to hurt us, we do not want to help them or share with them. We may not want to actually kill them, but we think we have the right to be angry with them or to hold on to the memory of what they did that was wrong. But Jesus tells us that if we keep this commandment only with our friends, we are not keeping it as God wants us to keep it. **Read Matthew 5:43–48.**

A. ✒ The seventh commandment is: *You shall not commit adultery.*

MONDAY

When God created people, He first created just one man. God said it was not good for the man to be alone, so he created a wife for him. Adam was delighted with the wife God had made for him and Eve must have been very happy to meet Adam. Husbands and wives are God's gifts to each other. **Read Proverbs 18:22.** God intended for husbands and wives to have a special relationship with each other, closer than any relationship they have with other people. He meant for husbands and wives to be each other's best friends. God intended for husbands and wives to spend their whole lives together, with nothing separating them. The purpose of this commandment, "You shall not commit adultery," is to protect the special relationship that husbands and wives have with one another.

TUESDAY

Most of us have many friends. Some of our friends are male and some are female. From all the people in the world, each person is to choose only one to have as a husband or wife. Once we have made that choice and married that person, we may not treat anyone else in the same special way we treat the person we have married. Marriage was God's idea. He wanted men and women to live together in a way that would honor Him and be good for them. So God ordained marriage as a way to protect the special relationship between a husband and wife. **Read Matthew 19:4–6.**

WEDNESDAY

Being married is not always easy. That is because both husbands and wives are sinners. No matter how much they love each other and no matter how much they want to do what God wants them to do, sometimes sin will get in the way of having a happy marriage. All marriages are difficult sometimes. Some marriages are difficult most of the time. When the problems in a marriage come, people sometimes feel like giving up. They may want to stop living together.

God ordained marriage to prevent husbands and wives from leaving each other when it is hard to be married. When a man and a woman get married, they make a covenant with each other. A covenant is an agreement to remain faithful to each other always, whether things are easy or hard. No one *has* to get married, but God's Word tells us that once two people have made a marriage covenant with each other, breaking it is sin. The prophet Malachi wrote to the Israelites, telling them why God was not pleased with their worship. He said it was because they were unfaithful to their marriage covenants. **Read Malachi 2:13–14.**

THURSDAY

Read Malachi 2:16. This verse tells us two things God hates, divorce and violence. Divorce is ending a marriage. When people get a divorce, they stop living together as husband and wife. Unfortunately, many people see divorce as the way out of an unpleasant situation. When married people do not get along well or when things are not as enjoyable in married life as they thought they would be, people may see divorce as a solution. Divorce hurts both the husband and the wife. It especially hurts the children of the marriage. When many families are ending in divorce, as in our country, it hurts the whole country. Because of these important things, people should not choose divorce. But more important than all these is the fact that God says He hates divorce. We should never want to do what we know God hates.

FRIDAY

This commandment tells us not to commit adultery. Adultery is treating someone other than a husband or wife in the special way that only a husband or wife should be treated. This is wrong because God intends for one man and one woman to be married to each other and to no one else all their lives. A married person commits adultery by treating someone else like a husband or wife. A person also commits adultery by divorcing a husband or wife in order to marry someone else. **Read Matthew 19:9.**

SATURDAY

Marriage is very important to God. He requires us to guard it carefully. With very few exceptions, He forbids people ending their marriages by getting divorced. And He forbids people committing adultery, or treating people to whom they are not married in the special way they would treat them if they *were* married to them. This matters so much to God because He designed the relationship between a husband and wife to be a picture of the relationship between the Lord Jesus Christ and His church. Marriages should show the world what Christ and His church are like. This cannot happen when people do not treat marriage as special in the way God says to treat it. **Read Ephesians 5:22–33.**

Q.71. WHAT DOES THE SEVENTH COMMANDMENT REQUIRE?

A. ✍ *The seventh commandment requires us and everyone else to keep sexually pure in heart, speech, and action.*

MONDAY

Men's bodies are different from women's bodies because God intended for husbands and wives to use their bodies to show love to one another. The relationship between a husband and wife is the closest human relationship there is. It is much closer than the relationship of parents with children or of friends with each other. Husbands and wives use their bodies to show love to each other in ways that other people may not do. When the answer to this catechism question says that we are required to be sexually pure, this is what it means.

We must be careful to use our bodies in this special way of showing love to another *only* with our husband or wife. A married person remains sexually pure by using his body to show love *only* to his wife. If he shows that kind of closeness to anyone else, he is no longer sexually pure. An unmarried person remains sexually pure by not using his body to show close, married love to anyone. He will wait until he gets married. If he never marries, he will not have that kind of closeness to anyone. It is only for husbands and wives. **Read Hebrews 13:4.**

TUESDAY

Unfortunately, people in America today no longer consider marriage special. Half the people who get married will divorce later. People in America often do not wait until marriage to show the love that only husbands and wives show each other. People today would say that it is natural for men and women to use their bodies to be close to each other and that it does not matter if they are married. This might be a good argument if you were talking about animals. An animal may have many different mates. Human beings, however, are not animals and it is sad when people do not realize that.

Human beings are made in the image of God. The relationship between a husband and wife is to be a picture of the relationship God has with His people. God makes a covenant with His people. He promises to be their God and to have them as His people forever. When a man and a woman get married, they make a covenant with each other. They promise to be husband and wife to one another and to no one else, as long as they live. It is not right for a man and a woman who are not married to one another to use their bodies to be close to each other. **Read Proverbs 2:16–17.**

WEDNESDAY

People today are confused about sexual purity. One reason for that is that so many people spend so much time watching television and movies and listening to popular music. The message these things give is confused. In almost every romantic movie, as soon as a man and a woman meet each other and think they might like each other, they begin to show the kind of love toward one another that God intends only for husbands and wives.

From watching most movies or listening to most popular songs, you would think that showing this kind of love is the way a man and a woman get to know each other. This is backwards! Using your body to show love to someone is *not* the way to get to know that person! First, two people should get to know each other well. If they see a Christlike character in each other, they may become good friends and begin to love each other. Then, they make a commitment to live together always as husband and wife. They belong to each other for life. Finally, they are free to use their bodies to display love toward one another. **Read 1 Corinthians 7:4.**

THURSDAY

Another reason people today are confused about sexual purity is that they have forgotten the purpose for which God made them. Do you remember the answer to the very first question of this catechism? "What is man's primary purpose? Man's primary purpose is to glorify God and to enjoy Him forever." People today think their primary purpose is to please themselves. So they use their bodies in whatever way they want to, doing what will bring pleasure to themselves. Our bodies were made for us to use to glorify God. This is especially true for Christians. God has given His Holy Spirit to live inside Christians. Our bodies are His temples and we should use them to honor Him. When Jesus died for us, He did not just die for our souls but for our bodies as well. Our bodies belong to Him. We must use them for His purposes, not for our own selfish ones. **Read 1 Corinthians 6:19–20.**

FRIDAY

Being sexually pure is more than just being careful of what we do with our bodies. The answer to this question tells us that we must also keep pure in heart and in speech as well as in action. Jesus said that even if a man did nothing wrong with his body but *imagined* in his heart doing things he should not do with a woman who was not his wife, that man had committed adultery in his heart (Matt. 5:28). God is not impressed by what we do on the outside. God requires us to have pure hearts. The best way to stay sexually pure in what we do is by being careful to keep pure in what we think about and in what we love. What we *do* comes out of what we *are* in our hearts. **Read Proverbs 4:23.**

SATURDAY

The apostle Paul reminded the Corinthian Christians that they were God's people. God has promised to have a relationship with His people that He does not have with anyone else. God's people should be careful to be pure in every way because of their thankfulness for this special relationship they have with God. They should also be careful to be pure because the God with whom they have this special relationship is holy. They should be afraid to do that which would displease Him. God's Word calls us to be careful in every way to keep both our bodies and our hearts pure. **Read 2 Corinthians 7:1.**

Q.72. WHAT DOES THE SEVENTH COMMANDMENT FORBID?

A. ✍ *The seventh commandment forbids thinking, saying, or doing anything sexually impure.*

MONDAY

When people break this commandment and commit adultery, they never do it suddenly, with no warning. People break this commandment because they have been *thinking* about what it would be like to break it. What we do always comes from what we have been thinking. God requires us to be pure in our thinking. That means that the things we put into our minds need to be pure things. **Read Philippians 4:8.** This verse describes the kinds of things with which we should fill our minds. We should choose the music we listen to, the books we read, and the television shows we watch based on how well this verse describes them. When we first see or hear something that we know is not pure, we do not like it and we think that it is wrong. The more we watch or listen, though, the less it bothers us. Little by little, we change our idea of what is pure and what is not. Instead of using God's Word to decide these things, we let the shows we watch and the music we hear tell us what is right and what is wrong.

TUESDAY

Read Job 31:1. Job had a wise idea. He knew that some things cause us to think impure thoughts if we spend time looking at them. He also knew that, once we begin, it is hard to *stop* looking at things that we should not see. So Job decided beforehand not to look at anything that would cause him to think impure thoughts. He said that he had made a covenant with his eyes. Job was committed to not looking at things that would cause him to think wrongly. When we wait until there is suddenly something in front of us that we should not look at, it is very hard to look away. If we have decided in advance what we will and what we will not look at, it will be much easier to turn away from the things that cause impure thoughts.

WEDNESDAY

We help each other think pure thoughts when we are careful about how we look. God made husbands and wives so that they are attracted to each other when they look at each other. That is right and good. But we need to be careful that we do not invite people to whom we are not married to look at us and think about our bodies. Some clothing draws attention to our bodies. Tight clothing or clothing that does not cover enough of our bodies may cause other people to look at us and think thoughts they should not think. We should always be sure that our clothing is modest and does not draw attention to our bodies. **Read 1 Timothy 2:9–10.** This verse is speaking to women, but men (and boys) also fail to dress modestly sometimes. They should also take care how they dress, not trying to draw attention to their bodies.

THURSDAY

The seventh commandment forbids us to act in a way that is sexually impure or to think thoughts that are not pure. It also forbids us to say things that are sexually impure. **Read Ephesians 5:3–4.** Bad language and "dirty" jokes are all around us. Most people do not think twice about using them. They do not see anything wrong with these things. Bad language and dirty jokes are ways people use their mouths for sexual impurity. This passage tells us that there should not be even a hint of sexual impurity among us because we are God's people.

FRIDAY

We want to be pure in what we say because God requires it of us. We also want to be careful of what we say so we can use our words for the purpose God had in mind when He created us able to communicate. The ability to talk to each other is one of God's best gifts

239

to us. He gave us this gift to use for His glory and for the good of other people. When we use our words in a way that is not sexually pure, we are doing exactly the opposite of what God intends for us. We are using our words to harm others rather than to help them. **Read Ephesians 4:29.**

SATURDAY

The Bible tells of a young man who was tempted to be sexually impure, but refused to give in to the temptation. Joseph worked hard as a servant in the home of an Egyptian soldier. Joseph's master trusted him. He put everything in his house under Joseph's care. The wife of Joseph's master thought Joseph was attractive. She wanted to do things with him that she should only have done with her husband. **Read Genesis 39:6–9.** Joseph would not listen to the woman. One reason was that he knew his master trusted him and he did not want to disappoint him. But the more important reason given is that it would be sin against God.

Q.73. WHAT IS THE EIGHTH COMMANDMENT?

A. ✒ The eighth commandment is: *You shall not steal.*

MONDAY

The first four of the Ten Commandments tell us how to act toward God. Those commandments warn us against stealing from God. We steal from God when we fail to give Him the worship we owe Him or when we give it to someone or something else. The last six of the Ten Commandments tell us how to act toward other people. This eighth commandment especially warns us against stealing from other human beings. We owe God reverence, worship, and obedience. To fail to give Him what we owe is to steal from Him. We owe people respect because they are made in the image of God. One way we show respect for people is by respecting the things that belong to them. We also owe love to people because God has commanded us to love others. One way we show love for others is by helping them to have what they need. **Read Romans 13:7–8.**

TUESDAY

God commands us to love others. He tells us that, when we show love to others, we keep the law. Sometimes we may wonder how to love someone. We can ask ourselves: What would I want someone to do for me if I were in that person's place? Jesus said that doing for other people what we would want done for us sums up all God's teaching on how to treat others. **Read Matthew 7:12.** We would not want someone to take something of ours or to borrow something of ours and never give it back. We would not like it if we paid someone to do a job for us and they did sloppy work that needed to be done over again. So we should not do any of those things to anyone else. But we would like it if someone shared their food with us if we had none. If we lost something valuable and someone else found it and returned it to us, it would make us happy. These are the kinds of things we should do for other people. When we do for others what we would like done for us, we keep the commandment to not steal.

WEDNESDAY

The same thing is true of the commandment not to steal as is true of all the commandments. God is not satisfied simply by what we do or do not do. He wants our attitude to be right. We may have never taken something that did not belong to us, but that does not mean we have kept this commandment. This commandment forbids greed. Greed is not being content with what we have and wanting more. **Read 1 Timothy 6:6–10.** The apostle Paul wrote these verses. He says that it is when people want to get rich that they fall into temptation and do what is wrong. He warns us that when we love money (or the things that money can buy), we will sin and get into trouble. An attitude of greed—wanting more and more—will cause us to take what does not belong to us because we want it so badly.

THURSDAY

One way to keep from being greedy is to understand what really makes us rich. Most people think that if they had enough money, they would be happy. Most people think that "enough money" is just a little more than what they have now—no matter how much they have now. We think that being rich is having the money to do what we want to do. Being rich is having a big house and a nice car. It is having the best clothes and buying things we will enjoy using. We could go on wonderful vacations and do exciting things if we were rich. And most people think that if they had all those things, they would be rich and they would be happy.

Read Proverbs 10:22 to see what really makes a person rich or wealthy. We will be content with what we have when we learn what things are really valuable. Money and things do not last long. We are really rich when we have the things that last forever. Only God can give us those riches. If we have put our faith in the Lord Jesus Christ to give us spiritual riches, such as peace with God and a home in heaven forever, we are truly rich. Even if we do not have much money or many things while we live on this earth, we have the blessing of the Lord that brings wealth.

FRIDAY

The opposite of greed is contentment. Greed is the attitude God tells us not to have when He commands us not to steal. Contentment is the attitude He wants us to have. Contentment is being satisfied and thankful for what we have, without letting what we do not have spoil it. God's children can be content with whatever they have because God has promised to give them everything they need. If we have to do without something that we think we need, it is because God knows we need something else instead. And while we go without it, God will give us the strength we need to trust Him. **Read Philippians 4:11–13.**

SATURDAY

Another reason we can be content with whatever we have is that we know that God controls everything. When we studied Question 7 of this catechism, we learned that God "has foreordained everything that happens." Nothing can happen unless God planned it to happen. Whatever our circumstances are—whether we have plenty or whether we have very little—they are exactly what God has chosen for us. Since we know that God loves us and that He has all wisdom, we know that the circumstances He has chosen are what is best for us. We can be content with what we have because what we have is what God has given us. Job was a rich man with a happy family. He had many blessings and he thanked God for them. Even when his children were killed and he lost all his possessions and his riches, he was still content. He knew that just as God was the One who had given him all he had, so it was God who had taken it all away. **Read what he said in Job 1:20–21.**

Q.74.

WHAT DOES THE EIGHTH COMMANDMENT REQUIRE?

A. ✑ *The eighth commandment requires that we lawfully acquire and increase our own and others' money and possessions.*

MONDAY

Instead of stealing the things we want, God tells us to work so we can buy them. When God created man, He gave him work to do. As soon as God made Adam, the Bible tells us He put him in the garden of Eden so he would "work it and take care of it" (Gen. 2:15). People are supposed to work. It is part of God's plan for them. The book of Proverbs is full of wisdom for everyday life. It tells us how to get the things we need or want. **Read Proverbs 14:23 and Proverbs 10:4.** According to God's Word, the way to have money to buy the things we would like to have is through hard work!

TUESDAY

Read Proverbs 28:19. When Solomon wrote the book of Proverbs, most of the people in his kingdom were farmers. Solomon says the farmer who works his land—the one who works hard all year to be sure he has a good crop growing—will have abundant food. He will have more than he needs so he can sell the extra. Although this is talking about farmers, it is true for all of us that we get what we need by working hard. The other person this verse talks about does no work because he keeps busy "chasing fantasies." He always looks for ways to get rich quickly. This is the boy who does not work hard in school because he is going to be an NBA player or the girl who does not care about her grades because she is going to be a famous model. These people are chasing fantasies and will not have what they need. They will only have poverty.

WEDNESDAY

Hard work earns us money. But there is a better reason than that for working hard and doing a good job. We should do the best we can at whatever we do for the glory of God. Remember the answer to the first catechism question: "Man's primary purpose is to glorify God and to enjoy Him forever." We should do all our work for the glory of God. Whether a man is a pastor or a car mechanic, he is to do the best he can at his work so that he will glorify God in it. Whether a woman is a homemaker or a nurse, she is to work hard and be diligent so God will be glorified. When a child studies for a math test or cleans his room, he should do it for God's glory. That means he will not do his work in a sloppy, half-hearted way, but will do it carefully and well. If people know that we say we love God, but they see us do our work poorly, what will they think of God? **Read 1 Thessalonians 4:11–12.**

THURSDAY

The commandment "You shall not steal" requires us to work hard for what we need and for the glory of God. It also requires us to be concerned about what others need. We must help others in any way we can to have what they need. Is the opposite of stealing *not* stealing? No, it is sharing. The opposite of *taking* things from people is *giving* things to people. By forbidding stealing, this commandment requires the opposite of stealing: sharing. We are to do good to people. That includes helping them to have more of what would be good for them to have. **Read Galatians 6:10.**

FRIDAY

We are to work hard so that we will have what we need. Then, once we have all we need, should we stop working and earning money? No, because if we continue to work, we will have more to share with others. We work so that we will glorify God by the good job that we do. We work to have what we need. And we work so that we will have money to share with those who do not have what they need. **Read Ephesians 4:28.**

SATURDAY

Because of sin, things in this world are not always fair and sad things happen. Because of sin, people have problems. There have always been people who are poor and do not have what they need. There always will be poor people, until Jesus comes again. When we have all we need, it is easy to ignore others who do not have what they need. Sometimes people are poor because they have not worked hard, as God says we should. But often people are poor because of things they cannot change. Such people need our help. God wants us to remember that the poor are human beings too. We must respect them because He made them in His image. He wants us to do whatever we can to help them. **Read Proverbs 17:5.**

Q.75. WHAT DOES THE EIGHTH COMMANDMENT FORBID?

A. *The eighth commandment forbids anything that either does or may unjustly take away money or possessions from us or anyone else.*

MONDAY

Read Exodus 22:1–6. The eighth commandment specifically forbids stealing. Stealing is more than robbing a bank with a gun or breaking into a locked house to take a VCR. Any time we keep someone from having what rightfully belongs to her or him, we break this commandment. Exodus 22:1–6 talks about stealing and how to punish a thief. Verses 5 and 6 talk about people who did not steal on purpose but whose careless actions caused others to lose what belonged to them. Such carelessness is a form of stealing. These verses command such careless people to restore to others what they caused them to lose.

TUESDAY

When we cheat, we unjustly take away money or possessions from someone else. Someone may give us back too much change when we buy something. If we realize what has happened and do not say anything, we cheat the person (or the store) out of money. This is stealing. If we find something someone else has lost and do not return it, we cheat him out of what is rightfully his and we steal. We cheat someone out of what is his when we borrow something and then fail to return it. We have not borrowed that thing; we have stolen it. When we damage property, we steal. People steal when they paint or write on or break another person's property.

Read Proverbs 20:17. Fraud is cheating. Fraud is tricking someone so that you get his money. Imagine putting something deliciously sweet into your mouth and, as you chewed it, having it turn into pieces of rock! This verse says that is what it is like to get things by cheating. At first you enjoy what you get. Because this displeases God, though, you can be sure that sooner or later you will suffer for it.

WEDNESDAY

How do you walk when your foot hurts badly? You limp slowly because you cannot put any weight on your sore foot. How do you chew when you have a painful tooth? You have to take very small bites of things that are soft because you cannot chew on the side of your mouth that hurts. **Read Proverbs 25:19.** If I count on you to do a job and you do not do it or you do it poorly, it is like I am trying to walk with a lame foot or trying to chew with a sore tooth. Imagine working out in the field on a hot August day. You have worked for hours in the hot sun. You are sweaty and dirty—and suddenly, snow falls! How refreshing!

Read Proverbs 25:13. If I count on you to do a job and you do it well, I am refreshed. What does all this have to do with the commandment not to steal? When someone pays me to do something, if I fail to do all of what I was paid for or if I do it poorly so that someone else will need to do it over, I am stealing from the one who paid me. We keep from breaking the eighth commandment when we take care to do the best job we can for work someone has paid us to do.

THURSDAY

Read Proverbs 22:1. Sometimes people steal things that are not money or the things money buys. This verse talks about the value of a good name or a good reputation. When a person has a good name, people hear his name and think of good things that are true about him. When someone has a good name, he has the esteem or respect of those who know him. The esteem and respect of others are worth more than money.

We can steal another's good name, however. All it takes to steal another's reputation is to tell people things about him that cause them to question his character. If we pass on things we have heard that are not good about someone, we contribute to stealing his good name. Those things may not be true or they may be only partly true.

When we tell them to others, people believe them and think less of the person we are talking about. When we hear bad things about someone else, we want to listen. Once we have heard, we want to tell others what we heard. Whenever we do these things, we break the eighth commandment because we steal someone's good reputation.

FRIDAY

We can steal from other people and we can also steal from ourselves. The answer to this catechism question says that we are forbidden to do "anything that either does or may unjustly take away money or possessions from *us.*" There are sinful ways we can lose our own possessions or money.

Read Proverbs 21:17. This verse describes the person who loves pleasure. He wants to have a good time all the time. He always has to have the best of everything. In Bible times, rich people used good wine and good oil. If a person really is not rich but loves the kinds of things rich people have, he or she quickly becomes poor. We can spend our money on many things that bring pleasure. We want to spend a little here on this good-tasting treat and a little there on having a good time with friends and a lot there on buying something fun to own. Suddenly, we have no money left.

Spending large amounts of money on things that bring pleasure wastes what we have. When we use too much of our money to buy what we *want,* we will no longer have money to buy what we *need.* When we fail to provide what we need for ourselves or when we waste what we have, we break the commandment to not steal.

SATURDAY

We have said that having right attitudes keeps us from breaking the commandment not to steal. If we are not greedy but content with what we have, we will not feel that we have to have more, so we will not go out and steal it. When we trust in God's providence, we will thank Him for what we have without demanding more. We will obey this commandment when we fear God. When we understand that God is holy and that He hates stealing and will punish it, we will take care not to break this commandment. No matter how much we might like to have more than we do have, we will want to please God even more. **Read Proverbs 15:16.**

Q.76. WHAT IS THE NINTH COMMANDMENT?

A. ✑ The ninth commandment is: *You shall not give false testimony against your neighbor.*

MONDAY

"Testimony" is a word used in the courtroom. A person has been accused of doing something wrong and is taken to court. Witnesses are called who either saw the crime committed or know something about the accused person. When a witness tells what he or she knows, we call it giving testimony. Courts can only work when all the witnesses tell the truth. If the witnesses give false testimony, the person on trial may be punished for doing something he did not do. Or someone who *has* committed a terrible crime may go free.

Especially in court, it is very important for people to tell the truth. If someone gives false testimony against an innocent person in court, that innocent person may suffer for something he did not do. If someone gives false testimony against a guilty criminal and he goes free, he may cause other innocent people to suffer.

God's people are always to tell the truth. God loves truth and hates falsehood. Whether we are in court or not, we must always speak what is true. **Read Zechariah 8:16–17.**

TUESDAY

Part of the Old Testament law told what to do when someone had done something seriously wrong. If the person who had committed the crime was proven guilty, everyone else was to throw stones until he died. The law said that the first person to throw a stone at him should be the person who had given testimony against him. The one who had gone to others, saying, "I saw this person commit a crime," was to throw the first stone (Deut. 13:9). This would help people realize how serious their testimony was. It was what they had said about this person that would cause him to be put to death.

What we say about other people *is* very serious. God requires us to speak carefully of others. Our careless words can hurt people badly. We need to be especially careful not to say about others what may not be true. **Read Proverbs 14:5.**

WEDNESDAY

When was the last time someone came to you to tell you something about someone else that made that person look bad? When you heard this bad thing about this person, did you find it really interesting? How long was it before you told someone else about it? Although we know it is wrong to do it, all of us love passing on the bad things we hear about others. Most of the time we pass on things that we do not know to be completely true. Saying something untrue that makes a person look bad is called slander. God forbids us from spreading slander. **Read Leviticus 19:16a.** Be careful about passing on the bad things you hear about others. You may be breaking God's commandment.

THURSDAY

Telling the truth about other people and telling the truth at all times is important to God. God loves truth. He speaks only what is true. Jesus, the Son of God, called Himself "the Way, *the Truth,* and the Life." Psalm 15 describes the person who can come near to God. **Read Psalm 15.** Look for the parts that talk about truth and about how we speak of others.

FRIDAY

People enjoy thinking of God's love. We may not find it as enjoyable to think about what God hates, but we should consider these things also so we can avoid them. Proverbs 6 lists seven things God hates. **Read the list in Proverbs 6:16–19** and find the three that have to do with this ninth commandment.

SATURDAY

People might give false witness or tell lies for many different reasons. They might do it because they will get money or something else they want if they do. People might give false witness or tell a lie to get attention by making a story more interesting. They might do so because they are afraid of getting into some kind of trouble. Whatever the reason for lying, it is never good enough when we realize that God hates lying and always punishes it. **Read Proverbs 19:5.**

Q.77.

WHAT DOES THE NINTH COMMANDMENT REQUIRE?

A. ✐ *The ninth commandment requires us to tell the truth and to maintain and promote it and our own and others' reputations, especially when testifying.*

MONDAY

What people believe about us is called our *reputation*. Someone may have a reputation as a hard worker. Or someone may have a reputation for being dishonest. Sometimes a reputation is based on fact. Sometimes, it is based on what people have said that may not be true. Our reputations are important. If we have a good reputation, others will respect us and will give glory to God, since we say we belong to Him.

This commandment calls on us to do all we can to protect our own reputations and the reputations of other people. We damage the reputation of someone else when we pass on the bad things we have heard about her or him. If we love others, we will not be quick to believe the bad things we hear about them and we will not want to pass those things on to someone else. If we know that someone we love really has done something he should not have done, we will want to talk to him about it before talking to others. We will want to find out why he did it. We will not quickly jump to the conclusion that he *intended* to do what was wrong. **Read 1 Peter 4:8.**

TUESDAY

Protecting the reputations of others does not mean we should not speak out for the truth. Loving others requires that we speak out when they do wrong. Love does not ignore wrongdoing. But there are loving ways to speak the truth. **Read Matthew 18:15–18.**

When we know that someone has done wrong, we should talk to him about it, but *only* to him. We must not talk to other people about it first. To protect the person's reputation, we should speak only to him. We should speak to him when he is alone, so others will not hear. We will hope that he will be sorry for what he has done and will change. But if he does not, we do not stop trying. We must love him enough to bring a few others with us to try to change his mind. If he still will not listen, we still do not give up. The Bible tells us that the next thing is to tell the church leaders and the church, who will also try to get him to give up doing wrong. If he continues to sin, we must not consider him a part of the church any longer. Of course, the church should always welcome someone back if he repents of what he has done wrong.

WEDNESDAY

We protect the reputations of others by being careful of what we say about them. We are also to protect others' reputations by being careful of what we *hear* about them. Because we are sinners, it is always interesting to hear reports of bad things about others. We may imagine that what we do is not wrong because *we* are not saying anything. Yet when we listen without stopping someone from ruining another's reputation, we sin. **Read Proverbs 18:8.**

"Choice morsels" are tasty little treats of food. A choice morsel is hard to resist. When we see a choice morsel sitting there looking delicious, we want to eat it. The bad things others say about people are like choice morsels. We want to hear it and it is very hard to tell someone, "No, I am not going to listen to that." Just like a choice morsel of food goes down into our bodies and becomes a part of us, so the bad things we hear about others stay with us and influence what we think of them. Even when we are not sure whether what we have heard is true, it stays in our minds and affects how we think of that person.

THURSDAY

When God's law forbids one thing, it commands the opposite. We must not eagerly listen to the bad things people have to say about others. We would never say that we want people to do evil, but the eager way we listen to evil reports about others makes it seem that we rejoice in evil. **Read 1 Corinthians 13:6.** We should

enjoy hearing *good* things about others, not reports of wrongdoing.
Read 3 John 3–4.

FRIDAY

Not only should we carefully protect the reputations of other
people, we should protect our own reputations as well. We should
not care so much about what others think of us that we would do
anything, even what is wrong, to make people think well of us. But
we *should* want people to think of us as honest, trustworthy, and
kind. We should want it enough that we are always careful to *do* what
is honest, trustworthy, and kind, even when it is not easy. If we are
always careful to do what is right and to avoid doing wrong, we will
keep a clear conscience. Then, even if people lie about us and say
that we have done what is wrong, it will soon be clear to all that it is
not true. **Read 1 Peter 3:15–16.**

SATURDAY

Everyone would like to have a good reputation. We like thinking that people have a good opinion of us. We enjoy knowing that
people will ask us to do a job because they are sure we will do it well.
But the most important reason for guarding a good reputation for
ourselves is not because *we* enjoy having it. The most important reason for protecting our reputation is that, if we are Christians, people see what we do and think of God. If we claim to be Christians
and have a reputation for lying or for being unkind, people think
less of God and He is dishonored. God is pure and holy and good.
We can never show people by our lives how good God really is, but
we should always carefully do as much good as we can. People will
give glory to God when we take care to live as we should. **Read
Matthew 5:14–16.**

Q.78. WHAT DOES THE NINTH COMMANDMENT FORBID?

A. ✒ *The ninth commandment forbids anything that gets in the way of the truth or injures anyone's reputation.*

MONDAY

God only speaks what is true. God created us to be righteous and holy. He created us to speak and to love the truth as He does. Adam sinned by listening to Satan's lie rather than obeying God's truth. As a result, all of us are born as sinners who love falsehood more than truth. When God saves us and causes us to be born again, He changes us so that we want to live for God and please Him. He gives us a new love for the truth. Christians show that God has changed their hearts when they avoid falsehood and speak only what is true. **Read Ephesians 4:21–25.**

TUESDAY

The ninth commandment forbids false testimony against our neighbor. It requires speaking the truth. The worst possible way we could give false testimony would be if we were to give false testimony about God. **Read Jeremiah 23:30–32.** Most people have their own ideas of what God is like. They like to tell others what they believe about God. If they tell something about God that is not true, it is not only lying, it is blasphemy. Many people speak to large crowds or write books claiming to speak for God. They tell anyone who will listen what God is like, but they tell what is not true about Him. Even some who claim to be Christian pastors say that God has said things He has not said, or they say untrue things about God.

How can we be sure our ideas of God are correct? How do we know that when we tell people what God is like we are not giving false testimony about Him? When people say, "This is what God is like," how do we know if what they say is true? The only way to be sure is by knowing what the Bible says. We cannot know just bits and pieces of it or we will have a faulty idea of what God is like. We need to study *all* of God's Word. We must study it often and know it well. The Bible is the only place where we can learn the truth about God.

WEDNESDAY

The ninth commandment forbids anything that would injure or hurt another's reputation. However, we should only go as far in protecting another's reputation as we can while still telling the truth. Because God values truth so much, we must value it as well. We should defend the truth, even if it means someone's reputation may be damaged. Yesterday we read about people who claim to speak for God but say what God never said. When we know that this is happening, God's Word requires us to let others know it.

We must protect others from believing what is not true about God by pointing out those who give false testimony about Him. This will damage the reputation of the person giving the false teaching, but it must be done. God's people must stand against falsehood and evil. They must not be afraid to speak out against those things that God hates. When someone refuses to listen to God's Word and continues to teach or to do what is wrong, we *must* say something. **Read Ephesians 5:8–11.**

THURSDAY

Yesterday's Bible reading told us that we are to "expose" the "deeds of darkness." God's Word requires us to point out when evil is being done. We must be willing to go to other Christians and remind them of what God's Word says when we see them doing wrong. This does not mean that we should eagerly watch everyone around us, hoping someone will do something wrong so we can say something about it. When we know someone is doing something that is sinful, we have a responsibility to say something. The one person I should most eagerly watch for sin is myself. **Read Matthew 7:3–5.**

FRIDAY

People often give false testimony about themselves. Until the Holy Spirit shows them how sinful their hearts are, they really believe they are good. Of course, this is false. If most people were asked, "Will you go to heaven when you die?" they would say yes. If you asked them, "Why do you think you will go to heaven?" they would say because they have tried to be good all their lives. They would give this false testimony about themselves because they do not realize how sinful they are. A young man gave this kind of false testimony about himself to Jesus. This young man honestly believed that he had perfectly kept all of God's commands all his life. So Jesus told him to do something that would show him he was not as good as he thought was. **Read this story in Mark 10:17–22.**

SATURDAY

Jesus told a story about two men. One of the two men gave false testimony about himself to God. He tried to tell God how good he was, but God did not even listen to him. The other man understood what he was really like. He told God the truth about himself (which, of course, God already knew). He told God he was a sinner and deserved nothing from Him. Jesus said that this man's prayer for mercy was heard and answered. **Read Luke 18:9–14.**

Q.79. WHAT IS THE TENTH COMMANDMENT?

A. ✍ The tenth commandment is: *You shall not covet your neighbor's house. You shall not covet your neighbor's wife, or his manservant or his maidservant, his ox or donkey, or anything that belongs to your neighbor.*

MONDAY

If we quickly read the first nine of the Ten Commandments without thinking much about them, we might think we are good people. We do not pray to statues or kill or steal. If we look at the Ten Commandments this way, we fail to consider our hearts. We do not see that we can also break the Ten Commandments by wrong thoughts and attitudes in our hearts. One purpose of this final commandment is to force people to look at their hearts so they will realize they are sinful.

Saul was a very intelligent man. He had spent his life using that great intelligence to study the law of God. Yet even with all that studying and all that intelligence, Saul did not realize he was a sinner. He thought he could keep God's law himself. After he saw his need for a Savior and put his trust in Christ, he said it was this tenth commandment that had showed him he was a sinner. Coveting is wanting something we do not have in a way that is wrong. We covet in our hearts where no one else can see. This commandment shows us that sin is not just how we act on the outside. Wrong thoughts and feelings in our hearts are sin just as well. **Read Romans 7:7.**

TUESDAY

When we know a person has murdered someone, we put that person in jail. When we know someone has stolen something, we put that person in jail as well. We all agree that murderers and thieves are lawbreakers. People often think they are law-keepers because they have never done anything that would send them to jail. They are not criminals so they must be good people. This is not how God sees it. God gave this law, "You shall not covet," for people who think they are good just because they have never gone to jail. All of us would have to admit that we have broken this law. All of us have been unhappy because we did not have something we wanted. We have felt jealous because of what someone else had or was allowed to do. God wants us to see that we all break this law. He wants us to know that even if this were the only law we had ever broken, we would be just as guilty as if we had broken every law there is. **Read James 2:10.**

WEDNESDAY

God tells us that His Word is like a mirror. We look into a mirror to find out how we look and what we might need to change. When we look into God's Word, we see the things that are wrong with us that we need to change. **Read James 1:22–25.** If I leave the breakfast table with egg on my face, other people may laugh when they see me, but I will not realize there is anything wrong. When I finally look in the mirror, I see the egg and am embarrassed because it was there all the time. We may not realize how sinful we are and so we feel no shame for our sin. When we stop and think about this commandment not to covet, we realize that even our wrong thoughts are sin. We see how many wrong thoughts we have had, and we become ashamed of how sinful we were all along, without knowing it. That is why God gave this commandment.

THURSDAY

Sometimes we cannot help what we think or feel. Someone says or does something to hurt our feelings, and, even if it is for just a moment, we feel anger and hatred toward that person. One difficult thing after another happens to us, and, even if it is just for a moment, we feel sorry for ourselves and wish things were easier. Others get something we had really wanted, and, even if it is just for a moment, we wish *we* had gotten it instead of them. If a thought or a feeling takes us by surprise so that we cannot help thinking or feeling it, is it still sin? Yes, it is.

We may think that God should not call something we do "sin" if we cannot help doing it. But God is holy. He will not be satisfied if we simply do our best. He will only be satisfied if we live lives of perfect obedience to Him. He wants us to do all we do for His glory. If we do not do that, we sin. **Read Galatians 3:10.**

FRIDAY

Is God harsh when He calls sin even thoughts and feelings we cannot help? No, this shows us God's mercy. By giving us a commandment that shows us how sinful our hearts are, God shows us how very much we need a Savior. A savior saves people from danger. A person in a swimming pool does not want to be saved unless he or she is really drowning. We will only want to be saved from our sin if we believe we are sinners. The commandment "You shall not covet" shows us our need for a Savior so we will turn to Christ to save us. Jesus invited those who felt burdened to come to Him for rest. It is knowing we are sinners that causes us to feel burdened. We need a commandment like this one to make us realize how burdened we are so we will call out to Jesus to save us. **Read Matthew 11:28–30.**

SATURDAY

The commandments of God show us how sinful we are so that we will turn to the Lord Jesus to save us. Once we have done that, the commandments of God should cause us to be grateful to Him. God's commandments are good and perfect. We break those good commandments, hundreds of times and in hundreds of ways. If we were to try to count all the times we have broken God's laws, we would find we cannot count that high. Yet God receives us as perfectly righteous when we put our faith in Christ. The law shows non-Christians how much they need a Savior. It shows Christians how much they have been forgiven. **Read Luke 7:36–47.**

Q.80.

WHAT DOES THE TENTH COMMANDMENT REQUIRE?

A. ✍ *The tenth commandment requires us to be completely satisfied with our own status in life and to have a proper, loving attitude toward others and their possessions.*

MONDAY

Our status in life is what we have and what we are compared to others. It includes our family, our race, and our background. It includes being rich or poor, male or female. Being healthy, smart, attractive, or good at sports is all part of our status. The commandment to not covet requires that we be completely satisfied with whatever we have in all those areas.

What a difficult commandment this is to keep! We want to complain when our health is bad. We feel disappointed when someone gets a first place ribbon at a race and we only got the second prize. To truly obey the tenth commandment is to be completely satisfied with whatever we have. We should be content with what we have because God gave it to us. Any talents, health, money, or possessions we have are all gifts from God that we did not bring with us into the world when we were born. **Read 1 Timothy 6:6–7.** Not only that, but whatever we have is more than we deserve. We were born sinners, rebels against God, but in His goodness He has given us good gifts. God made Jacob rich, but God also gave Jacob a life that was hard in many ways. **Read Genesis 32:10** to see what Jacob said about what God had given him.

TUESDAY

We can be completely satisfied with our status in life because God planned it for us. Back in Question 7, we learned that "the decrees of God are His eternal plan by which, for His own glory, He has foreordained everything that happens." Nothing about us is an accident. God planned where we would be born, what our noses would look like, who our parents would be, and what we would do well. God ordained every one of these things, as well as everything else about us and about what we have.

We also learned, in Question 11, that "God's providence is His completely holy, wise, and powerful preserving and governing every creature and every action." God controls everything that ever happens to us. God gives us everything we have. He takes away the things we lose. God makes no mistakes. Whether or not we understand *why* He gives what He gives and takes what He takes, we know we can trust Him. Job had been given many good things, and then he lost them all. **Read** what he said about it in **Job 1:21.**

WEDNESDAY

Some people believe that the good, happy things in their lives come from God, but not the sad or the hard things. It is hard to be content with your status in life if you think that bad things happen to you by accident. The Bible teaches that God causes hard things to happen to His children when He knows it will be good for them. Hard times can cause us to grow in ways that happy times cannot.

Read Psalm 119:75. Affliction is suffering. The writer of this psalm had suffering as part of his status in life. He knew that God had caused it and that whatever God did was what was best for him. **Read Romans 8:28.** Because God's providence rules over everything, with nothing left out, and because God's providence is completely holy and wise, we can be sure that everything about our status in life is what is best for us. That is why we can be content with whatever we are and have. To be dissatisfied with what we have shows that we do not trust God, and that is sin.

THURSDAY

We can be completely satisfied with our status because God has told us what matters the most. Money or talents or an attractive appearance or health are not the most valuable things in life. Most of us believe that if we just had a little more money or that one possession we really want, we would be satisfied. Maybe it is good health or prettier teeth that would satisfy us. These things cannot satisfy us. We were not meant to find our satisfaction in riches and things or perfect health and beauty. God made us to know and love and glorify Him. Only when we have what we need to love and glorify God will we be truly satisfied.

A man came to Jesus, unhappy because his brother would not share with him. He wanted Jesus to tell his brother to share. Instead, Jesus tried to show him that, even if he had the money he wanted from his brother, he would not have anything that was really important. **Read this story in Luke 12:13–21.**

FRIDAY

We can be content with our status in life because whatever we have is a gift from God and is more than we deserve. The things that would change our status—more money or better looks or a stronger body—do not have true and lasting value. One very good reason for God's children to be satisfied with what they have is this: God's children have God Himself. God has promised His people, "I will be your God." Having God, there is nothing else we could want or need that would make our lives any better.

A man named Asaph wrote the 73rd psalm. He wrote this psalm when he was struggling with the sin of coveting. **Read Psalm 73:2–3.** Whom did Asaph envy and why? As he looked at the wicked, it seemed to Asaph that they had everything—even things he did not have, although he had always tried to please God. **Read verses 4 and 12.** By the end of the psalm, Asaph realized two things. First, God will destroy the wicked in His anger. All the things they have enjoyed in this life will not help them. Besides that, Asaph realized that what he had *right now* was better than anything the wicked had, because Asaph had God.

A portion is the part someone gets. You may get the largest *portion* of a pie. In Bible times, the oldest son got the largest *portion* of what his father had. Asaph learned that God Himself was *his* portion, and that God would be his portion *forever*. **Read Psalm 73:23–26.**

SATURDAY

We have seen that the commandment to not covet calls us to be completely satisfied with our status in life. It also calls us to "have a proper loving attitude toward others and their possessions." Jesus told us that whatever we would like others to do for us, we should do for them (Matt. 7:12). That is the proper loving attitude we should have toward others and their possessions.

Read Romans 12:9–16. If we like to be honored or if we like to win first place, we should rejoice for others when they receive an honor or win a prize. Since we would enjoy having certain things, we should be pleased when others have them. If we wish we were more attractive or in better health, we should be glad for others who are. Again we see, when we look at this commandment, how badly we fail to keep God's laws. It is so much easier and more natural for us to be jealous of people than to be happy for them. How very sinful our hearts are. We break the laws of God in so many ways. How much we need a Savior!

Q.81. WHAT DOES THE TENTH COMMANDMENT FORBID?

A. ✍ *The tenth commandment forbids any dissatisfaction with what belongs to us, envy or grief at the success of others, and all improper desire for anything that belongs to someone else.*

MONDAY

God requires us to be content with what we have. He is angry when we covet what He has not given us. God had set the Israelites free from slavery in Egypt. He led them to the land He had promised to give them. There were no grocery stores along the way where the many Israelites could buy food. They would have starved to death, but God provided for them. He caused bread to fall out of heaven for them. It was called manna. It would fall in the night and every morning when the Israelites got up, there was fresh manna on the ground. All they had to do was to go out with baskets and gather it.

From the description the Bible gives of the manna, it must have been very tasty. You would think the Israelites would have thanked God. Out in the middle of nowhere, He had provided food for so many people. However, the Israelites were sinners like we are. They were thankful enough at first, but they became dissatisfied. Day after day, the same old food, they complained. **Read what they said in Numbers 11:4–6.** God sent quail, birds that can be eaten, to the Israelites' camp. Thousands of them flew very low over the camp, making it easy for the Israelites to catch them for food. God was angry with the Israelites, though, because of their dissatisfaction over the manna. **Read verses 33 and 34** to see what happened because of God's anger.

TUESDAY

Every good story has a mean and nasty villain. One of the best stories in the Bible is the story of Esther, the Jewish queen who saved her people from destruction. The story has one of the meanest, nastiest villains ever—the wicked Haman. Haman got the king to agree to have all the Jews everywhere put to death. It was all because there was one Jewish man, Mordecai, who would not bow to Haman when he walked by. Haman was the perfect example of a person breaking the commandment to not covet. Haman was not content with what he had. Because of it, he wanted evil things to happen to other people. The king had made Haman the second highest ruler in the land. Haman was rich and powerful and had everything he could possibly want. He was unhappy, however, because *one* person did not honor him as he wanted to be honored. **Read** what Haman whined about in **Esther 5:10b–13.**

WEDNESDAY

Psalm 112 describes the righteous man and the blessings that will come to him. It says he will always be secure. The righteous man will always trust the Lord. He will have enough to share with the poor. **Read Psalm 112:10** to see how the wicked man reacts to the blessings of the righteous man. This wicked attitude is forbidden by the tenth commandment. We are forbidden to feel envy or grief at the success of others. We may read Psalm 112 and agree that the wicked man is wrong to feel envy. But we often do the same thing. Someone else succeeds and we feel jealous. We wish *we* had succeeded. Perhaps someone we do not like very well receives praise for something. We are unhappy about it because we do not think he or she deserved it. This is a difficult commandment to keep. It forces us to take a good look at our attitudes and see how sinful they often are.

THURSDAY

The tenth commandment also forbids all improper desire for anything that belongs to someone else. There is a story of an Israelite king and his desire for the vineyard of another man. **Read 1 Kings 21:1–2.** At first, there was nothing wrong with King Ahab's desire for the vineyard. It was close to his palace and would make a good garden. He offered to buy it or trade for it, even being willing to pay more than it was really worth. However, Naboth, the owner of the vineyard, did not want to sell it. Now Ahab's desire became an improper one. **Read verses 4–6.**

Ahab's response was childish. We often behave in the same way. In spite of all we have, there is one thing—often something small and unimportant—that we want now. If we cannot get it, we become irritable and angry, pouting about what we cannot have. When we do this, we show that our desire was not a good, healthy desire, but an improper one. Our attitude is sinful and, if we are not careful, we will go even further in our sin. Ahab did. **Read 1 Kings 21:8–16** to see what he did.

FRIDAY

Ahab's envy and improper desire led to murder. The tenth commandment is very important because it deals with our thoughts and our attitudes. Everything we do, whether good or bad, begins as a thought or an attitude. Sinful thoughts and attitudes become sinful actions if we do not stop them. **Read James 4:1–3.**

SATURDAY

The Ten Commandments are much more difficult to keep than they seem when we first read them. When God tells us *not* to do something, He requires us to *do* the opposite. When He commands us not to kill (which seems easy enough), He commands us to love—perfectly and all the time. He commands us not to worship other gods and to worship Him—perfectly and all the time. When we stop and think about the Ten Commandments, we realize that they are much too difficult for us to keep. Just in case we miss the point, God included this commandment to not covet.

We must always be perfectly satisfied with what we have. We must rejoice about the good things that happen to others just as we would if they had happened to us. This commandment makes it perfectly clear that we are lawbreakers. God considers those who break His law as His enemies and He is angry with them. **Read Psalm 5:4–6.** The Ten Commandments, and especially the tenth one, show us what a dangerous position we are in if we have not put our faith in the Lord Jesus Christ to save us from God's anger at our sin.

A. ✒ *Since the fall no ordinary man can perfectly keep the commandments of God in this life but breaks them every day in thought, word, and action.*

MONDAY

When we take the time to study the Ten Commandments, we see how many times and in how many ways we break them every day. When God tells us *not* to do certain things, He tells us *to do* the opposite of those things. Once we understand this, we see that we cannot do all God wants us to do. When God commands us to *behave* in certain ways, He also commands us to *think and feel* in certain ways. If we realize that, we realize that we cannot keep God's commandments perfectly.

Read James 3:2. James says that we all sin in many ways. He uses the things we say as an example of that. If you consider all the Ten Commandments, thinking only of whether you keep them in what you say, you will find that you sin in many ways. Have you ever talked through part of a Sunday school lesson or a sermon? Then you have broken the commandment to keep the Sabbath holy. Have you ever been rude to someone in authority? If so, you have broken the commandment to honor parents. Have you ever called someone a name? By not showing love, you have broken the commandment to not kill. Have you ever spoken unkindly to someone about another person? Then you have stolen that person's reputation and broken the commandment not to steal. Just as James says, we sin with our mouths in many ways. But we not only sin by what we say, we also sin by what we want, what we like and do not like, what we think, and what we feel, as well as by what we do. Clearly, none of us keeps the commandments of God.

TUESDAY

Did it surprise God when no human being could keep His commandments? Of course not. God knew when He gave His law that no one would be able to keep it. Then why did He give us pages and pages of commandments? God's purpose was to show us how desperately we need Christ. When we read His commandments, we see what God Himself is like. We see how holy a person would have to be in order for God to accept him or her. When we compare ourselves with what God says He wants in His commandments, we realize that we are not nearly holy enough for Him to accept us. God's commandments show us that we could never please Him by keeping them. We need to have someone who can keep God's commandments for us. We need someone who will take the punishment for the commandments we have broken. God gave us His law and His commandments so we would see that we need a Savior. **Read Galatians 3:24.**

WEDNESDAY

Read Romans 8:7–8. Before we become Christians, we do not keep God's commandments because we cannot keep them. Until God changes our hearts, we will not want to do what God wants us to do. It is different once we are Christians. Then, God has changed our hearts so that we want to do what pleases Him. God has also given us His Holy Spirit to live inside us and make us able to do what is pleasing to Him. However, we are still not able to keep God's commandments perfectly because there is still sin left in our hearts. When we do what the Holy Spirit inside us wants us to do, we keep God's commandments. When we do what the sin inside us wants us to do, we break God's commandments. As long as we live as Christians on this earth, we should be always growing in learning to obey the Holy Spirit and to refuse to do what our sinful natures want us to do. **Read Galatians 5:16–18.**

THURSDAY

Since Christians know that Jesus has kept the law in their place and since they know they could never keep God's commandments perfectly themselves, can they stop trying? Are Christians free to live however they like? Absolutely not! People who claim to be Christians claim to belong to the kingdom of the Lord Jesus Christ. Jesus is their King. They must obey the King and keep the commandments of God! Jesus said His people should aim at being perfect, as God is perfect. **Read Matthew 5:48.** When Christians sin (and they will), Jesus is the One who comes between them and God's anger because Jesus has already taken that anger on Himself. **Read 1 John 2:1–2.**

FRIDAY

The answer to this catechism question says that no one can keep the commandments of God perfectly *in this life*. Does that mean that people *will* be able to keep God's commandments perfectly in another life? The Bible tells us that when Jesus comes again to take His people to be with Him in heaven, they will be "glorified." Part of being glorified is being made perfect and able to keep from sinning forever. Finally, God's people will be like Jesus. Then they will be able to keep God's commandments perfectly. **Read 1 John 3:2.** Even believers who have already died, whose spirits wait in heaven for their bodies to rise from the dead, have already been made perfect and are able to keep from sinning. **Read Hebrews 12:22–23.**

SATURDAY

The answer to this catechism question says that no one can keep God's commandments perfectly. Jesus kept God's commandments perfectly. The answer says that no *ordinary man* can keep God's commandments perfectly. To say someone is an "ordinary man" is to say that he is only human and nothing more. Jesus, of course, was more than human. He was perfectly human, but He was also God. While we cannot keep from sinning, Jesus could not sin. It is impossible for God to sin. Jesus is God, so it was impossible for Jesus to sin. We can trust Him completely because He perfectly obeyed God's law in our place. We can go to Him for help when we are tempted because He was also human and knows what it is like to be tempted. **Read Hebrews 4:14–16.**

Q.83. ARE ALL SINS EQUALLY EVIL?

A. *In the eyes of God, some sins in themselves are more evil than others, and some are more evil because of the harm that results from them.*

MONDAY

To break even one of God's commandments makes us guilty before God and places us under His anger. We may see something as a small sin, but since all sins are against God, there is no such thing as a small sin. All sin makes us guilty of being lawbreakers. But the Bible tells us that some sins will be punished even more severely than other sins, because in God's eyes, they are more evil. What kinds of sin are more evil than others?

All sins are against God, even sins that are against other people. After David murdered Uriah so that he could marry Uriah's wife, he confessed his guilt to God by saying, "Against You, You only, have I sinned." Sometimes when people sin, they intend harm only against other human beings. They do not think about God at all. Other sins, however, are deliberately against God, as when people curse God or try to make others stop worshiping Him. Sin that is deliberately against God is worse than sin in which someone only means to hurt another human being. **Read 1 Samuel 2:17, 23–25.**

TUESDAY

Sins intended against God are more evil than sins intended against other human beings. Some sins against people are more evil than other sins against people. A sin against another is more evil depending on how much harm it does to the person. In the Ten Commandments, the commandments that forbid us to sin against others go in order of forbidding the most harm (you shall not murder) to the least harm (you shall not covet). It is more evil to take a man's life than to harm his marriage. It is more evil to harm a man's marriage than to steal his property. **Read Proverbs 6:30–35.**

WEDNESDAY

Another thing that makes some sins more evil than other sins is the position of the person committing the sin. God has made some people leaders to others. People look up to them as leaders and watch their example. When people in leadership positions sin, others may follow them. People see leaders doing something that God has forbidden and think there is nothing wrong with it since, after all, this leader is doing it. Parents, teachers, church leaders, and others in positions of authority must be especially careful not to set a harmful example. **Read James 3:1.**

THURSDAY

Some sins are more evil than others because of who it is committing the sin. When a Christian sins, his sin is more evil than the same sin would be if a non-Christian committed it. There are several reasons for this. First, the Christian knows that sin is sin, while the non-Christian may not realize it. Then, too, God has given the Christian a changed heart so he can obey God, while the non-Christian cannot do what pleases God. The Christian has the Holy Spirit living inside him, showing him what he should do and giving him the power he needs to do it. The non-Christian has no such help. Finally, the Christian represents Christ. People look at him and think, "This is what Jesus is like." When he sins, he brings dishonor to Christ. All these things make the sins of a Christian more evil than the same sins committed by a non-Christian. **Read Romans 2:23–24.**

FRIDAY

Growing up in a Christian home is a great privilege. It gives you many advantages that other people do not have. You grow up knowing who God is and what He requires of you. You grow up learning the gospel and knowing that God has provided a Savior so you may be justified by faith. Growing up in a Christian home also carries great responsibilities. The more you know about who God is and what He wants, the less excuse you have for sinning. The Bible teaches that those who fully know what they should do and refuse to do it will be punished much more severely than those who do not have such knowledge. **Read Luke 12:47–48.**

SATURDAY

The children of Christian parents grow up as a part of the people of God. They join God's people when they gather to hear His Word and to worship Him. God's people teach and minister to them when they teach and minister to each other. Children of Christian parents grow up hearing the gospel over and over. They grow up knowing that God gave His Son as a sacrifice for sin and that the only way for sins to be forgiven is by faith in Him. As children grow up in a Christian church, they grow up with the people of God praying for them.

After all that, a child raised in a Christian home may still refuse to put his faith in the Lord Jesus Christ. He may choose instead to live in sinful rebellion against God. This is a sin much more evil than the sins committed by a person who grew up with no one to teach him about the Lord Jesus Christ. As you grow up in a Christian home, be grateful for the privileges you have, but do not take them lightly. Understand that God will judge your sins more severely than the sins of others. Be sure your faith is in Christ to bear that judgment for you. **Read Hebrews 10:26–31.**

Q.84. WHAT DOES EVERY SIN DESERVE?

A. ✍ *Every sin deserves God's anger and curse, both in this life and in the life to come.*

MONDAY

In Question 16, we learned that when Adam sinned, he acted as the representative of the whole human race. When Adam sinned, all of us sinned in him and fell with him. In Question 19, we learned that, because of that, all mankind is under God's anger and curse. This question and answer teach us that we are under God's anger and curse, not only for the sin of Adam, but for our own sins as well. God holds all mankind guilty for what Adam did. Even if that were not so, we each sin against God ourselves, many times every day. Since every one of those sins earns God's anger and curse, each of us is completely guilty before God because of our own sin.

So we are guilty before God and deserve His punishment for two reasons. First, because we are guilty in Adam, and second, because we are guilty ourselves for choosing to disobey God. The only hope any of us have is to stop thinking we are good enough and to admit that we are hopelessly guilty before God. Once we realize we are sinners, we can turn to Christ who alone can save sinners from God's anger and curse. **Read 1 John 1:8–10.**

TUESDAY

Why does this answer say that *every* sin deserves God's anger and curse? People often sin against us and we forgive them. In fact, God tells us to forgive the things people do to hurt us. When people do especially horrible things, or when they commit the same sin over and over, we might find it hard to forgive them. But we let little sins go. Should not God do the same? Should *every* sin deserve His anger and His curse?

A sin against God is quite different from a sin against another human being. To sin against a human being is to sin against another sinner. To sin against God is to sin against the Holy One who has never committed any sin. When we sin against God, we sin against the One who has given us everything we have, including the very life we live and air we breathe. When we sin against God, we sin against the Ruler of all, who deserves absolute obedience. A sin against such a God as this is terribly wicked. That is why our sins earn us His anger and curse. **Read Psalm 2:1–3.**

WEDNESDAY

Most people find the smell of a skunk very offensive. However, other skunks do not seem to mind the smell. Our sins are wicked and highly offensive to the holy God. They do not seem so bad to us, however, because we are sinners. Some famous people become famous for the very reason that they live immorally and boast about it. God calls this sin. Working long hours to earn more and more money so that important things are left undone, is very common, but God calls it sin. Bad language and joking about things we should treat with respect are in almost every movie or television show we see. In his letter to the Ephesian church, Paul lists all these things as examples of sins that God will punish. These things may not seem so bad to us because they have become so familiar, but God is deeply offended over all such sin. **Read Ephesians 5:3–7.**

THURSDAY

Our sins earn us the anger and curse of God both in this life and in the life to come. Part of God's curse on sin in this life is that those who choose it become steadily more and more wicked. The more they sin, the more they love to sin. They do what they want to do when they sin, without realizing what they are becoming. These are people who have no desire to know and obey God; they would rather serve sin. So God gives them what they want as part of His curse on them. **Read Romans 1:28–31.** The more they sin, the more they earn the wrath and punishment of God in the next life. **Read 2 Thessalonians 1:8–9.**

FRIDAY

Read Revelation 20:11–15. All of us are under the anger and curse of God because, in Adam, all of us sinned. We have all gone beyond Adam's sin to earn the anger and curse of God for ourselves by our own sins. Every sin deserves God's anger and curse. Even if we had sinned only once in a lifetime, we would have earned God's punishment. Of course, we do not sin once in a lifetime; we sin every day. We do not sin only once a day, but many times every day. All those sins are recorded and God will judge us for them. Only those whose names are written in the Book of Life will escape the punishment those sins deserve.

SATURDAY

We begin life guilty before God because of the sin of Adam. We continue our lives, sinning every day and adding to our guilt. We are hopelessly condemned as lawbreakers who deserve to be punished by God forever. God has provided the only way of escape from His just judgment. That way of escape is faith in His Son, who took the curse and punishment sin deserves. Those who believe in the Lord Jesus Christ will escape God's judgment. Those who refuse to believe in Him are still under God's anger and curse and will have to experience it all for themselves. **Read John 3:36.**

Q.85.

WHAT DOES GOD REQUIRE FROM US TO ESCAPE HIS ANGER AND CURSE, WHICH WE DESERVE FOR OUR SIN?

A. *To escape God's anger and curse, which we deserve for our sin, God requires from us faith in Jesus Christ and repentance unto life along with diligent involvement in all the external ways Christ uses to bring us the benefits of redemption.*

MONDAY

God is full of mercy. He made us and gave us everything we need. When we turned our backs on Him by choosing to sin, He did not owe us anything except anger and judgment. Because of His great mercy, however, He provided a way of escape so we could come back to Him. God has not only given us a way to escape the curse we deserve; He has made a way for us to have all the blessings He would have given us if we had perfectly obeyed Him. If we want to have God's forgiveness, we must do what He requires. God is not so eager to forgive that He will forgive people no matter what. He will forgive only those who do what He requires them to do to be forgiven.

God has provided a substitute in His Son. He gave His Son to live a life of perfect righteousness in our place and to die in our place, taking our curse for us. To be forgiven, God requires that we put our faith in His Son. There is no other way that He will pardon and accept us. **Read Acts 13:38–39.**

TUESDAY

God requires faith in Christ from us. He also requires our repentance. To repent is to turn from our sinful actions, thoughts, and attitudes and turn to God. When we repent, we stop loving what is wrong and begin to hate it and to be ashamed of it instead. God's promise of forgiveness is only for those who repent. We cannot continue to love and cling to our sin and expect God to forgive it. Repentance is "unto life" because to turn from sin is turning from death and to turn to God is turning to life. **Read Acts 20:21.**

WEDNESDAY

God can do whatever He wants to do in any way He chooses to do it. He chooses to do some things in certain ways. He could do them in other ways, but He chooses to do them in these ways. Creating life is an example. God made the first human being from the dust of the earth and the second human being from his bone. Every human being since then has been born to a mother and father. God does not have to create new human beings that way, but He *chooses* to do it that way.

God has chosen to use specific things to bring His people to salvation. That is what this question and answer mean by "the external ways Christ uses to bring us the benefits of redemption." Christ has accomplished our redemption. He has done everything needed to save us from God's anger. Some people enjoy the benefits of Christ's redemption while others do not. Some people have their sins forgiven and enjoy peace with God. These benefits come to people through "external ways Christ uses." Those external ways include hearing the gospel preached, prayer, and the sacraments (baptism and the Lord's Supper). God requires of us "diligent involvement" in these "external ways" He has chosen to use. **Read Hebrews 10:19–25.**

THURSDAY

God requires us to hear His Word preached, especially the gospel. It is as His people hear the gospel proclaimed that the Holy Spirit works in their hearts to produce faith in Christ. God could choose to bring people to faith in Christ through dreams or through voices from heaven or through any other way, but He has chosen to do it through the preaching of the gospel. This brings honor to His Son. As God's people hear the gospel preached, God gives them faith to believe in Jesus. Once they are believers, God wants His people to go regularly to hear the gospel preached. He will use this to cause them to grow in knowing Him, loving Him, and being like Him. **Read 1 Corinthians 15:1–2.**

FRIDAY

We do not become Christians because we pray a certain prayer at a certain time. We become Christians by faith in Christ alone. God uses prayer to bring us to repentance and faith. A person may begin to see that he has sinned against God and made Him angry. He realizes that he must turn from sin if he wants to be saved, but he is not sure that he can. That person can ask God to give him repentance so he can turn from his sin and be forgiven. A person may hear that God requires him to have faith in Christ. He may be afraid that he does not have true faith in Christ. He can pray and ask God to give him the faith he needs.

A man in the New Testament said something to the apostle Peter that showed the wicked thoughts of his heart. Peter told him how wicked his heart was, then told him to repent and seek forgiveness. **Read Acts 8:22–23.** Once we are Christians, prayer is one of the ways God has chosen by which we will grow in holiness. God requires that we be diligent in our use of prayer.

SATURDAY

God also requires of us diligent use of the sacraments: baptism and the Lord's Supper. These things do not save us. They show how God saves sinners, and God uses them to bring us the benefits of being saved. Baptism and the Lord's Supper are not things God's people may participate in or neglect as they please. God requires that His people be baptized and that they participate in the Lord's Supper. **Read Acts 2:38 and 1 Corinthians 11:23–26.**

Q.86. WHAT IS FAITH IN JESUS CHRIST?

A. ✑ *Faith in Jesus Christ is a saving grace, by which we receive and rest on Him alone for salvation, as He is offered to us in the gospel.*

MONDAY

The answer to the previous question told us what God requires from us to escape the anger and curse we deserve for our sin. We learned that God requires us to have faith in Jesus Christ. Our faith does not save us. The Lord Jesus Christ saves us. He did everything that needed to be done to save us from the anger and curse of God. Faith is the way we reach out and receive all that Christ has done for us.

If I were starving to death, someone might offer me food. I would reach out with my hand to take the food I was being given. My hand would not save me from starving; the food would save me. My hand is just what I use to accept the food that is being given to me. That is what faith is like. The faith does not save us; what Christ did for us saves us. The faith is what we use to reach out and take what Christ did for us and make it ours. **Read Romans 3:22–24.**

TUESDAY

God requires us to have faith in the Lord Jesus Christ to escape the curse our sin deserves. What Jesus has done in our place is what saves us. Faith is the way we reach out and receive for ourselves what He has done. Faith in Christ is not something we work up on our own. If it were, then we could say that we are saved because of something we do. Faith in Christ is the gift of God. **Read Ephesians 2:8–9.** God requires faith from us, and then He Himself gives us that faith so we *can* escape His curse.

WEDNESDAY

For centuries, God had promised to send a Savior. He gave many clear prophecies telling what this Savior would be like. When the promised Savior came, He did many miracles that should have convinced anyone that He was the One God had promised. Yet many did not receive Him as the One promised by God. That is because only those to whom God has given faith can receive Christ as the promised Savior. **Read John 1:10–13.**

THURSDAY

The faith that God requires rests in Christ alone for salvation. We must trust Christ alone to save us from God's anger. Many people believe that God will save them *if* they believe in what Jesus did for them *and* work hard to please God. They think that if they put their faith in Christ, God will be less angry at their sin, but they must still do more. They think they must also do good works of their own to take away God's anger. Before the apostle Paul put his faith in Christ, he worked hard at doing good works. He tried to carefully keep God's laws. Once God gave him faith in Christ, he understood that he was to trust in Christ alone. All the good things he had worked so hard at doing did not matter to him anymore. He knew that *Christ alone* plus nothing, would save him from God's anger at his sin. **Read Philippians 3:4–9.**

FRIDAY

True faith receives Jesus Christ. But it must receive Him as He is offered in the gospel. People have many different ideas about what it means to receive Christ. Some think that receiving Him adds something a little extra to their lives to make life better and happier. Others want to receive Him as the cure for loneliness or sadness. Some people think of receiving Jesus as receiving One who gives them power to triumph over life's problems.

Jesus may do all these things for His people. But this is not how He is offered to us in the gospel. In the Bible, the gospel offers us Christ as a Savior from sin. God did not send His Son so He could make us happy or keep us from loneliness or help us with our problems. God sent Jesus to save us from the sin that had separated us from God. True faith in Christ understands that we are sinful and that, before anything else, we need a Savior. True faith receives Jesus Christ as He is offered in the gospel: as a Savior from sin. **Read** in the book of Acts these examples of how the apostles offered Christ to people as a Savior from sin: **Acts 2:38; 3:19–20; 10:42–43.**

SATURDAY

God requires faith in Jesus Christ for us to escape His anger and curse for our sin. That faith is not something we do to earn God's salvation. It is the way we reach out and receive what Christ has earned for us. Faith in Christ is a gift from God. The faith that God gives makes us able to receive Christ as He is offered in the gospel, as a Savior from sin. True faith in Christ trusts in what Jesus has done in our place, plus nothing else, to save us from God's anger at sin. Who has this faith in Jesus Christ that God requires?

God chose some to be His before He created them or anything else. God has always known and loved His people. He does everything needed to save them. He requires faith in Christ and then He gives them that faith. God makes sure that all those whom He has chosen believe in Jesus Christ. **Read Acts 13:48.**

Q.87. WHAT IS REPENTANCE UNTO LIFE?

A. ❧ Repentance unto life is a saving grace, by which a sinner, being truly aware of his sinfulness, understands the mercy of God in Christ, grieves for and hates his sins, and turns from them to God, fully intending and striving for a new obedience.

MONDAY

In order for God to forgive our sin, He requires of us faith in Christ *and* repentance unto life. We cannot continue in our sin as though it does not matter and expect God to forgive it. True repentance is a necessary part of being saved from God's anger at our sin. It is not enough to simply say we believe in Jesus, or to raise our hand when someone asks who wants to "accept Christ." Jesus came as *a Savior from sin.* We must be deeply sorrowful for our sin and want to turn from it to God with all our hearts. Otherwise, our faith is not in Christ as a Savior from sin. Repentance for sin and faith in Christ as a Savior from sin always go together. This kind of repentance is called "repentance unto life." When we repent, we are sad and sorry because of our sin. Usually sadness and sorrow make us feel badly for a while and then go away. Repentance is sorrow that brings life, because it makes us turn away from sin and turn to Christ to have that sin forgiven. **Read 2 Corinthians 7:9–10.**

TUESDAY

Repentance is a saving grace. It is something God gives to His people. On our own, we would not repent of our sin. Our hearts are sinful and they like being sinful. The Bible says that the hearts of all people are like stone. They are not sorry at all about sin. Before anyone can repent, that person must be given a new heart. God promised that He would give new hearts to His people. **Read Ezekiel 36:26–27.** Like faith in Christ, repentance is not something that we could come up with on our own. Like faith in Christ, repentance is required by God for salvation. And like faith in Christ, repentance is a gift that God gives to those whom He has chosen to be His people. **Read Acts 11:18.**

WEDNESDAY

This catechism question tells us that when a sinner repents, he will "grieve for and hate his sins." To grieve for sins is to feel very sad and sorry that we have committed them. Sometimes people realize they have not been as good as they should have been and they feel embarrassed because of what others will think. This is not repentance. When we repent, we are sorry, not that we have dishonored *ourselves* by our bad actions, but that we have dishonored *God*. Sometimes people realize that they have done what is wrong and their conscience makes them feel bad. Then they are sorry because they feel guilty. When we really repent, we are not sad because we have hurt our own consciences or feelings, but because what we have done has wounded Christ. When we repent, we come to hate our sins. The very things we used to enjoy doing so much, we think about now with hatred and disgust. We see *ourselves* as hateful and disgusting too, because we have done what God hates. **Read Isaiah 64:5–7.**

THURSDAY

In order to repent, a person needs to understand how sinful he is. He needs to be troubled about that sin so he will turn from it. Before he can repent, a person must also see how merciful and forgiving God is. That will cause him to turn to God. **Read Psalm 51:1–2.** The answer to this catechism question tells us that a person must understand "the mercy of God in Christ." God offers us His mercy only in Christ. If anyone thinks that all he has to do to be forgiven is just to feel bad about sinning or to tell God "I'm sorry," he is wrong. Our faith must be in Christ as the One who took the punishment for our sin. That is the only way God will forgive it. God is holy and just and never forgives sin that has not been punished. He offers us mercy and forgiveness only because Christ has been punished for our sin.

FRIDAY

Repentance is more than just a feeling. Judas felt bad about turning Jesus over to His enemies. He felt so badly that he killed himself. But Judas did not repent. He did not turn from his sin and turn to God. When a person repents, he hates his sin and no longer wants to have anything to do with it. When a person repents, he turns to God, asking for His mercy and forgiveness. A person who truly repents wants to begin to obey. All these things are part of turning from sin and turning to God. **Read Isaiah 55:6–7.**

SATURDAY

The end of the answer to this catechism question tells us that truly repenting includes "fully intending and striving for a new obedience." It would not be repentance if we said we were sorry but planned to go right back to our sin. A person who has been given a changed heart by God no longer wants to sin. Now he wants to obey God. He will not be able to obey God perfectly, because he is still a sinner. But he will have God's Holy Spirit living in him to make him want to obey and to make him able to obey. That is why we call it a "new obedience." Before a person has the Spirit of God living in him, he cannot please God. A person who truly repents and turns to Christ in faith will want to obey God and will try hard, with the Holy Spirit's help, to do so. **Read 1 John 2:3–6.**

Q.88.

WHAT ARE THE ORDINARY, EXTERNAL WAYS CHRIST USES TO BRING US THE BENEFITS OF REDEMPTION?

A. *The ordinary, external ways Christ uses to bring us the benefits of redemption are His regulations, particularly the word, sacraments, and prayer, all of which are made effective for the salvation of His chosen ones.*

MONDAY

Imagine a father who is away on a trip. He has been wanting to buy a horse for his son. While he is away, the father sees the perfect horse for his son. So he buys it for him. The father has paid the full price for the horse. Nothing more needs to be done to make the horse the boy's horse. But because the boy is at home, in a different state, he cannot enjoy the benefit of having a horse. So the father hires a truck and a trailer as the way to bring the horse to the boy. Now the boy can enjoy all the benefits of having the horse that his father bought for him.

The Lord Jesus paid fully to redeem His people when He died on the cross. Nothing more needs to be done to redeem them. But the benefits of being redeemed need to be brought to God's people. The Lord Jesus has chosen ways to bring those benefits to us. This answer lists those ways. The Word of God, the sacraments (baptism and the Lord's Supper), and prayer are the "ordinary, external ways Christ has chosen to bring us the benefits of redemption." As we read and hear God's Word, as we pray, and as we receive baptism and communion, we enjoy the benefits of the redemption Christ bought for us.

The apostle Paul wrote to Timothy, giving him instructions about prayer, worship, and preaching and teaching God's Word. He told him that using these things would result in salvation for Timothy and for those to whom he ministered. **Read 1 Timothy 4:15–16.**

TUESDAY

Salvation is more than knowing you would have gone to hell but now you will go to heaven because you believe in Jesus. Salvation includes having sins forgiven, being made right with God, and becoming God's children—things that happen when a person becomes a believer in Christ. Salvation also includes things that are still happening now or will happen in the future. Our salvation includes growing less sinful and more like Jesus. Using what God has provided will cause those who have trusted in Christ to grow in knowing God and becoming holy people. God will use those same things to bring His people who are still unbelievers to faith in Christ. **Read Jude 20–21.**

WEDNESDAY

The Lord Jesus has chosen to use certain things to bring us the benefits of redemption. Because He is the Lord, He is the One who chooses what He will use. In His Word, He tells us clearly what things He has chosen to use. He then commands us to use those things. We cannot expect people to put their faith in Christ or to grow in Christlikeness unless they use what Jesus tells them to use. **Read Matthew 28:18–20.** Sometimes Jesus chooses to use something other than the things listed in this answer to accomplish His purpose in someone. For instance, Jesus has commanded us to preach the gospel. That is what He uses to bring people to faith in Himself. But when the apostle Paul was converted, it was because he saw a bright light and heard a voice from heaven. Usually, however, Jesus uses His Word as we have it in the Bible to bring people to faith.

THURSDAY

The answer to this question lists the "ordinary, external ways Christ uses to bring us the benefits of redemption." The first thing listed is "the word." God has given us His Word in the Bible. The Bible is not like any other book. Because the Bible is the Word of

God, it is alive. It has power. It can change people. God uses His Word to cause unbelievers to put their faith in Christ. As non-Christians read the Bible or as they hear a faithful pastor preach from God's Word, the Holy Spirit causes them to see the truth of what they read or hear. He changes their hearts so they can put their faith in Christ.

The Bible causes change in Christians too. We can never know all there is to know in God's Word. No matter how well we know it or have studied it, we should always be studying it even more. We should come to God's Word willing to let it change us. When we do, God will use it to cause us to become less controlled by sin and more like Jesus. **Read James 1:21–25.**

FRIDAY

Sacraments are things that Christ has commanded His people to do, promising to bless them when they do them. Christ gave His people two sacraments: baptism and the Lord's Supper. Sacraments are things we can see that remind us of spiritual things we cannot see. Sacraments celebrate things that have already happened. At the same time, they also celebrate what God continues to do for His people. **Read 1 Corinthians 11:23–25.**

SATURDAY

The Lord Jesus has also commanded us to pray. He uses prayer in our salvation. God uses the prayers of His people to bring others to faith in Christ. When a person begins to be aware that he is a sinner who needs a Savior, God will often give him a desire to pray and to seek God. In these ways God uses prayer to bring non-Christians to faith in Christ. Once we are Christians, there is so much growing we have to do! We are still sinners who are far from being like Jesus. God commands us to pray that He will change us. He commands us to pray that we will grow in holiness. God uses the time we spend in prayer to make us more like what He saved us to be. **Read 1 Timothy 2:1–4.**

A. ◠ *The Spirit of God causes the reading and especially the preaching of the word to convince and convert sinners and to build them up in holiness and comfort through faith to salvation.*

MONDAY

Jesus promised His disciples that He would send the Holy Spirit. The Holy Spirit would convince people that they were sinners who needed a Savior. God's Spirit is the One who converts, or changes, people so that they stop loving sin and put their faith in Jesus for forgiveness. The Holy Spirit has a tool that He uses to do this. His tool is the Bible, the Word of God. The Spirit of God uses the Word of God to bring non-Christians to faith in Christ. **Read 2 Timothy 3:14–15.** The Spirit of God also uses the Word of God to cause Christians to grow in holiness. A non-Christian who never hears or reads the Word of God will probably not become a Christian. A Christian who never hears or reads the Word of God will probably not grow in holiness.

TUESDAY

People have not always had the Scriptures in their own language so that they could read it for themselves. Many people all over the world today do not have God's Word in a language they can understand. We should thank God for giving us His Word in our language. Even more than that, we should thank God for giving us His Word at all. The Bible is a treasure we should be diligent to use.

Not only has God given us His Word so we can read it, but He has given us pastors and teachers to explain it to us as well. God has chosen the preaching of His Word as the main thing He uses to bring unbelievers to faith in Christ. **Read 1 Corinthians 1:21.** He also uses the preaching of His Word to convince His people of the sin that is still in their hearts. He uses the preaching of faithful pastors to call His people to grow in holiness. Of course, many people claim to faithfully preach God's Word when they say things that are not in it at all. God requires each of us to know the Scriptures for ourselves so we know whether the things a preacher says are true or not. **Read Acts 17:11.**

WEDNESDAY

The Holy Spirit uses God's Word to convince people that they are sinners who need a Savior. As people read about God in the Bible, they see how great and holy He is. As they read the laws He has given us, they see how hopeless it is for any of us to keep His laws perfectly, as He requires. God's Word shows non-Christians that they are sinners who have made God angry by their sin. Left to themselves, they may think they are good people. When they compare themselves with others, they may think they are better than other people. When God causes non-Christians to compare themselves with His Word, they see that they are miserable sinners who must have a Savior.

Once people put their faith in Christ for salvation, they are still sinners who must say "No" to sin every day. They have to learn to live in obedience to the Lord Jesus. Again, it is the Word of God that the Holy Spirit uses to show His people the sin that is still in their hearts so that they will turn from it. **Read Hebrews 4:12.**

THURSDAY

The Holy Spirit is the One who convinces people of their sin. He is also the One who converts them. To "convert" means to change. When the Holy Spirit converts a person, He changes that person from an unbeliever to a believer. He changes an enemy of God into a child of God. Again, it is God's Word, the Bible, that He uses to convert people. It is in God's Word that we learn about Jesus, the Savior God provided. The Bible shows us that Jesus is the Son of God who came to die in our place. It tells us that Jesus has done all that needs to be done to save us so that all we have to do is to put our faith in Him. This is the gospel. It is as people hear the gospel preached that the Holy Spirit converts them, or changes their hearts, so that they can believe it. **Read Acts 4:1–4.**

FRIDAY

The Spirit of God uses the Word of God to convince and convert sinners. Once people are converted and believe in Jesus, there is more that must happen. Christians must become more and more like Jesus until, finally, when they go to be with Him in heaven, they will be made perfect. Again, the Holy Spirit is the One who causes this to happen. He works in the lives of God's people to make them what God wants them to be. And, again, it is the Word of God that the Holy Spirit uses to cause this to happen. He uses God's Word to build up believers. It causes them to know God better and better and to live more completely for Him. **Read Acts 20:32.**

SATURDAY

The Bible makes it clear that God's purpose has always been to have people who would be His own special people. These people would have to be holy because God is holy. When God saves us, it is not so we will go to heaven or so we will be happy. God saves us so we will be holy. God uses His Word to make us holy. As we spend time studying it, it changes our minds. Our thoughts become like God's thoughts instead of being sinful. The way we think changes the way we talk and the way we behave. In this way, as we grow to know God's Word, we also grow in holiness. **Read 2 Timothy 3:16–17.**

Q.90.

HOW IS THE WORD TO BE READ AND HEARD IN ORDER TO BECOME EFFECTIVE FOR SALVATION?

A. *For the word to become effective for salvation, we must pay careful attention to it, prepare ourselves, and pray for understanding. We must also receive it with faith and love, treasure it in our hearts, and practice it in our lives.*

MONDAY

God's Word is unlike any other book in the world. Because it is the Word of God, it has the power to make great changes in people. It can change people who hate God into people who love and live for Him. It can change people from being selfish and wicked to being loving and holy. God's word is "effective for salvation." God uses His Word to bring people to faith in Christ and to make them like Jesus.

That does not mean the Bible is magic. God's Word is not like a magic formula that makes things happen whenever someone uses it. We must read and hear God's Word in certain ways if it is going to be effective for salvation. Sometimes, when people grow up in Christian homes, they develop a know-it-all attitude about God's Word. They think they have heard all that the Bible contains, and they do not want to hear it again. Such people do not realize the danger they are in. Because they hear and read the Bible often, they mistakenly believe they are Christians who are pleasing to God.

Jesus told a parable to show the different kinds of people who hear and read God's Word. He said that a farmer planting seeds is like a preacher preaching God's Word. Some seed falls on hard ground and does not sink in; birds come and eat it. This is like people who hear the Word and immediately forget it. Some seed falls on rocky ground and starts to grow, but has no root. It soon dies. This is a picture of people who believe at first, but when obeying God becomes hard, they give up. Other seed falls in thorny places. It starts to grow, but then the thorns choke it out. These plants represent people who start to obey God's Word, but become distracted by things in the world. Finally, there is the seed that falls on good soil and produces a good crop. **Read Luke 8:15** to see what kind of person this is like.

TUESDAY

The first thing anyone must do if he is to be saved by God's Word, is to receive it with faith. As a person hears or reads God's Word, he needs to believe that it is indeed *God's* Word, and not just the opinion of another human being. God's Word will tell him that he is a sinner who has made God angry. He may not like hearing that, but he must receive what God says about him with faith or he cannot be saved. God's Word will tell him that there is no way he can remove his sins and God's anger. It will also tell him that God has given a Savior, the Lord Jesus Christ, who took the sins of His people on Himself and was punished for them. God's Word will command the person reading or hearing it to put his faith in Christ alone. It will show him that only Jesus can save him from his sin and from God's anger at it. As long as a person refuses to believe that this is what God says about him and about how to be right with God, he will never be saved. He must receive God's Word *as* God's Word, agree with it, and do what it says. **Read 1 Thessalonians 2:13.**

WEDNESDAY

The answer to this question tells us that we must pay careful attention to God's Word. This means that we need to make time and take the trouble to get to know it very well. When children (or teenagers or adults) say, "I already know this," and act bored with the Bible, they show that they really do not understand much at all about God's Word. Books show what is in the mind of their authors. The Bible shows us what is in the mind of God, who is infinite. Just as we could never begin to understand all that God is, so we can never get to the end of knowing and understanding all that the Bible says.

There are people who have studied the Scriptures all day every day for years. In some cases, it is their *job* to know what the Scriptures teach, so they spend almost all their time studying them. Even at the end of their lives, such people will probably say that there is still so much left for them to learn and discover in God's Word. If we want God's Word to do its work in our lives, we must be diligent students of it. We must never think we know all of it we need to know. We must work hard at studying it every day of our lives. **Read Proverbs 2:1–5.**

THURSDAY

If we want God's Word to do its work in us, we must prepare ourselves for reading or hearing it. We can do several things to prepare ourselves. Before we go to church and before we sit down to read our Bibles, we should pray, asking God to help us understand His Word. Without the Holy Spirit showing us what God means in His Word, we will never spiritually understand it. So we prepare ourselves by praying for understanding. When we are getting ready to go to church to hear God's Word preached, we should also spend some time asking God to speak to us through it. As we listen to the sermon, we should listen for anything God would want us to change. **Read James 1:21.**

FRIDAY

God's enemies have no interest in His Word. When God has given a person a new heart, that person will have a new love for God's Word. If a person acts bored when the Bible is studied, it may be that he or she has not yet been born again and does not have a God-given love for God's Word. God's children will love His Word. They will treasure it. If they had to choose between many things that they have or could have—even important things—and a copy of the Bible, they would want a Bible. **Read** these verses that tell how Job and David felt about God's Word: **Job 23:12; Psalm 119:72, 131.**

SATURDAY

If God's Word is going to be effective for salvation and do God's work in our hearts, we have to read and hear it in certain ways. We have to pay careful attention to it. We should prepare ourselves to hear and read it by confessing and forsaking our sins and by praying for the Holy Spirit to give us understanding of it. When we read or hear God's Word, we must receive it with the faith that it truly is the Word of God. God wants us to love His Word and treasure it in our hearts. Finally, if God's Word is going to change us, we must not just *know* what it says. We must *do* what it says. We must practice it in our lives. **Read James 1:22–25.**

HOW DO THE SACRAMENTS
BECOME EFFECTIVE MEANS OF
SALVATION?

A. *The sacraments become effective means of salvation, not because of any special power in them or in the people who administer them, but rather by the blessing of Christ and the working of His Spirit in those who receive them by faith.*

MONDAY

There are two sacraments: baptism and the Lord's Supper. This question and answer explain how God uses these sacraments in our salvation. It is not "because of any special power" in the sacraments themselves. Being baptized is not like waving a magic wand. Eating the Lord's Supper does not magically make good things happen. Both baptism and the Lord's Supper must be received with faith. One man in the New Testament was baptized because everyone else was being baptized. But we see in the story about him that he was interested only in what he could get. He did not have genuine faith in Christ. Even though he had been baptized, if he did not repent, he would perish. **Read his story in Acts 8:9–13, 18–23.**

TUESDAY

God uses the sacraments as effective means for salvation. But this is "not because of any special power . . . in the people who administer them." Some people think there is special power in the priest or the minister who is doing the baptizing or serving the bread and wine. This is not true. When the Lord's people obey Him, the Lord Himself blesses them. There is no special power in any priest or pastor or elder to save people. **Read 1 Corinthians 3:6–7.**

WEDNESDAY

If there is nothing magical in baptism or the Lord's Supper and if the person administering these sacraments has no special power, what is it that makes these things effective for salvation? It is "because of the blessing of Christ." It was Jesus Himself who gave us baptism. At His last meal with His disciples, He gave His disciples the Lord's Supper. When the Lord's people use what He has given them, He blesses them. It is the blessing of Christ that makes the sacraments effective for salvation. **Read Acts 2:38–39 and 1 Corinthians 10:16.**

THURSDAY

Because the Lord Jesus gave us the sacraments, He blesses them when we use them. The Holy Spirit, also, works inside those who receive the sacraments by faith. Water baptism shows that the Holy Spirit baptizes people into the body of Christ and makes them members of Christ's body forever. When believers share the bread and wine in the Lord's Supper, they share in Christ and in His Spirit. **Read 1 Corinthians 12:13.**

FRIDAY

Baptism and the Lord's Supper are not for everyone. God gave them only to His people. They are effective as means of salvation only for "those who receive them by faith." Many people have eaten the Lord's Supper. It does them no good if they do not understand what it means and have never put their faith in Jesus. Many people have been baptized. If they never believe the gospel, they will die in their sins anyway, even though they have been baptized. **Read Mark 16:15–16.**

SATURDAY

Fairy tales often tell of magic rituals, such as rubbing the lamp in which a genie is living. In the fairy tales, whenever the ritual is performed, even when someone does it by accident, the magic happens. The sacraments are not like magic rituals. God did not intend for the sacraments to be used all by themselves. They are to be used with God's Word. The Lord Jesus Christ commanded His people to be baptized and to eat the Lord's Supper. He gave promises of blessing to go with each of the sacraments. **Read** these two verses, looking for what is promised in each of them. **Matthew 26:26–28 and Acts 2:38.**

Q.92. WHAT IS A SACRAMENT?

A. ✍ *A sacrament is a holy regulation established by Christ, in which Christ and the benefits of the new covenant are represented, sealed, and applied to believers by physical signs.*

MONDAY

Read Genesis 17:1–2, 9. The word "sacrament" comes from a word that Roman soldiers used long ago. It meant a very serious promise that a soldier would always remain faithful to his general and do what the general commanded. This word could also mean the promise the general made to remain faithful to the soldiers under his command. The Lord Jesus Christ has made a covenant with His people. He has promised them certain things that He will be sure to give them. His people have made a covenant with Christ. They have promised to trust in Him, obey Him, and remain faithful to Him all their lives. The sacraments remind us of the promises Christ has made to us and of the covenant we have with Him.

TUESDAY

"A sacrament is a holy regulation established by Christ." A "regulation" is a law or a rule made by someone in authority. The Lord Jesus Christ is the King of His church. He makes the rules the church must obey. King Jesus is the only One who can make such rules. There are two regulations or rules Jesus made for the church. He gave them to His disciples and commanded that they be obeyed always. Jesus gave one of those rules, or regulations, as He ate His last meal before dying. He was eating with His disciples. As He broke the bread into pieces and as He passed the cup around, He told them always to eat bread and drink wine in remembrance of Him. God's people celebrate the Lord's Supper as one of the sacraments because Jesus has commanded us to do so. **Read 1 Corinthians 11:23–25.**

Jesus gave the other regulation just before He went back to heaven. He commanded His disciples to go into all the world, making more disciples and baptizing those who became His followers. That is why baptism is the other sacrament. The Lord Jesus commanded it. **Read Matthew 28:18–19.**

WEDNESDAY

Each sacrament has two parts. There is the physical part, which we see or feel or taste. There is the true, spiritual thing of which it is a picture. This part of the sacrament is invisible. When a person is baptized, he or she sees and feels the water. Those who are watching also see the water. They see the baptized person get wet. But what baptism represents cannot be seen. It represents being united to Christ. Jesus' death for sin counts as though the person baptized by faith has died himself or herself. As Jesus rose from the dead and became alive again, so the baptized believer has new life by being united to Christ and has the power to live for God. **Read Romans 6:4.**

When believers take the Lord's Supper, they eat and drink ordinary bread and wine. These are things people depend on for everyday life. The believer taking these in the Lord's Supper sees, feels, and tastes real bread and wine. These things represent something that cannot be seen, felt, or tasted. The person eating the Lord's Supper depends on Christ's broken body and poured-out blood to give eternal life. **Read John 6:54.**

THURSDAY

Read 1 Corinthians 11:26. People remember those they love who have died. Sometimes, people visit the graves of dead friends or relatives and put flowers on them. The Lord's Supper is more than that. It is not just a memorial for someone who has died. For a believer, eating the Lord's Supper is a way of growing to know and trust Christ better. It is a way of appreciating and receiving all that Jesus accomplished for His people by dying on the cross. Both baptism and the Lord's Supper are more than just pictures. They *are* pictures of what Christ does for His people. But Jesus also uses them to actually do things for His people. He uses the sacraments to cause His people to grow into what He wants them to be.

FRIDAY

In some ways, the sacraments are like God's Word. Both the sacraments and God's Word were given to us by God. Both will cause us to grow in grace when we use them. The one who receives either the sacraments or God's Word must receive them with faith. The Holy Spirit uses both the sacraments and the Word of God to produce change in His people's hearts. God's Word is important and so are baptism and the Lord's Supper. In some ways, though, these things are very different. God does not use the mere act of baptism or the Lord's Supper to convert unbelievers. God uses His Word to bring unbelievers to faith in Christ. It is when a non-Christian hears God's Word with faith that he or she becomes a Christian. Neither being baptized nor taking the Lord's Supper will make a non-Christian into a Christian. **Read John 5:24.**

SATURDAY

The sacraments are different from God's Word because of who will benefit from them. God's Word is to be preached to all. When God's Word is preached to those who are a part of the church, it comforts them and it causes them to grow stronger in Christ. When God's Word is preached to those who are not part of the church, God will use it to show them their sin and to show them Christ as Savior. The sacraments are only for those who are in the church. Baptism and the Lord's Supper strengthen and encourage God's people, but they do nothing for those who are not His people. God's Word, on the other hand, has value for both believers and unbelievers. God uses His Word to cause faith in someone who did not have it before. He uses the sacraments to strengthen the faith of those who believe. **Read Romans 10:17.**

Q.93.

WHAT ARE THE SACRAMENTS OF THE NEW TESTAMENT?

A. ❧ *The sacraments of the New Testament are baptism and the Lord's Supper.*

MONDAY

God has always made covenants with His people. When God makes a covenant with people, He promises to do certain things for them. He commits Himself to them. He also requires certain things of the people with whom He has a covenant. All through the Old Testament, God made covenants with His people. One of the earliest covenants God made was with Abraham. When God made the covenant with Abraham, He told Abraham that he was to be circumcised. Circumcision is a small operation performed on men and boys. All the men in Abraham's household were to be circumcised, as well as all the boys born in his house. This would be a sign and a seal that they were under a covenant with God. It would be something they could see on their bodies that would mark them as belonging to God. **Read Genesis 17:9–10.**

A little later, God made a covenant with His people when Moses was their leader. One of the things God required of His people then was that they celebrate the Passover meal every year. This was to remind them of how God had saved them from slavery in Egypt. Exodus 12 gives instructions on how the Israelites should celebrate the Passover. **Read** what God said at the end of these instructions in **Exodus 12:24.**

Circumcision and the Passover were sacraments God gave His people as signs and seals of the Old Testament covenant.

TUESDAY

When Jesus came, God made a new covenant with His people. This new covenant is a much better covenant than anything God's people had before. It has better promises and better benefits. When God replaced the old covenant with this new and better one, He replaced the signs and seals of the covenant as well. Instead of the Passover, we now have the Lord's Supper. Instead of circumcision, we have baptism.

Under the old covenant, a man who was not an Israelite might want to serve the one true God and become one of the people of God. That man was to be circumcised. When Jewish parents had a little boy, they were to circumcise him. Circumcision was something done to a person only once. It showed that a person was joining the people of God. Now he would be included in God's covenant with His people. **Read Genesis 17:11.**

Under the new covenant, baptism has replaced circumcision. Like circumcision, baptism is done to a person only once. Baptism shows that a person is joined to the people of God, as circumcision showed the same thing. Like circumcision, baptism shows that a person is included in the new covenant Christ has made with His people. **Read Galatians 3:26–28.**

WEDNESDAY

Circumcision was an operation that cut and removed a small piece of skin. It reminded sinful human beings of the need to cut off their sinful nature. A person cannot cut out and remove sin from his own heart. God has to do it for him. When a man was circumcised, it showed that he wanted his sin to be removed. It showed that he trusted God to do that for him. Sometimes a person's body was circumcised, but in his heart, he had no desire to stop sinning. In that case, the circumcision of his body did no good at all.

In the same way, baptism stands for death to a person's old, sinful way of life. When someone chooses to be baptized, he is saying that he no longer wants to live in rebellion against God. His sinful nature has died with Christ on the cross. God will work in him to make him more and more able to live for Him instead of for sin. Like circumcision, baptism is something done to a person's body. If someone has no desire to stop sinning and to live for God, baptism does him no good. **Read Colossians 2:11–12,** noticing that it talks about both circumcision and baptism.

THURSDAY

The big event of the Old Testament was God's deliverance of His people, the Israelites, from slavery in Egypt. Pharaoh was determined to keep the Israelites as slaves. God was determined to free them and lead them to the land He had promised them. God sent ten different plagues on the Egyptians before Pharaoh would let them go. The last plague was the death of the firstborn son in every Egyptian family. At last, Pharaoh allowed the Israelites to leave Egypt. But then he changed his mind. He set out after them with his army. When Pharaoh trapped the Israelites at the Red Sea, God caused the waters of the sea to split apart so that it was dry down the middle. Then God's people crossed on dry land. When the Egyptians tried to follow, the waters came back together and they drowned.

God commanded the Israelites to spend a week each year celebrating this event. Part of the celebration included eating the Passover feast. They were to do this regularly, over and over, as long as they lived. **Read Exodus 12:14.**

God's deliverance of the Israelites from Egypt was a great event. But it was a small thing compared to God's deliverance of His people from sin. That is the big event of the New Testament. God's people under the new covenant no longer celebrate salvation from the Egyptians by eating the Passover. Now they celebrate their salvation from sin by eating the Lord's Supper. Like Passover, the Lord's Supper is not to be done only once, but is to be celebrated regularly, over and over, until the Lord returns.

FRIDAY

The name "Passover" came from what happened during the last of the ten plagues of Egypt. God warned that He was going to kill the firstborn son of every family in the land of Egypt. He did not want to include the families of the Israelites in this plague. So He gave them a way to escape from the angel of death He would send. God told His people to kill a lamb in the evening. They were to take some of its blood and paint the blood on the doorposts of their homes. When the angel of death came during the night, he would see the blood on the doorposts and "pass over" their houses.

Any people who were not Israelites, even Egyptians, could do the same thing and be just as safe from the angel of death. The lamb that was killed was the Passover lamb. It died so Israelites would not have to die. Each year, when God's people celebrated the Passover, they would kill a lamb and eat it. They ate the Passover meal as a reminder of what great things God had done for them.

The Passover lamb was a picture of the Lord Jesus Christ. He died so that God's people would not have to die. When God comes to judge people's sin, He sees the blood of His Son that paid for sin and He passes over His people, instead of judging them. We no longer eat the meat from the Passover lamb. Now we eat bread that Jesus said stands for His body and we drink wine or juice that Jesus said stands for His blood. **See** what the Bible calls Jesus in **1 Corinthians 5:7b.**

SATURDAY

In the Old Testament sacraments of circumcision and the Passover, people could see and taste and feel physical things that pictured spiritual things. These sacraments were not magic. They showed that God had made a covenant with the people who used them. Circumcision and the Passover demonstrated people's trust in God to keep His part of the covenant. These things showed that God's people intended to be faithful to Him. Without faith in God and obedience to Him, these Old Testament sacraments were useless. The same is true of baptism and the Lord's Supper now. They show our faith in Christ to save us and our commitment to serve Him always. Without faith and obedience to Christ, the New Testament sacraments are useless. What today's Scripture reading says about circumcision is true of the New Testament sacraments as well. **Read Romans 2:28–29.**

Q.94. WHAT IS BAPTISM?

A. ✍ *The sacrament of baptism is a washing with water in the name of the Father, the Son, and the Holy Spirit, which is a sign and seal that we are joined to Christ, that we receive the benefits of the covenant of grace, and that we are engaged to be the Lord's.*

MONDAY

No one can be one of God's children as long as sin is in the way. A person must be freed from sins before he or she can receive the blessings of belonging to God. The Lord Jesus Christ came to free His people from their sins. He died on the cross to pay for all the times they had made God angry by breaking His laws. His blood is worth enough to pay for all His people's sins. With their sins out of the way, God's people are free to love and serve Him. **Read Revelation 1:5–6.**

TUESDAY

The blood of Christ washes the hearts of His people. It cleans away all their sin. When people are baptized, their bodies are washed or sprinkled with water. This is a picture of what has happened to the hearts of those who truly believe in Jesus. Their hearts have been washed clean by the blood of Jesus Christ. Sin no longer separates God from His people. Now they can come to God, sure that He will welcome them. **Read Hebrews 10:22.**

WEDNESDAY

People are baptized in the name of the Father, the Son, and the Holy Spirit as Jesus commanded. The Father, the Son, and the Holy Spirit each has a part to play in saving a person from sin. A new

Christian must believe in God as He has revealed Himself in the Bible. That means the person being baptized must believe in God the Father and live in obedience to His commands. He or she must believe in God the Son and serve Him as Lord, and must also believe in God the Holy Spirit and want to do His will. **Read 1 Peter 1:1–2.**

THURSDAY

God has made a new covenant with us, His people. Baptism is the sign and seal of the covenant. In this covenant, God promises many wonderful benefits. Adoption by God Himself and life that lasts forever are only two of them. There are many more. Jesus earned all these benefits for His people. We receive them because we are joined to Him. His life of perfect obedience and His death for sin count as if we had done them ourselves. Baptism is the sign and seal that we have been joined with Christ so that the blessings He deserves belong to us as well. **Read Romans 6:3–4.**

FRIDAY

One of the benefits Jesus earned for His people and gives them in the new covenant is membership in His church. Baptism announces that a person now belongs to the people of God. Another benefit of the new covenant is forgiveness of sin. A person who is baptized because of faith in Christ is a person whose sins are forgiven. **Read Acts 2:38.** Another benefit believers have in the new covenant is that they have been made new. They have new hearts to love God and hate sin. They will live new lives and will grow more like Jesus every day. **Read Titus 3:4–5.** Baptism is a sign and seal of all these benefits Christ has earned for His people.

SATURDAY

Baptism marks people as belonging to the Lord. A person being baptized takes on the responsibility to be the Lord's servant for the rest of his life. He is bound to serve, follow, and obey Christ. This is what the answer to this question means when it says baptism is a sign and seal that "we are engaged to be the Lord's." After baptism, a person should live as one who wants to please Christ in all that he or she does. **Read Romans 6:4, 11.**

Q.95.

A. ⚶ *Those who are not members of churches should not be baptized until they have publicly stated that they believe in Christ and will obey Him, but the infant children of church members should be baptized.*

MONDAY

Baptism shows that a person is being joined to the Lord and to His people. A person who is not joined to the Lord or to His people should not be baptized. Baptism is something we can see that tells us of something we cannot see. It tells us that the person being baptized is now included in the covenant Christ makes with His people. Any person who is not under that covenant should not be baptized. **Read Ephesians 2:12.** A person who wants to be baptized must be sure he believes in Christ and wants to obey Him. He must not just believe privately, in his heart, but he must state it publicly, for others to hear and know. That is why, when someone desires to be baptized, the pastor will ask if he has put his faith in Christ as his only Savior. The pastor will also ask if the person intends to follow Christ all his life. The pastor does not want to baptize someone who does not belong to Christ.

TUESDAY

The sign of the covenant in the Old Testament was circumcision. To God's Old Testament people, circumcision was very important. A person was not included in God's covenant if he was not circumcised. When Jesus came, He made a new and better covenant. He gave baptism as the sign of this new covenant. One day, Peter was preaching the good news about Jesus to men who had never been circumcised. As he was speaking, the Holy Spirit came upon the people who listened. They began to speak in other languages and were praising God.

This surprised Peter and his friends. They would never have thought that the Holy Spirit would come upon uncircumcised people. If the Holy Spirit were inside these people, these people were included in Christ's new covenant—even if they *were* uncircumcised. Peter had these new believers baptized. He gave them the sign of the new covenant, even though they did not have the sign of the old one. That is because, under the new covenant, anyone who repents and believes is to be baptized. **Read Acts 10:44–48.**

WEDNESDAY

The answer to this catechism question teaches that people should not be baptized unless they believe in Christ and will live for Him. But it also teaches that when Christian parents have a baby, they should baptize that baby while he or she is still a very young baby. This is because baptism is a sign of the covenant God has with His people. In the Old Testament, little babies who were born to God's people received the sign of the covenant, circumcision.

Many places in the Bible tell of God making a covenant with His people. If you read all these verses, you would find that God often told His people, "My covenant is with you *and with your descendants (or children and grandchildren)."* When God gave Abraham circumcision as the sign of His covenant, He commanded Abraham to circumcise his children. When a baby boy was born into the family of any of God's people, that boy was to be circumcised when he was still a very young baby. **Read Genesis 17:10–12.** When Old Testament parents circumcised their baby boys, they were being obedient to God. The parents were saying that this child was born under God's covenant. They promised to raise him as one of God's people. The parents were showing that they trusted God to make their child able to keep God's covenant by faith.

THURSDAY

When God made a covenant with Abraham, it was not only with Abraham, but also with Abraham's descendants—his children, his grandchildren, and his great grandchildren. He promised not only to be Abraham's God, but the God of his children and his grandchildren as well. **Read Genesis 17:7.** God said the covenant He made with Abraham would be an everlasting covenant. As the Old Testament story continued, God made other covenants with people. Each new covenant was this same everlasting covenant God had made with Abraham, but clearer and fuller.

Finally, when Jesus came and made a new covenant with His people, it was the final and perfect covenant. It did not take away the covenant God made with Abraham, because God had said that covenant was an everlasting covenant. The new covenant makes the one that God made with Abraham fuller and better. God included the children of believing parents in the covenant He made with Abraham. Christian parents who baptize their young babies do so trusting that God includes their children in the new covenant.

FRIDAY

Christian parents who baptize their babies want to show that their children belong to the people of God. Christian parents believe that God will work in their children to bring them to faith in Christ. They promise to teach them about Jesus and train them to keep His covenant. Christian parents who baptize their children know that their children must put their faith in Jesus for themselves. If their children never do this, they will never be Christians.

Even when believing parents circumcised their children under the old covenant, they did not think that circumcision automatically made their children right with God. They knew that real circumcision was something God did in the heart. **Read Deuteronomy 30:6.**

SATURDAY

The men who wrote this catechism question said that baptism is for those who repent and believe *and* for the little babies of believing parents. Other Christians believe that baptism is only for those who repent and believe. Since little babies cannot repent and believe, these Christians would say babies should not be baptized at all.

We must be careful not to base our understanding on just a few verses in the Bible about a subject like this one. We should always want to study and know what the whole Bible teaches about something. Then we can have a truly biblical understanding. **Read Proverbs 2:1–6.**

Q.96. WHAT IS THE LORD'S SUPPER?

A. *The Lord's Supper is a sacrament in which bread and wine are given and received as Christ directed to proclaim His death. Those who receive the Lord's Supper in the right way share in His body and blood with all His benefits, not merely physically but by faith, and become spiritually stronger and grow in grace.*

MONDAY

The Lord Jesus gave us the Lord's Supper as a sacrament. During the last meal He ate with His disciples, He broke bread and gave it to them, telling them it was His body broken for them. He passed a cup of wine around the table, telling them it was His blood poured out for them. Jesus told His disciples that His blood was poured out for the forgiveness of sins. Then He told them to eat bread and drink wine in remembrance of Him until He would come again. Like baptism, the Lord's Supper is a sign and a seal of the covenant God makes with His people. It is a sign of the covenant, meaning that when we eat it, we are showing that we are included in God's covenant. We are among God's people and our sins have been forgiven. It is also a seal of the covenant, so that eating it brings us grace and forgiveness each time we eat it.

Why did Jesus choose to make eating bread and drinking wine a sacrament? Our bodies cannot live without bread and other food. We must receive the food God has provided or we will die. We cannot live spiritually apart from the Lord Jesus Christ. Jesus called Himself the Bread of Life. We must receive Him as the Savior God has provided if we want to have eternal life. Jesus said that His flesh is the bread He gives so we can have life. **Read John 6:48–51.**

TUESDAY

When God brings us to repentance and faith, we believe in His Son, Jesus. Right then, once and for all, God forgives all our sin. He forgives the sins we have committed in the past and He forgives the sins we have not yet committed. There is nothing we can do to lose God's forgiveness. We can do nothing to make God's forgiveness a little more complete. We do not stop sinning, however. We sin every day, in many ways. Because God has changed our hearts so that now our first desire is to please God, we feel guilty and sad when we sin. God, in His goodness, has given us the Lord's Supper as a reminder that Jesus has fully paid for all our sin and that God has forgiven us. As we come to the Lord's Table, we look carefully at how we have been living to see in what ways we have sinned against God. As we come in faith and eat the Lord's Supper, we once again receive Christ and His forgiveness. **Read Matthew 26:26–28.**

WEDNESDAY

At the end of the day, if you have worked or played hard and eaten nothing since lunchtime, you feel hungry. Your body grows tired and weak. When you eat something, your body feels refreshed. You grow strong again and have new energy. When you eat the right kinds of food every day, that food nourishes your body. It causes your body to grow strong and healthy.

The Lord's Supper does the same things for the spirits of God's people that good food does for their bodies. Sometimes we grow weary or discouraged as we live for God. The Lord's Supper refreshes Christians, like food refreshes our bodies. We are encouraged and strengthened by eating it. God gave us the Lord's Supper to nourish us spiritually. When Jesus was on earth, He spoke with people who did not understand that their spirits needed Him in the same way that their bodies needed food. These people were only concerned with food for their bodies. They were not looking for food for their souls. These people saw Jesus feed five thousand people from a little boy's lunch of bread and fish. They followed Jesus, hoping He would give them more food for their bodies. **Read** what Jesus told them in **John 6:26–27.**

THURSDAY

In the Lord's Supper, God's people take the bread that has been broken and eat it. They take the cup that has been poured out for them and drink it. As they do this, God's people receive the body and blood of Christ. Believers do not depend on themselves for what they need, but they humbly receive what God has given. When people first put their faith in Christ, they trust in the Savior God has provided for the forgiveness of their sin. When they regularly eat the Lord's Supper, they continue to trust in Him and to feed on Him by faith. **Read John 6:28–29.**

FRIDAY

Those who share in the Lord's Supper are joined to Christ. Those "who receive it in the right way share in His body and blood with all His benefits." All that Jesus did while He was on earth in a human body counts as though His people had done it themselves. He lived a life of perfect obedience to God. His people are joined to Him, so all the rewards He earned for His obedience belong to His people as well. Jesus died to pay for sin. His people are joined to Him, so all the punishment He received counts as though His people had received it. God will never punish them. When God's people eat the bread and drink the wine in the Lord's Supper, they receive, by faith, the benefits He earned for them. **Read John 6:53–56.**

SATURDAY

When believers participate in the Lord's Supper, they "proclaim His death." This does not mean simply that God's people are announcing to the world that Jesus died a sad and terrible death. Sometimes when innocent people die in a bad accident, people will observe a few moments of silence for them at special events. When important leaders die, the flag is lowered for several days. These are ways of remembering people's deaths and showing respect for those who have died.

The Lord's Supper is not like this. It is not simply a memorial. When God's people "proclaim His death" at the Lord's Supper, they announce to everyone their faith in what Jesus did when He died.

They proclaim, by their actions, that when Jesus died on the cross, He died for the sins of His people. By eating the Lord's Supper, God's people show their confidence that the death of Jesus was enough to save them from their sin. **Read 1 Corinthians 11:26.**

Q.97.   WHAT IS THE RIGHT WAY TO RECEIVE THE LORD'S SUPPER?

A. 〰 *The right way to receive the Lord's Supper is to examine whether we discern the Lord's body, whether our faith feeds on Him, and whether we have repentance, love and a new obedience—so that we may not come in the wrong way and eat and drink judgment on ourselves.*

MONDAY

There is nothing magical about eating the Lord's Supper. We must receive it in the right way if it is to help us grow. The Lord's Supper is not magical, but it is holy. It is a holy time of celebration and of renewing our commitment to our Lord. The Bible warns us against eating the Lord's Supper in an unworthy manner. This means taking it lightly and failing to treat it as something very serious. Because it is something so special, there are things we should do to get ready for it. The Bible tells us to examine ourselves before we come to eat the Lord's Supper. There are certain things we should look for in ourselves each time we prepare to take it. **Read 1 Corinthians 11:27–28.**

TUESDAY

One important thing to look for in ourselves before we take the Lord's Supper is understanding. That is what the answer to this catechism question means when it says we are to "discern the Lord's body." Do we understand that the bread represents the body of Christ, broken for His people? Do we understand that the juice represents Jesus' blood, poured out to pay for their sins?

Sometimes young children want to eat the Lord's Supper just because it is food and everyone else is eating it. The Lord's Supper is not refreshment time. Parents must not allow children to eat it until they understand the death of Christ for sin and how the bread and juice show us that. Sometimes people may eat the Lord's Supper because they want to do what the people around them are doing. Some adults may believe the bread and juice themselves will do them some good. Of course, this is not true. People should not participate in the Lord's Supper without understanding what it really is. **Read 1 Corinthians 11:29.**

We must also examine ourselves for faith. Does our "faith feed on Christ"? Do we trust in the Lord Jesus Christ to give us all we need to be pleasing to God and to make us grow? People who have never put their faith in Christ should not take the Lord's Supper. **Read 2 Corinthians 13:5.**

WEDNESDAY

The answer to this catechism question says we should also examine ourselves to see "whether we have repentance." God brings repentance to the heart of every person He saves. If people have never repented of sin, they are not Christians at all. If they have never been sorry for sin and turned away from it, they should not eat the Lord's Supper. Even after God has changed our hearts so that we repent and put our faith in Jesus, the sin in our hearts does not just go away. We still disobey God sometimes. Every day we sin and need to repent again. Before the Lord's Supper, we should take the time to think through our everyday lives, looking for the sinful things we do and the sinful attitudes we have. Whatever we see, we must confess to God. Then we must decide, with God's help, to stop doing that thing. **Read Lamentations 3:40.**

THURSDAY

Before eating the Lord's Supper, we must also examine ourselves for love. Left to themselves, people have a natural hatred for God in their hearts. When Jesus changes a person's heart, He takes away that hatred and replaces it with love for God. A true Christian will love God and want to please Him. The Bible tells us that true Christians will also love other Christians. If people do not love God or God's people, they are not Christians at all and should not eat the Lord's Supper. Even after God puts a new love for Himself and for His people into a believer's heart, people still sin against each other. It often happens that Christians hurt each other or make each other angry.

Before the Lord's Supper, we should especially examine ourselves to see if we hold any unloving attitudes in our hearts. We should ask ourselves whether we have done anything that was in any way hurtful to another. If so, we should go to the person we have hurt and ask forgiveness before eating the Lord's Supper. Perhaps someone has done something to hurt us. We should forgive her or him in our hearts before coming to the Lord's Table. **Read 1 John 4:19–21.**

FRIDAY

The Lord's Supper also reminds us to examine ourselves to see if we have "a new obedience" to Christ. Before Jesus saved us, we were rebels against God. We did not want to do the things He required of us. But when Jesus saves us and changes our hearts, He gives us a new desire to obey God. If we are Christians, we will want to know what God's Word says so we can obey it. Those who do not care if they obey God should not eat the Lord's Supper. They are probably not Christians. Of course, even true Christians who know God's Word and want to obey it will fail sometimes. Before taking the Lord's Supper, Christians should examine themselves for their failures to obey God. They should confess these to God as sin and ask for His help to obey. **Read 1 John 2:3–6.**

SATURDAY

The apostle Paul wrote to the Christians in Corinth and told them they were wrong in how they received the Lord's Supper. The Corinthians were eating the Lord's Supper while they were angry with one another. They were sinning as a way of life, without repenting before coming to the Lord's Table. They were treating the Lord's Supper as just another meal time. Paul rebuked the Corinthians for this. He told them that some of them were sick and some of them had died because God was judging them for how they received the Lord's Supper. God takes the Lord's Supper very seriously. He has commanded us to keep it, and He wants us to take it seriously as well. **Read 1 Corinthians 11:17–18, 20–21, 30.**

Q.98.   WHAT IS PRAYER?

A. *Prayer is offering our desires to God in the name of Christ for things that agree with His will, confessing our sins, and thankfully recognizing His mercies.*

MONDAY

Many people have wrong ideas about prayer. Most people believe they can talk to God whenever they want to and He will listen. Such people believe it is God's job to listen to prayers and to answer them. They may go for years without talking to God at all. Then trouble comes and they pray for help, expecting God to answer them. These people do not realize that God does not listen to everyone's prayers.

Read Proverbs 15:8, 29. God does not listen to the prayers of the wicked. He hates their prayers. Since all people are sinners, can no one pray to God? Those who have put their faith in Jesus come to God with Jesus' righteousness. God hears their prayers because their sins have been forgiven and they come with the righteousness of His Son. Unbelievers who have never put their faith in Christ are still in their sins. They cannot expect God to hear their prayers.

The Bible teaches us what prayer is. It instructs us how to pray so that God will listen. When we pray as God tells us to in His Word, God uses prayer as a means to our salvation.

TUESDAY

The answer to this catechism question gives us a biblical definition of prayer. It begins by telling us that, in true prayer, we offer our desires to God. Desires are our wishes for the things we want. What kind of desires do we offer to God? We offer Him those desires "that agree with His will." There are plenty of things we want, and God does care about the little details of our lives. However, when we pray, we are not to pray mostly about winning tomorrow's game or having good weather for our party. When we come to God in prayer, we must ask for the things God has told us in His Word that He wants for us. These are things like love and forgiveness for others, a true knowledge of God, and holiness. God has given us many examples of prayers in His Word. It is helpful to read them and then to pray for the same things for which these Bible prayers ask. **Read** one of these Bible prayers in **Colossians 1:9–10.**

WEDNESDAY

Notice that the answer to this question tells us to offer our *desires* to God. A desire comes from the heart. Sometimes we just say words when we pray, without thinking about what we say. This is wrong because God does not want words only from us. He wants our prayers to Him to be from the heart. When we pray aloud, we should pay attention and think about what we say. We must not just say the same thing we always say when we pray. When another person prays, especially if he or she prays for a long time, it is easy to let our minds wander to something else. It is easy, but it is wrong. When someone else prays, we must listen and agree with what he or she says. Most people find prayer difficult. It is hard work to pray sincerely and to keep alert in our prayers. We must keep growing in prayer, because God has commanded us to pray. The more we pray, the more we will grow in Christlikeness. **Read 1 Thessalonians 5:16–18.**

THURSDAY

The only way we can offer our desires to God is "in the name of Christ." That does not mean that the words "in Jesus' name" are some kind of magic formula that we tack on to our prayers before we say "amen." Have you ever heard a policeman in a movie say, "Halt, in the name of the law?" The policeman is telling the person that it is not just one man telling the person to stop. Behind the policeman stands the whole law. If the person keeps running, he does not merely disobey one man; he disobeys the law of the land.

When we come to God "in Jesus' name," we tell God that we do not expect Him to accept us or hear us because of who we are. After all, we are great sinners. God does not hear the prayers of sinners. We expect God to accept and hear our prayers because the Lord Jesus Christ stands behind us. We come asking for what we need in the name of the One who always obeyed God perfectly, even to the point of dying on the cross. Of course, it is only the person who has put her or his faith in the Lord Jesus as Lord and Savior who can pray in Jesus' name. When we come in His name, we are sure God will hear us and answer us. **Read Ephesians 3:11–12.**

FRIDAY

When we pray, we ask God for those things He has told us in His Word He wants us to have. We also confess our sins to God. If we want to grow as Christians, we will find it very helpful to examine our hearts every day, looking for sinful attitudes. Whatever we find, we should immediately confess to God, admitting that it is sin. We should ask Him to cause us to hate the sin we see in ourselves. If we are faithful to do this every day, it will help us a great deal in learning to live for God instead of for ourselves. There is another reason that it is important to confess our sins to God. He tells us in His Word that He will not listen to the prayers of His children when they hold on to sin and do not forsake it. **Read Psalm 66:18.**

SATURDAY

Thanksgiving is another important part of prayer. God is so good to us. If you were to list all the ways that God is good to you during just one day, it would be a long list. Those of us who are God's children have all the blessings He has given us in Christ for which to be thankful as well. For us, even the sad and hard things should cause us to give thanks. The hard things in our lives are the very things Jesus uses to make us grow more like Him. We must faithfully look for the things for which we ought to thank God and then thank Him for them. When we do, we will grow a great deal in godly character. **Read Philippians 4:6.**

Q.99. HOW DOES GOD DIRECT US TO PRAY?

A. ✐ *The whole word of God, but especially the Lord's prayer, which Christ taught His disciples, directs our prayers.*

MONDAY

The word "prayer" has come to mean many things to many different people. To some people, prayer is thinking hard about someone. To others, prayer is wishing for something. Some people see prayer as a way to think or say whatever they are feeling, even if it is sinful. Many people do not think at all when they pray. They simply say whatever is on their minds at the moment. Others believe they pray when they chant memorized words—whether or not they are paying any attention to what the words say.

We should want to know what Scripture has to say about anything we do. This is especially true of worshiping and serving God. The Bible has a great deal to say about prayer. It gives us many examples of prayers. The Holy Spirit Himself gave us the words of the prayers that are in the Bible. Instead of praying according to the mood or feeling we have at the moment, we should allow God's Word to direct our prayers. That is where we learn God's will. God has promised to hear those prayers that agree with His will. **Read 1 John 5:14.**

TUESDAY

When we come to the Bible, allowing it to direct our prayers, we learn that we should not ask for just anything. We are to ask for those things that God wants for us. We should pray for the things that have value to God. People often think of prayer as a way to get what they want. That is not why God gave it to us. He gave us prayer as a way to learn what *He* wants for us. As we pray for the things God wants for us, we will learn to want them too. We should not use prayer selfishly.

When we prepare to pray for something, we should stop to ask ourselves, "Why do I want this?" If God answers this prayer, will His Word be honored? Will one or more of His people become more godly? When we ask ourselves, "Why am I praying for this?" if the only answer is, "Because I really want it," we have no business praying for that thing. **Read James 4:2–3.**

WEDNESDAY

When we look to the Bible to direct our prayers, we need to consider all of the Bible's teaching on prayer. A verse in the book of Matthew says, "Ask and it will be given to you . . . for everyone who asks receives." If you read that verse alone, you might get the wrong idea about prayer. You might think you could ask for anything at all and God would give it to you, like a genie from a bottle granting wishes. However, we know from Monday's verse that God hears us when we ask for things that are according to His will. Jesus says in another verse that God will give us what we ask for in Jesus' name. In other words, when we come to God asking for what Jesus would have asked for, God will give it to us. **Read Luke 11:9–13.**

Jesus promised the Holy Spirit to His followers. God tells us in His Word that He wants His children to be controlled by the Holy Spirit and to have His fruit in their lives. This is an example of something we can ask for in Jesus' name, knowing God will hear and answer.

THURSDAY

We are to use all of God's Word to direct us in our praying. We should especially use the Lord's Prayer to show us how to pray. That is because Jesus gave it to us for the specific purpose of teaching us how to pray. One day Jesus was praying, as He often did. When He had finished, His disciples said to Him, "Lord, teach us to pray." Jesus' answer was the Lord's Prayer. Jesus knew better than anyone how to pray. Jesus had spent all eternity with God the Father. He knew Him and knew what was pleasing to Him. Jesus was perfect and sinless, so His prayers always honored God. God always listened to Jesus' prayers. Read what Jesus said about His prayers when He was raising Lazarus from the dead. **Read John 11:41–42.**

FRIDAY

There are two ways we can use the Lord's Prayer: as a prayer itself and as a pattern for prayer. We can use it as a prayer by saying it exactly as it is. People in a worship service will often say the Lord's Prayer together. When we do that, it is easy to say the words without thinking about what we say because we have them memorized. It is always wrong to pray without thinking. As we say the words of the Lord's Prayer, we should be thinking about each word and about what it means. Whenever we pray to God without thinking about what we say, we take His name in vain. We call on His name as we begin our prayer, then we pray without paying attention. To say words in prayer without meaning them from our hearts is not reverent and it dishonors God. The Bible warns us against saying empty words that do not have our hearts and minds behind them. **Read Matthew 6:7–8.**

SATURDAY

The second way we can use the Lord's Prayer is by using it as a pattern or a model for how we should pray. When we do that, we do not use the exact words of the Lord's Prayer. Instead, we follow the example given in the Lord's Prayer and we ask for the same things. The remaining questions and answers of the catechism show us what each part of the Lord's Prayer asks for or says. They give us examples of how we can use the Lord's Prayer as a pattern when we make up our own prayers, using our own words. **Read Matthew 6:9–13.**

A. ✍ *The beginning of the Lord's prayer* (Our Father in heaven) *teaches us to draw near to God with completely holy reverence and confidence, as children to a father who is able and ready to help us. It also teaches us that we should pray with and for others.*

MONDAY

Most fathers love their children. Fathers are proud of their children and want what is best for them. It is natural for fathers to love their children, because their children are part of them. Because they love their children, fathers want to give them good things. When a man adopts a child, he chooses to be a father to a child who does not have one. That father chooses to be the one who will pay for whatever the child needs. He will take care of and love and protect that child until the child is grown. Adopting a child who is not his own is a very loving thing for a father to do. When an adopted child goes to his father to ask for something he needs, he can be sure his father will listen to him. His father has already shown that he loves him by adopting him in the first place.

God has chosen to be a Father to His people. He has adopted us. He has chosen to be the One who will always love us, protect us, and give us what we need. Jesus taught us to think of God as a loving Father. He taught us to call Him, "Our Father." When we come to God to pray, we can be sure He will listen to us because He is our Father who loves us. **Read Romans 8:15–16.**

TUESDAY

When a self-centered, disrespectful child comes to his father, the child demands his father's attention right now. If his father is speaking with someone else, this child is not polite enough to wait to speak. He screams at his father, perhaps even pulling on him or hitting him to get his attention. This child does not ask for what he wants; he demands it rudely. It is wrong for a child to treat his father in this way. A child is to honor his father and mother. Children should speak politely to their parents and show them respect. When we come to God with our prayers, we can come freely, as children come to a father. As *respectful* children coming to a father, though, we must speak to God in a way that honors Him. When we pray, our prayers should not sound as though we think we can give God orders. Instead, we ask God respectfully for what we need. **Read Malachi 1:6.**

WEDNESDAY

When a spoiled child comes to his father, the child knows exactly what he wants and he will not settle for anything else. If the father will not give what he wants when he wants it, this child will cry and scream angrily. He will try to make his father give it to him. A wise, obedient child will not act like this. A wise child knows that his father is wiser than he is. He will tell his father what he needs and will trust his father to do what is best for him. If his father tells him he cannot have what he wants, he will accept that without complaining. When we pray to God as our Father, we should not be like spoiled children. We should bring our needs to God in prayer and trust Him to give us what we need. If He does not give us what *we* think we need, we will not complain. Instead, we will accept what He does give and be content. **Read Psalm 131.**

THURSDAY

Jesus' first words in the Lord's Prayer, "Our Father," teach us that we can come freely to God like children coming freely to a father. These first words also remind us that we come to a *heavenly* Father, not an ordinary one. Our Father, God, is "in heaven." He is our Father, so we may come with confidence. At the same time, there is a great distance between us and our heavenly Father, so we must also come with reverence. God is in heaven and we are on earth. God is the great, majestic, and holy God, while we are sinful creatures. Our attitude in prayer is to be, not only respectful, but reverent as well. **Read Ecclesiastes 5:2.**

FRIDAY

When children come to a human father with their needs, he may be a harsh, unloving father who does not care about them. He may be able to meet their needs but does not want to do so. Our Father in heaven is not like that. We know that God is willing to give us, His children, whatever we need. We are sure of this because He has already given us what was most costly for Him to give, His own Son. **Read Romans 8:32.**

When children come to a human father with their needs, the father may want to give them what they ask for, but he may be unable to do it. They may be asking for something he does not have. Or they may be asking him to do something that is too hard for him to do. We know that nothing is too hard for our Father in heaven. Not only is He able to do whatever we ask, He is able to do more than we could even imagine. **Read Ephesians 3:20–21.**

SATURDAY

These opening words of the Lord's Prayer teach us that we may come confidently to God because He is our Father. They teach us that we must come reverently to God because He is our God. These first words teach us one more thing. Jesus said we should call God "*Our* Father in heaven." If we were thinking only of ourselves, we would say "My Father." We will say "Our Father" if we are thinking of others too. Many people believe that worship and prayer are private things. They believe they do not need churches and other people. They think they can worship and pray all by themselves and please God. This idea does not come from the Bible. When the Lord Jesus saves a person, He saves her or him to be a part of His church. He requires us to worship and pray together. He requires us to pray *with* other believers and to pray *for* other believers. **Read Ephesians 6:18.**

Q.101.

FOR WHAT DO WE PRAY IN THE FIRST REQUEST?

A. *In the first request* (hallowed be your name) *we pray that God will enable us and others to glorify Him in everything He uses to make Himself known and that He will work out everything to His own glory.*

MONDAY

Whenever there is a prayer time at church or at home, people bring their prayer requests. Listen sometime to how many of our requests have to do with making us or someone else more comfortable in this life. Our prayers ask for health for sick people and for safety for travelers. We pray for people to have good jobs to earn the money they need. We even ask for people to "have a good time" when they are about to do something. God is concerned about all these details of our lives. However, there is something we should notice about prayer requests from this prayer Jesus gave us as a model.

There are six requests in this prayer. Only one of them is concerned with making us comfortable in this life. The other five requests have to do with spiritual things. In the Lord's Prayer, Jesus taught us to pray for spiritual things that will last forever, not for physical things that can last only a little while.

The first request is for God's name to be hallowed. This is a request that we know God will answer, because we know God wants His name to be honored. **Read Malachi 1:11.** Remember the third commandment, "You shall not misuse the name of the Lord your God." The catechism says that God's name includes His "names, titles, qualities, regulations, word, and works." God's name stands for all these things. To hallow God's name is to treat all these things with reverence and to honor God in them all.

TUESDAY

When we pray, "Hallowed be your name," we ask for God to receive the honor and glory He deserves. We ask God to make us and others able to glorify Him. There is nothing wrong with asking for good health or for other things our bodies need. Much more of our prayer time, though, should be spent in asking God to help us glorify Him. When we pray for others, too, most of our prayers should be for those things that would make them able to live for God's glory.

One way we dishonor God is by sinning. If we say we are God's people and then sin, we bring dishonor on God's name. **Read Romans 2:23–24.** We hallow God's name or glorify Him when we confess our sins to Him and turn from them. If, each day, we check to see what sins from that day we need to confess to God, we will hallow His name. We should ask God to give to us and to those we love hearts that are troubled when we sin against Him.

WEDNESDAY

We hallow God's name or give Him glory when we walk in His truth. **Read Psalm 86:11.** When we walk in God's truth, we study the Bible regularly. We believe and love what we read in God's Word and then we obey it carefully. It is ridiculous to say we want God's name to be honored if we do not honor it ourselves by obeying God in our everyday lives. God's children are eager to see God receive the honor He deserves. They read the Scriptures to see how to live for His glory. Then they ask Him to help them to do what it says so that His name will be hallowed.

THURSDAY

We hallow God's name or give Him glory when we praise and worship Him. It is possible to *think* we are worshiping God and praising His name when we really are not. We do this when we worship God without really knowing what He is like. It is possible to think we know what God is like and to pray to the god we have in our minds, when this is not what God is like at all. God has shown us what He is like in His Word. If our idea of God does not agree with what the Bible says, our idea of God is wrong. When we worship this god we have in our minds, we are not worshiping the true God. We hallow God's name in our worship when we find out from His Word what He is like and praise Him for it. **Read Psalm 96:1–8.**

FRIDAY

When we pray, "Hallowed be your name," we ask God to help us want His glory more than anything else. A true child of God should do everything he does for the glory of God. Because we are still sinful, it often happens that our own sinful desires get in the way. It often happens that we are more concerned about ourselves than about God's glory. By praying, "Hallowed be your name," we ask God to change our hearts so that honoring Him will be the most important thing to us. When the apostle Paul wrote a letter to the Philippian Christians, he was in jail for preaching about Jesus. He knew he might be killed. He wrote to the Philippians that he would be content either to live or to die. What he really wanted was to honor God, whether it was by his life or by his death. **Read Philippians 1:20.**

SATURDAY

When we pray, "Hallowed be your name," we ask God to "enable us and others to glorify Him in everything He uses to make Himself known." When we pray this, we also ask God to "work out everything to His own glory." We often see things around us that make us think God's enemies are winning. It often looks as though the things that go against God's will are the very things that keep happening. It is comforting to remember that God has promised in His Word that He will work out all things so that He will receive praise and glory. When we pray for Him to do this, we know that we are praying for something that He will do. **Read Ephesians 1:11.**

Q.102. FOR WHAT DO WE PRAY IN THE SECOND REQUEST?

A.   *In the second request* (your kingdom come) *we pray that Satan's kingdom may be destroyed, that the kingdom of grace may be advanced, with ourselves and others brought into and kept in it, and that the kingdom of glory may come quickly.*

MONDAY

The Bible teaches us that all people are, by nature, members of the kingdom of Satan because all people are sinful. God created man to serve Him as Lord and King. When the first man chose to obey Satan rather than God, all mankind came under the rule of Satan. Satan is not the rightful king over God's people, and he is not the rightful king over God's world. The Lord Jesus came to destroy the works of the devil. **Read 1 John 3:8.** In the second request of the Lord's Prayer, we ask God to destroy the kingdom of Satan. We ask Him to destroy it in the hearts of His people now and to destroy it completely and forever at the end of time. We ask God to replace the kingdom of Satan with the kingdom of Christ, both now, in our hearts and, later, in the entire universe.

TUESDAY

The Lord Jesus is the King of kings. There is no king as great as He is and there never will be. When He first came to earth, Jesus established a kingdom of grace. This is a kingdom in the hearts of His people. He changes the hearts of His people so they will stop hating Him and choose Him for their King. He sends His Spirit to live inside them so they will have the power to obey Him. The Jews of Jesus' day knew God had promised to send a King and set up a

331

kingdom. They expected an earthly king, like David or Solomon had been. Jesus' kingdom of grace is not a place where people can go. It is not something that can be seen. For now, Jesus rules in and through His people. **Read Luke 17:20–21.** Part of what we ask for when we ask for God's kingdom to come is that Jesus' kingdom of grace would advance or grow.

WEDNESDAY

When we pray, "Your kingdom come," we ask for God's kingdom of grace to advance. This is the kingdom Jesus established in the hearts of His people when He first came. By praying for it to advance, we pray for more people to come into it. God knows the people He has chosen. He will save every one of them from Satan's rule and will bring them all into His kingdom. God has chosen to use the prayers of His people as one of the ways He does His will. He commands us to pray for the salvation of others. God uses the preaching of His Word and the prayers of His people to cause His kingdom to advance. He turns people from their sins and Satan's kingdom to obedience and the kingdom of His Son. **Read Acts 26:17–18.**

THURSDAY

God's kingdom advances when people are added to it and it grows larger. It also advances when God keeps His people in His kingdom and causes them to grow in holiness. God's kingdom advances in each of our hearts when we become more like Jesus. When many of God's people grow in holiness, His whole church grows in holiness. This is part of what we ask for when we pray, "Your kingdom come." **Read 1 Thessalonians 5:23–24.**

FRIDAY

Jesus rules in the hearts of His people now, but His rule is not perfectly obeyed. That is because our hearts are still sinful. Sin is the enemy of God inside Christians that keeps them from obeying Him completely. Satan is another enemy of God, outside Christians, always tempting them to follow him instead of God. God has promised that, in His timing, Jesus will come again. This time He will establish a kingdom of glory. This kingdom will be perfect because He will destroy all His enemies. The hearts of His people will no longer have any sin. Satan will be thrown into a lake of fire, where he will stay forever, along with all of God's enemies. Nothing and no one will remain to fight against God. His kingdom will be perfect and glorious. When we pray, "Your kingdom come," we ask for Jesus to return soon to destroy His enemies and rule with no one to resist Him. **Read Psalm 68:1–3.**

SATURDAY

The world is not nearly so wonderful a place now as it was before sin entered it. Still, God gives us many wonderful things to enjoy. Sometimes, we can become rather comfortable in this world. However, God's people see the pain and suffering caused by sin. They see things turn ugly that God created to be beautiful. They see God's enemies fight against Him and, sometimes, it looks like those enemies are winning. The thing that troubles God's people the most is seeing the sin in their own hearts. They know how much God has done for them. They know how much they owe Him. God's people know they should love Him perfectly, but they do not. Instead, they sin against Him every day. More than anything else, this makes God's people weary of this world. This is what causes them to long and pray for God's kingdom of glory to come quickly.

The last book of the Bible describes the hatred God's enemies have for God. It describes how desperately they fight against Him. Then it describes their destruction. Finally, Revelation tells about God's perfect kingdom of glory, free of all sin, sorrow, and death. The people of God long for this kingdom to come. In the Lord's Prayer, Jesus teaches us to pray for it to come quickly. **Read Revelation 22:12–15, 20.**

Q.103. FOR WHAT DO WE PRAY IN THE THIRD REQUEST?

A. *In the third request* (your will be done on earth as it is in heaven) *we pray that by His grace God would make us have the capability and the will to know, obey, and submit to His will in everything, as the angels do in heaven.*

MONDAY

When we pray for God's will to be done, we may mean one of two things. We may be asking Him to help us to do His will as He has told it to us in the Bible. The person who is truly a Christian has a strong desire to please God. He wants to do what God wants him to do. He knows that on his own, he can never do God's will, so he asks for help. If a person claims to be a Christian but is not concerned with knowing and doing God's will, he has no right to make that claim. The one who truly belongs to the Lord is eager to obey Him. **Read Matthew 7:21.**

TUESDAY

The other kind of God's will we can pray for is His will in working out all circumstances for His own purposes. We call this God's *providence.* God, in His providence, arranges all the details of every person's life for the good of His people and for His own glory. When we pray for God's will in this sense, we ask for something that He will do, whether or not we ask Him. By asking Him to do His will, we are not asking for something so much as we are telling Him that we accept whatever He chooses as best. We admit that He is great, all-wise, and all-powerful. We tell Him that we want Him to use us and to do to us whatever He knows to be the best. **Read 1 Peter 4:19.**

WEDNESDAY

Because of sin we cannot know God's will or understand His Word on our own. He has told us His will for us in His Word. In the Bible, God has given us commands, promises, and examples. Left to ourselves, we would never rightly understand His will. One thing we ask for when we pray "Thy will be done in earth as it is in heaven" is for God to give us understanding of His will. We ask for God to bless us when we hear and study His Word, so that we will learn from it what He wants us to know. We ask Him to cause us to grow in the knowledge of His Word and of His will. Because we are praying to "*Our* Father in heaven," we include others in our prayer. We ask God to make His will known and understood to others, as well as to ourselves. **Read Colossians 1:9.**

THURSDAY

Because of sin we cannot know and understand God's will on our own. Not only that, if we knew God's will, we would not want to do it. Again, that is because of the sin in our hearts. The sin in our hearts causes us to want to do what *we* want to do and not what God wants us to do. Our sinful hearts, left to themselves, see God as the enemy and want to disobey Him. When we ask for God's will to be done on earth as it is in heaven, we ask God to cause our hearts to want Him alone as our King. We ask Him to weaken sin in our hearts and strengthen our love for Him. These are things God has promised to do for His people. **Read Ezekiel 36:26–27.** God uses our prayers to make our hearts want to do His will. In our prayers, we should ask God to give us and others hearts that want to obey Him.

FRIDAY

When we pray for God's will to be done, we are asking God to make us able to know, understand, and want to do the commands He has given us in His Word. We also ask God to work all things out for the good of His people and for His glory. Of course, God will do this anyway. When we pray for it, we agree to accept God's will for us and for His world, whatever it is. Whatever God's choices are for us, we will trust Him and not complain.

When God works out our circumstances so that we have happiness and good health, we will see that all our blessings are from Him and we will give Him thanks. When God works out our circumstances so that we have to endure sad or difficult things, we will again see these things as coming from Him. We will not grumble, but will trust Him to do what is best and will try to be faithful to obey and please Him even in the hard times. **Read 1 Peter 3:16–17.**

SATURDAY

In this request, we ask for God's will to be done. We also say *how* we want God's will to be done. This request asks that God's will be done here on earth as the angels do it in heaven. In heaven, all the angels always do the will of God. We should pray that we and others would obey God always, in all places. In heaven, the angels do God's will instantly. They do not question it, and they do not need time to "get into the mood" to obey. They obey immediately. Our prayer should be that we and others would obey God's commands as soon as we know what they are. The angels in heaven never grow tired of obeying God, as we sometimes do. By asking for God's will to be done on earth as it is in heaven, we are asking that we and others would be strengthened to *keep* doing God's will. **Read Psalm 103:20–21.**

Q.104. FOR WHAT DO WE PRAY IN THE FOURTH REQUEST?

A. ✍ *In the fourth request* (Give us today our daily bread) *we pray that we may receive an adequate amount of the good things in this life as a free gift of God and that with them we may enjoy His blessing.*

MONDAY

When we pray for our daily bread, we are not asking for bread only. "Our daily bread" means any of the things that we need to live. It includes all our food, our water, our clothing, and our shelter. This is the only one of all the requests in the Lord's Prayer that asks for things for our bodies. All the other requests are concerned with spiritual things. Because there is only one request concerning things for our bodies, we see that our prayers should be concerned mostly with spiritual things. Still, since there *is* this request for physical things, we see that these things matter to God. In His goodness, He gives us what we need for our bodies. **Read Psalm 145:15–16.**

TUESDAY

At first glance, it might seem that asking God for physical things is selfish. Really, though, prayer for what we need gives worship to God. When we ask God for the things we need for everyday life, we admit that we depend on Him for all we need. It is a way of saying that we know we cannot live without Him and that all we have comes from Him. To ask God for what our bodies need is to show that we know He is the Creator who makes and cares for everything that exists. Asking God humbly for what we need is a form of worship. **Read Psalm 65:9–13.**

WEDNESDAY

By asking God for our daily bread, we ask just for what we need. Most of us here in America have much more than our daily bread. Our cupboards and refrigerators have enough food in them to last us for at least a week. Often, fathers or mothers have jobs that provide them with enough money for a week or more. This prayer request asks only for enough food for one day at a time. The Christian attitude toward things is to want only what we need and to trust God to decide what we really need. He has promised to give His people what they need. Sometimes we ask God for something we think we need, but we still find ourselves having to do without it. When that happens, we can trust that God would give us that thing if it were really what was best for us. **Read Proverbs 30:7–9.**

THURSDAY

God is good. He is generous with His gifts. The Bible tells us that God sends His sun on the evil and the good and causes it to rain on the righteous and the unrighteous. God is so good that He freely gives to animals, birds, fish, and people all that they need to live. He gives food and possessions even to people who never ask Him for them. So why should we include these things in our prayers? For one thing, although God generously gives many things to many people, He gives His promise to supply needs only to those who depend on Him. **Read Psalm 34:9–10.** Another reason to ask God for what we need is that asking shows that we know and worship God as the One who provides for His creatures.

FRIDAY

We pray for our daily bread because that is how it becomes a blessing to us. It is not just our daily bread and the things our bodies need that we want; we also want God's blessing as we use those things. When we eat food, we want to remember that it is a gift from God. We want to eat with a grateful spirit. When we enjoy good health, we want to be thankful for it and to use it to serve God. In asking God for our physical needs, we are asking Him for spiritual blessings with them as well. **Read Deuteronomy 28:1–8.**

SATURDAY

All that we have is a gift from God. Here in America, most of us have so much, we sometimes forget that it all comes from Him. Most of us have more than our daily bread. We have enough to last us for weeks and more keeps coming. So we forget that we would have nothing if God did not give it. Giving thanks before we eat is one way to remind ourselves that all we have comes from God. We do the same thing in the worship service when we sing, before taking the offering, "Praise God from whom all blessings flow." Remembering to thank God for physical things reminds us that He gave them to us. **Read Matthew 15:35–37.**

A. ✐ *In the fifth request* (Forgive us our debts, as we also have forgiven our debtors), *encouraged by God's grace, which makes it possible for us sincerely to forgive others, we pray that for Christ's sake God would freely pardon all our sins.*

MONDAY

A debt is something we owe to someone else. If I agreed to pay money for something sold to me, and I still have not paid it, it is a debt. God is our Creator and we owe Him obedience. We do not obey God as we should. Instead, we sin against Him. We owe a debt to God's justice. The only way we could pay our debts would be by suffering punishment forever for breaking God's laws.

God graciously provided another way for His people's debts to be paid. He gave His only Son, Jesus, to take the punishment for the laws they had broken. He gave His only Son to live a life of perfect obedience in the place of His people. The death of Christ has paid the debt His people owed. Christians can come to God in Jesus' righteousness. When we ask God to forgive our debts, we are not asking Him to ignore them. We are asking Him to forgive them because Christ has paid them for us. **Read 2 Corinthians 5:21.**

TUESDAY

Read Psalm 51:1. When we ask God to forgive our sins, we do not ask because we deserve it. We cannot do enough good things to make up for the sinful things we do. We ask God to forgive us because we know He is gracious and forgiving. Since God shows mercy to sinners who do not deserve it, we can ask Him to show mercy to us and forgive our debts. Anyone could pray for forgiveness. But the only prayers for forgiveness that God answers are the prayers of those who trust in Jesus and what He did on the cross.

WEDNESDAY

Our sins deserve punishment. The Lord Jesus Christ suffered in our place. Jesus took on Himself all the anger of God and the judgment that our sins deserved. **Read Isaiah 53:4–6.** When we pray, "Forgive us our debts," we ask God to count Jesus' death and suffering as punishment for our sins. We ask that God would no longer hold us guilty because Jesus has paid for what we have done wrong.

THURSDAY

When we become Christians, the Holy Spirit comes to live inside us. He gives us the power to say "No" to sin. He gives us the power to obey God. Our hearts are still sinful, though, and they continue to cause us to sin until we die or until Jesus returns. Even with the Holy Spirit living inside us, we will still sin. We will sin every day. Each evening we should ask God to show us the sins we have committed that day. We should ask God to forgive us the debts or sins of each day. **Read Hosea 14:2.**

FRIDAY

Because the Holy Spirit lives inside Christians, Christians cannot have peace and rejoice while they sin against God. God hates sin. Once we are His children, sin troubles us too. When we sin, we know we have done something displeasing to our Heavenly Father. When we ask God to forgive our sins, we ask Him to give us back the peace and the joy that we had before we sinned. We ask Him to assure us (or make us sure) that He has forgiven us and does not hold our sins against us. **Read Psalm 51:8–12.**

SATURDAY

One of the hardest things for people to do is to forgive those who have hurt them or who have wronged them in some way. God requires us to forgive each other. He gives the Holy Spirit to His children. The Holy Spirit makes it possible for us to forgive others. It is an amazing thing when sinful human beings can forgive each other! By God's grace, we can do it. Surely God, who is not sinful but holy, will forgive us when we come to Him in the name of Jesus who paid for all our sins. Since God's grace makes us able to forgive each other, we can be encouraged that He will freely forgive us. **Read Matthew 6:14–15.**

Q.106. For What Do We Pray In The Sixth Request?

A. ✍ *In the sixth request* (And lead us not into temptation, but deliver us from the evil one) *we pray that God would either keep us from being tempted to sin or support and deliver us when we are tempted.*

MONDAY

The Holy Spirit comes to live inside us when we become Christians. He changes our hearts so that now we want to do what is right. He gives us the power to *not* do what we want to do when we know it would be wrong. However, our hearts continue to be sinful until the day we die. We still want to sin. To a Christian, it often feels like there is a war going on inside him. There *is!* The war is between new desires to please God and old desires to sin and please self. **Read Galatians 5:17.**

We must be very careful and very watchful because we so easily fall into sin. The Bible tells us that the devil is always looking for an opportunity to cause us to do what is wrong (1 Peter 5:8). It also tells us that our own hearts are desperately wicked and will trick us into sinning and telling ourselves that it was not sin at all (Jer. 17:9). Being careful is not enough, though. If God does not protect us from sin, all our efforts are useless. That is why Jesus taught us to pray, "And lead us not into temptation, but deliver us from the evil one."

TUESDAY

Of course, God never tempts anyone to do wrong. He does choose all the circumstances of our lives for us. He controls everything that happens. When we pray, "Lead us not into temptation," we admit that God controls all things and we depend on Him. We ask Him to so arrange all that happens to us that we will not be tempted. We know that even Satan can do nothing except what God allows him to do, so we ask God to hold Satan back from tempting us. **Read John 17:15.** We know how easily we sin, so we ask God not to place us in situations where we will be tempted and perhaps give in to sin. **Read Psalm 19:13.**

WEDNESDAY

Sometimes, God knows it will be best for us to face a situation where we will be tempted to sin. He knows this is one way we grow strong in faith and learn to trust and obey Him more fully. So sometimes He places us in circumstances where Satan is allowed to tempt us or where it would be easy to sin. He has promised that the temptations He allows will never be more than we can resist. **Read 1 Corinthians 10:13.** God has promised that when we are tempted or when Satan is allowed to trouble us, God will give us grace. He will give us all we need to resist the temptation and to keep obeying Him. **Read 2 Corinthians 12:7–9.** When we pray, "Deliver us from evil," we ask God for the strength to resist and not give in to sin when we are tempted.

THURSDAY

When we ask God to keep us from temptation and to deliver us from sin when we are tempted, we must be sincere. If we are sincere, we will be diligent to keep ourselves from being tempted or from giving in to sin. We should watch our hearts carefully. We should know what things are especially hard for us, which sins especially tempt us. Then we must be careful to avoid those things. It is foolish to see how close we can come to sinning without really sinning. When we are serious about asking God not to lead us into temptation, we will not walk into it on purpose! If we know that we have a weakness for a certain sin, we should stay away from the activities or the people that encourage us to commit that sin. The apostle Paul told his young friend Timothy to flee—to run away from—the things that caused him to want to do what is evil. Instead, Paul told him to work hard at building those things into his life that are pleasing to God. **Read 2 Timothy 2:22.**

FRIDAY

As we read before, Satan eagerly looks for opportunities to get us to sin. Because our hearts are sinful, we easily cooperate with Satan. We must take care not to do that. One of Satan's favorite temptations that he uses with God's people is that of tempting them to hate each other or to be angry with one another. Satan knows that God wants His children to love each other. He knows that the world watches Christians to see if what they say is true. If Christians cannot get along with each other, non-Christians will not listen to what they say. When Christians are angry with each other, they will not work together and they will not be able to do much to help God's kingdom grow. For all these reasons, Satan works especially hard at causing Christians to dislike each other and quarrel with one another.

People *will* sin against us. They will hurt us and make us angry, because they are sinful, just as we are. We help Satan when we refuse to forgive people for the wrong they do to us. If we are serious when we ask God to deliver us from the evil one, we must not leave any room in our hearts for Satan to do his work of dividing God's people. We must be sure to forgive and keep on loving others, even when we do not feel like it. **Read Ephesians 4:26–27.**

SATURDAY

Because God's Spirit lives inside us and because we want to please God our Father, this sixth request should be important to us. We should want to do all we can to make sure that we will not be tempted, or that if we are tempted, we will not sin. During times when we are not facing temptation, we should be working hard to prepare ourselves for the temptations that will come in the future.

Christians should think of themselves as soldiers in training. Soldiers would be foolish to do nothing but eat and sleep when they will soon face a difficult battle. Soldiers will make sure their weapons and their armor are in good order. They will work hard at getting in good shape to be as strong as possible. Good soldiers will always be training, becoming more skilled in fighting. In the same way, Christians should work diligently every day to get to know God's Word better. They should spend time in prayer. Christians should encourage other Christians and be encouraged by them. They should practice doing those things God has commanded. Then, when strong temptations hit, the temptations will not take them by surprise. Because they have been diligent, they will be strong and better able to resist. **Read Ephesians 6:13–18.**

Q.107. WHAT DOES THE CONCLUSION OF THE LORD'S PRAYER TEACH US?

A. *The conclusion of the Lord's prayer* (for yours is the kingdom and the power and the glory forever) *teaches us to be encouraged only by God in our prayers and to praise Him by acknowledging that kingdom, power, and glory are His. To show that we want to be heard and have confidence that we are, we say* Amen.

MONDAY

God's people should be encouraged to pray. They can be sure that they are welcome to come to God to ask for the things they need. God's children can be bold to ask even for things that seem impossible. However, there is only one reason that God's people can be so confident when they pray. The reason Christians can be encouraged to pray is not because they have been good and have been pleasing to God. God does not hear or answer prayers because people deserve it. He hears and answers prayers because of who He is. God's people can be encouraged to pray because they know what God is like. God wanted His people to be able to pray to Him. By giving His Son, God has made a way for people to come to Him in prayer. When God's people come in the name of God's Son, they can be sure they will be welcomed. **Read Daniel 9:18.**

TUESDAY

The final words of the Lord's Prayer remind us of who God is. They remind us that we can pray to Him with confidence because He is able and willing to answer our prayers. The Lord's Prayer reminds us that the kingdom belongs to God. He is the King over all.

He controls all things and can do whatever He pleases with all of creation. We can ask for His will to be done and for our sins to be forgiven. We can ask for our daily bread and for God to keep us from sin. God can give us these things because He rules everything. God can cause every detail to work out so that our prayers are answered, if the answers are what He knows to be the best. The Lord's Prayer also reminds us that power belongs to God. All power is His. He can do whatever He wants to do, so we can be sure that He can do the things we ask. **Read Ephesians 3:20–21.**

WEDNESDAY

Not only is God *able* to answer our prayers, He is *willing* to do what is best for us. If all power belonged to God but He did not care about His people, He would not answer their prayers. But the final words of the Lord's Prayer remind us that all glory belongs to God. He is glorious in His goodness and delights in giving to those He loves. He is glorious in His faithfulness and will always do what is best for His people. When we ask God for what we need in prayer, we can be encouraged because we know that our glorious God will either do what we ask or will do something even better. We know He is willing to bless His people. **Read Matthew 7:7–11.**

THURSDAY

Prayer is not just for asking for things from God. In prayer, we also thank God for what He has given and give Him praise. It is easy to remember to pray when there is something we want badly. It is not as easy to remember to thank God for the answer when He sends it. The Bible tells us that we must combine our requests when we pray with thanksgiving for what God has done for us. **Read Philippians 4:6–7.**

FRIDAY

The final words of the Lord's Prayer teach us that we can be encouraged to pray because the kingdom, the power, and the glory belong to God. We know He can and will hear and answer our prayers. These words are also words of praise, and they remind us to give thanks when we pray. When we pray, we should praise God because He is the Lord of all. We should praise Him because He is almighty and can do anything He pleases. He also deserves our praise because His glory is so great. These final words of the Lord's Prayer remind us to come to God, not just for what we can get, but to come to Him to give praises. **Read 1 Chronicles 29:10–13.**

SATURDAY

At the end of the Lord's Prayer, as at the end of all prayers, we say, "Amen." "Amen" means "Let it be so," or "It shall be so." By saying, "Amen," we are saying that we are confident God will hear and answer our prayers. The Bible tells the story of Hannah, who desperately wanted a child. She had not been able to have a child. This made her so sad that she often cried and went without eating. Everyone who knew her could tell how troubled she was. One day she went to the Tabernacle and prayed long and hard that God would give her a child. Eli, the priest who served at the Tabernacle, encouraged her to believe that God had heard her. Hannah's response showed her confidence that God would answer her prayer. **Read 1 Samuel 1:17–18.**